MW01148031

DESERET'S SONS OF TOIL

A History of the Worker Movements of Territorial Utah
1852 - 1896

J. Kenneth Davies

Olympus Publishing Company • Salt Lake City

Manufactured in the United States of America.

This publication was produced through the
cooperation of:

Utah State AFL-CIO
Allied Printing Trades Council of Utah
International Typographical Union Local Number 115
Web Pressmens Union Local Number 28
Mailers Union Local Number 21
Graphic Arts International Union Local Number 511
Printing Specialties and Paper Products Union
    Local Number 541

Library of Congress Cataloging in Publication Data

Davies, Joseph Kenneth, 1925-
    Deseret's sons of toil.

    Includes bibliographies and index.
    1. Church and labor--Utah--History. 2. Church of
Jesus Christ of Latter-Day Saints. 3. Trade-unions--
Utah--History. I. Title.
HD6338.2.U52U82   261.8'5   76-26459
ISBN 0-913420-64-6

Contents

List of Tables

Acknowledgments

The author is indebted to a number of people and institutions who have contributed to this volume. The late Professor Elmer Miller of Brigham Young University initially provoked the interest of the author in the study of labor unionism in general and the Utah labor movement in particular. A master's thesis, "The Utah County Labor Movement," was prepared in 1953 under his direction. Next were Professors Spencer D. Pollard and E. Bryant Phillips of the University of Southern California under whom a doctoral dissertation, "The Development of a Labor Philosophy within the Church of Jesus Christ of Latter-day Saints," was written in 1957–59.

Dr. Leonard Arrington, now Historian of the Church of Jesus Christ of Latter-day Saints, unselfishly made his personal files on labor in Utah available to the author in the early 1950s. These files of notations were made during his careful examination of the *Journal History* in the archives of the above-named church in preparation for his authoritative work *Great Basin Kingdom*.

The staffs of the following libraries and archives have been most helpful in assisting the author in collection of data: Brigham Young University, University of Utah, AFL-CIO, United Brotherhood of Carpenters and Joiners, Catholic University, International

Typographical Union, the Church of Jesus Christ of Latter-day Saints, the Utah Historical Society, and the Salt Lake and Weber county libraries.

Dr. Larry Wimmer, economic historian at Brigham Young University, read the initial draft of this volume and made many insightful suggestions which resulted in considerable revision. Many of the author's research assistants and students contributed to the grubby work of reading thousands of issues of newspapers and other publications over the past twenty years. In addition, a number of secretaries have typed and retyped the thousands of pages from which this material was finally developed.

Brigham Young University, through its financial support over the years of the author's research and writing efforts, has been of great help. In addition, the University of Utah and the Utah AFL-CIO have helped in the financial backing of this book.

The author is grateful to the thousands of men and women who pioneered in the development of a viable labor movement in Utah. Without them, the history would not have been lived. Especially important was Robert Gibson Sleater, the unsung hero and father of the Utah labor movement. He lived and breathed unionism at tremendous personal sacrifice, earning a living as a typographer while still pioneering Deseret's union movement, from at least 1868 to 1905, a period of some 37 years.

And no married man could accomplish much without the help and forbearance of his wife. For these virtues, the author is grateful to his wife, Pauline Beard Taylor Davies, a descendant of several of Utah's most illustrious pioneers.

Provo, Utah
1976

1

Introduction — An Overview

In a study of the development of a labor philosophy within the Church of Jesus Christ of Latter-day Saints, which I made between 1949 and 1959, a uniqueness was identified that cried for understanding. It was found that local and regional church leaders (bishops and stake presidents) and the most active church members tended to be well educated, Republican, and strongly biased toward white collar occupations, with little membership in labor unions. The Stake presidents (church hierarchy is broken down into many segments — all explained later) indicated greater tendencies in these directions than the bishops and the most active members. In turn, the bishops and the most active church members were more strongly oriented toward these characteristics than the general membership, and the general membership was more strongly oriented than the most inactive church members. Or, stated another way, the completely inactive church members were more likely to be less educated, Democratic, and members of the working class, with substantially more union membership than was true for the leadership and most active members of the church. These characteristics may be clearly seen in Table 1.

It was also found that the attitude of these groupings toward labor unions followed the pattern that might be expected from the data in

Table 1

Characteristics of Selected Groupings of Latter-day Saints

(1959; percent)

Category	Stake President	Bishop	Most Active	General Membership	Most Inactive
Under twelve years of schooling	32.1%	38.9%	50.9%	62.6%	70.3%
College graduate	42.8	25.0	23.1	14.4	10.1
Republican oriented	89.3	55.6	58.4	40.8	31.3
Democratic oriented	10.7	22.2	24.1	38.3	48.3
Skilled and unskilled workers		16.7	14.9	37.5	44.5
Union membership		16.7	18.8	21.4	27.7

Source: J. Kenneth Davies, "The Development of a Labor Philosophy within the Church of Jesus Christ of Latter-day Saints" (Los Angeles: University of Southern California, 1959), pp. 289–360. Doctoral dissertation.

Table 1. Leaders were less likely to look upon Christianity and unionism as compatible than was a member, as seen in Table 2.

Table 3 compares the attitudes of these five groupings on three vital labor-related issues. Stake presidents were generally opposed to organizing workers into unions, strikes, and union shops. While bishops and the most active members supported organizing workers, they rejected the other two union activities. The general membership and the most inactive members supported all three.

Interestingly, all groups — stake presidents, bishops, general membership, the most active, and the most inactive — were strongly positive toward the bargaining of workers with their employers over wages, hours, and working conditions, ranging from 75 to 96 percent positive responses. The difference in attitude toward workers who bargain with employers and the attitude toward unions and union-related activities indicates an antagonism toward labor unions which is stronger for stake presidents than for bishops, and stronger for bishops than for active church members. The most active are more antagonistic toward unionism than the general membership, and the general membership more antagonistic than the most inactive. However, the general

Table 2

Positive Responses as to Compatibility of Christianity and
Unionism in Selected Groupings of Latter-day Saints

(1959; percent)

Category	Stake President	Bishop	Most Active	General Membership	Most Inactive
Always compatible	3.7	5.7	17.5	22.2	23.1
Never compatible	3.7	2.9	3.7	2.2	0.7

Source: J. Kenneth Davies, "The Development of a Labor Philosophy
within the Church of Jesus Christ of Latter-day Saints" (Los
Angeles: University of Southern California, 1959), pp. 289-360.
Doctoral dissertation.

membership and the least active, based upon the three issues illustrated in
Table 3, are generally positive in their attitudes toward labor unions.

The facts presented here do not show how Mormons (Latter-day
Saints) compare with non-Mormons. In 1959–60 I engaged in an unpublished study in North Carolina in which a comparison was made of
certain labor-related questions among the ministries of various churches
in that state. In terms of the feeling of absolute compatibility of church
and union membership, the Latter-day Saint (LDS) local church leaders
were found to be less certain of such compatibility than the leaders of the
Judaic, Roman Catholic, Methodist, Church of Christ, Presbyterian,
Episcopalian, Lutheran, Wesleyan Methodist, Moravian, Friends,
African Methodist, Nazarene, Pentecostal, Evangelical Reformed,
Congregational, Disciples of Christ, Free-Will Baptist, and Southern
Baptist churches. The LDS leaders were significantly more receptive to
unions in these terms than the leaders of the Greek Orthodox, the Christian and Missionary Alliance, the Seventh Day Adventist, Christian
Science, and Brethren churches. In terms of having a "good" attitude
toward unions, all church leaderships had a more favorable attitude than
the LDS leaders. While on some specific issues LDS leaders were not
relatively as antagonistic as on these questions, nevertheless they were
generally much more negative toward unions and union activities than
the overwhelming majority of Judeo-Christian church ministries.

A team of researchers — Richard Wirthlin and Bruce Merrill — discovered in 1968 that in Utah 83 percent of the Mormons interviewed

Table 3

Positive Responses on Acceptability of Selected Union-Related
Activities for Selected Groupings of Latter-day Saints

(1959; percent)

Category	Stake President	Bishop	Most Active	General Membership	Most Inactive
Organization of workers into unions	43.9	75.0	66.2	60.2	67.1
Strikes	39.3	47.3	47.2	53.1	61.0
Union shop	35.7	44.4	41.9	52.2	59.1

Source: J. Kenneth Davies, "The Development of a Labor Philosophy
within the Church of Jesus Christ of Latter-day Saints" (Los
Angeles: University of Southern California, 1959), pp. 289–360.
Doctoral dissertation.

favored right-to-work laws (which is usually interpreted as being anti-
labor), while only 69 percent of those who are not members of the LDS
church favored such laws. They also found that active church members
were much more likely to favor such laws than inactive members.

From the foregoing, it may be concluded (1) that the Latter-day
Saints as a body have developed a philosophy of labor which has strong
anti-union overtones, and (2) that the more active a church member is,
the more likely he or she is to be opposed to unions. However, this theme
should not be overplayed, for as shown below, most Latter-day Saints
feel that unions and Christianity are usually or always compatible
(Davies, 1959, pp. 289–360):

Status of Member	Percentage
Stake president	55.6%
Bishop	71.4%
Most active	67.1%

| General membership | 72.4% |
| Most active | 76.2% |

In addition, it is important to recognize that there are many active Latter-day Saints who are dedicated unionists. In a study conducted in 1965 (also unpublished), I found that Mormons in Utah are filling their proportionate share of union officership positions, with 73.6 percent of the state's union officers responding to a questionnaire being Mormon and with many holding church positions — bishops, bishop's counselors, clerks, stake missionaries, teachers, and leaders in the various priesthood quorums. Evidently these Latter-day Saints themselves have been able to accommodate their church and union activities.

Recognizing the complexity of the issue of the relationship of the church to unions, I concluded that a better understanding could be developed if a detailed study were made of the historical roots to the issue.

The casual student of the history of Utah and the Mormon church might easily conclude that the contemporary attitude comes because of a lack of experience with the labor movement, for there has been almost nothing published about Utah's labor movement. There have been several masters' and doctoral studies, but for some reason their information and conclusions have not become a part of either religious or secular published history. This has been a serious neglect, for unionism has played a significant role in both Utah and church history, and Utah unionism in turn has played an early and significant role in the development of the American labor movement.

For the church, the story began in Nauvoo, Illinois, when groups of workers formed worker guilds, using a Glasgow spinners' song: "The working man's only protection . . . is Union . . . / Union walls are high and grand / Union walls are nobly manned / Union walls are made to stand / against the strongest Foe."

Aside from the spinners, there were tailors, smiths, boot and harness makers, coopers, wagon makers, printers, and actors who had some form of organization, most likely of the master-journeyman-apprentice variety. By some accounts, the actors were organized in Salt Lake as early as 1850, three years after the arrival of the first Mormon pioneers, and the typographers or printers in 1852. By 1861, some fifty crafts were organized, a number of them appearing to be very much unionlike. Until the mid-1860s, these workers organizations evidently had the sponsorship and the encouragement of the General Authorities (leaders) of the church, including the church president, Brigham Young. They were controlled by active, endowed Mormons, and some of them required church membership. (The term "endowed" refers to a special religious ordinance reserved for those church members who conform to certain religious requirements beyond those expected of persons who were merely baptized into the church.)

However, as workers came into conflict with their employers, including church leaders, this encouragement disappeared. On the whole, church leaders in the 1860s and '70s advocated a low-wage policy which workers found difficult to accept. In 1864, organized workers began to take unionlike action to protect their wages, the theater workers even negotiating with Brigham Young. By 1868, at least one group of workers, the typographers, had become associated with a national union organization, although others may have been so affiliated as early as 1861.

Utah's first known strike occurred in 1871 when members of Mormon-dominated Deseret Local 115 of the International Typographical Union struck against the anti-Mormon spokesman for the apostate Godbeite[1] movement, the Salt Lake *Tribune*, for dismissing two members of the local union. The following year, Robert Gibson Sleater (see chapter 8), an active, endowed, polygamous member of the church and a charter member of Local 115, was elected one of the vice presidents at the convention of the International Typographical Union. (As with endowment, polygamy was generally reserved for the more faithful church members.)

Thus it may be seen that Utah unionism finds its roots early in the history of the church as well as the Territory. While the early guilds were encouraged by church leaders, possibly as an institution for church control of the more secular activities, and were Mormon dominated almost from their beginning, they began the process of secularization. First the requirement of the typographers — that members of that guild be church members in good standing — was dropped. Then workers began to confront church leaders, as employers in the mid-1860s, on the question of wages. By 1868, at least one local had become associated with a national union which would require the local to accommodate itself to the requirements of the national body, eventually bringing it into direct conflict with the church.

---

[1]William H. Godbe was a prominent Mormon businessman who attempted to provoke a change in the church politico-economic policy of nonintercourse with non-Mormons.

With the coming of the railroads and the opening up of mining, non-Mormons in great numbers entered the previously isolated Mormon valleys of "Deseret," bringing with them their union ideas. By 1874, non-Mormon workers had become significant enough to dominate a workers' meeting that had been called to try to do something about the depression of that period; yet Mormons played an important role in that meeting. With the depression, union activity became almost nonexistent except for the typographers. But with the renewal of economic growth in the 1880s Utah unionism was reborn as miners, telegraphers, and railroad workers, followed by craft after craft, organized into union locals or engaged in strikes.

At least by 1884, and possibly even earlier, the Noble Order of the Knights of Labor, a polyglot national union group hoping to get all workers under its banner, began to organize local assemblies in Utah. That summer the first known local assembly had an outing at Grass Creek (near Coalville, Utah), with members possibly from the nearby railroad town of Echo and possibly the silver mines of Park City (some twenty miles east of Salt Lake City). Mormons apparently controlled this assembly. It was followed by assemblies in Ogden, Salt Lake City, Logan, and a number of mining and smelting communities in the Territory.

In 1887, a district assembly was organized with Salt Lake City as district headquarters. However, beginning that year, the Knights of Labor organization sank into decline throughout the nation and the Territory. Its demise in the Territory may have been hastened, although probably not significantly, by its conflict with church leaders. Too frequently, Knights of Labor activities were punctuated by violence and moblike activity. The Utah Noble Order of the Knights of Labor allowed itself to become embroiled politically, many of its members publicly becoming associated with the anti-Mormon Liberal Party (dedicated to the destruction of Mormon political and economic power as well as polygamy, considered by Mormons at that time to be of supreme religious importance). While this involvement was soon dissipated, it left behind its effects. The church leaders, through the *Deseret News* (the Mormon-controlled local newspaper), counseled church members not to become involved with union organization, and attempts were made by the Knights to exclude Mormons from the Noble Order's membership.

The Mormon reaction to the increasing numbers of "Gentiles" (non-Mormons) in Deseret[2] was retrenchment. In 1868 the church began

---

[2]Mormon country of the later half of the nineteenth century.

a cooperative program which sought to isolate Mormons economically from their Gentile neighbors. It was followed in the depression of 1874 with the church's United Orders and in 1877, upon Brigham Young's demise, by the Zion's Boards of Trade. Under these programs, Mormon workmen were expected to devote their secular activities to the building up of "Zion" — the Mormon expression for "Kingdom of God on earth." Thus the more active Mormon workers probably dissociated themselves from the budding union movement, leaving it largely in the hands of non-Mormons, apostates, and the less faithful. The sole known exception was the typographers union which remained controlled by Mormons until 1886, serving as a bridge between the Mormon and Gentile worlds.

However, with the antipolygamy raids of the mid- and late 1880s, the church economic system collapsed. The few remaining cooperatives and United Orders either ceased to exist or became privately owned — with the most notable exception of Zion's Cooperative Mercantile Institution (ZCMI). However, while ZCMI remained with the church, it essentially became a profit-oriented business organization, losing its "cooperative" characteristics.

With the demise of the church's economic system, Mormon workmen were thrown into an economic limbo. The church's economic system had given them some protection from exploitation. With a secularized capitalistic economy, which came to characterize Utah, they no longer had that protection. Whereas they had been working to "build up Zion," they were now working for capitalists, Mormon and non-Mormon, and thus working to build up private wealth — as well as to satisfy their own needs. They increasingly came into conflict with their employers — the church, Mormons, and non-Mormons. This conflict, combined with economic growth, produced a burgeoning of unionism in 1888 and 1889. In the former year, Utah unionists, under the leadership of R. G. Sleater, held their first Labor Day parade. The following winter, Sleater organized the Utah Federated Trades and Labor Council, dominated by Mormons, and attended the fall meeting of the three-year-old American Federation of Labor in Boston. Unionists who had previously been associated with the Knights of Labor now became members of the growing number of trade unions, and by 1890 there were at least 24 local unions in Salt Lake City and another eleven in Ogden, with an unknown number of railroad, miner, and smelter locals throughout the Territory.

As the unions grew in number and power, they began to exercise a union principle — that unionists should not work alongside non-unionists — enforcing the demand with strikes and boycotts. This principle came into conflict with the church, for it frequently meant that Mormons who were discouraged from joining unions were denied jobs. For Mormons, it was a denial of free agency — a cardinal religious principle. When in 1890 the typographers, now controlled by Gentiles, tried to compel the *Deseret News* to become a closed shop, employing only union personnel, the resulting confrontation caused a complete rupture between the unions and the church.

Sleater, Utah's grand old man of labor, made a last-ditch effort to prevent the rupture. He organized the Workingmen's Party in 1890 which collaborated with the church's People's Party in a combined effort to prevent the anti-Mormon Liberal Party from gaining control of the Salt Lake County elections. The effort was abortive, and Sleater, who apparently had not consulted with other union leaders, was defeated as head of the Utah Federated Trades and Labor Council — and non-Mormons took over. Even many of his beloved typographers turned against him.

In 1893, the Federated Trades and Labor Council became officially chartered by the American Federation of Labor, only to find itself almost destroyed in the depression starting that year, along with many of the local union organizations — as was true throughout the country. However, with statehood and economic recovery in 1896, Utah unionism was to rise again, this time under the name of the Utah Federation of Labor, and with the ubiquitous and enduring Robert Gibson Sleater appropriately as its first president. By that time Utah labor, which had begun as a religiously motivated and controlled guild movement, had become as secularized as Utah's political and general economic life.

References

Davies, J. Kenneth, "The Development of a Labor Philosophy within the Church of Jesus Christ of Latter-day Saints." Los Angeles: University of Southern California. 1959. Doctoral dissertation.

Wirthlin, Richard, and Merrill, Bruce D. "The L.D.S. Church As a Significant Political Group in Utah; 'Right to Work,' " *Dialogue*, Summer, 1968, pp. 129–33.

2

A Unique
Church History
1820 to 1896

No contemporary institution can be fully understood in the absence of a knowledge of its historical and institutional evolution, as well as its philosophical inheritance. While most of the LDS philosophy and many of its institutions come from its theology, which is held by church members to be of direct divine origin through revelation, there have been wide enough differences in political, social, and economic concepts among members of the church that the student of the LDS or Mormon culture recognizes that there must be another element of influence — basically the historical evolution of Mormon society as it has related to elements and institutions outside the church itself. To understand Utah labor of the nineteenth century requires an understanding of the Mormon culture and history.

Pre-Utah Period (1820 to 1847)[1]

The pre-Utah period of the church was dominated by one man — Joseph Smith — and most of the general theological and organizational pattern later followed by the church was laid down within

---

[1]Several major references serve as the basis for this chapter (see "references" at the end of the chapter): Joseph Smith, six volumes; Joseph Fielding Smith, 1946; Neff, 1940; Arrington, 1958; Bancroft, 1890; and B. H. Roberts, 1930.

his short lifetime. There has been some rationalization, change, and addition in church practice since his time, but of all the church leaders, he is looked to as the most authoritative. His claim to prophetic leadership is found in his reported visits with and instruction from heavenly personages, starting at the age of fourteen with God and the resurrected Christ, and continuing until his death at 38 years of age.

The church was organized in 1830 in New York under the direct divine command and direction to Joseph Smith. This claim to divine communication produced intense loyalties on the part of his adherents, and the faithful followed him with zeal seldom equaled. It also resulted in charges of quackery, delusion, dictatorship, and so on, from those outside the church and from members who became disillusioned or disaffected. One of the results of these reported heavenly visits was a unique, authoritative, scriptural base, originating through the president of the church. Local leaders may receive revelation and inspiration for their areas of responsibility, but such must fit with that coming from the president of the church. In addition, church members might receive personal divine guidance, but it too must conform to church doctrine in its application. While members might seek guidance from church leaders, they would have responsibility for their own decisions.

The Latter-day Saints looked upon their centers of settlement as Zion — "places of gathering." In each of these places of gathering they hoped to practice their peculiar brand of religion which, until the closing decade of the nineteenth century, included a high degree of communitarianism. Their peculiarities, cohesiveness, separativeness, and perhaps lack of tact often produced resentment, hatred, and fear on the part of their neighbors, and they were driven from Ohio and Missouri to settle in Illinois. There the Mormon Nauvoo was built, with farms, a temple, a university, stores, manufacturing establishments, hotels, and homes. But once again, problems with neighbors and political jealousy resulted in the imprisonment of their prophet-leader and in his martyrdom by a mob in 1844. Finally, the Latter-day Saints were driven from Illinois in 1846 under the leadership of Brigham Young who led them to the Salt Lake Valley in 1847. One of the pertinent results of these mobbings was a fear of mob action, of apostates, Christian ministers, and Gentile government officials who often led or condoned these mob activities.

For members to survive the mobbings required the spirit and practice of cooperation and brotherhood. However, the brotherhood that was developed was not strong enough to permit the practice of their revealed

Law of Consecration, which called for equality in earthly things, for any period of time.

In the attempted implementation of the Law of Consecration, Joseph Smith (pp. 364–65) had given some interesting instructions:

> . . . [M]an is bound by the law of the Church to consecrate to the Bishop before he can be considered a legal heir to the kingdom of Zion; and this, too, without constraint . . . . [E]very man must be his own judge how much he should receive and how much he should suffer to remain in the hands of the Bishop. . . . The matter of consecration must be done with the mutual consent of both parties; for to give the Bishop power to say how much every man shall have, and he be obliged to comply with the Bishop's judgment, is giving to the Bishop more power than a king; and upon the other hand, to let every man say how much he needs, and the Bishop be obliged to comply with his judgment, is to throw Zion into confusion, and make a slave of the Bishop . . . . [T]here must be a balance or equilibrium of power between the Bishop and the people, and thus harmony and good will may be preserved among you. . . . Therefore, those persons consecrating property to the Bishop in Zion, and then receiving an inheritance back, must reasonably show to the Bishop that they need as much as they claim. But in case the two parties cannot come to a mutual agreement . . . The case must be laid before a council of twelve High Priests . . . .

Here may be seen established in the operation of the church the principle of determination of contracts by mutual consent, which can take place only when there is a "balance or equilibrium of power." It was recognized that to give all power to the bishop would make him a virtual dictator with power that could easily be corrupted, a possibility that LDS scriptures (*Doctrine and Covenants*, 121:39) recognized: "We have learned by sad experience that it is the nature and disposition of almost all men, as soon as they get a little authority, as they suppose, they will immediately begin to exercise unrighteous dominion."

On the other hand, men by nature are selfish and, if left to make decisions alone with respect to material things, would not always act for the good of the whole. Under this system the bishop and members were to try in brotherly love to reach an amicable agreement; but if such were not possible, the case was to be laid before a "council of High Priests" acting as a board of arbitration. It was better to be judged by such a church system of jurisprudence than by their enemies.

Political Developments in the Territorial
Period (1847 to 1896)

With the intrusion of the Saints into the desert lands of the Great Salt Lake Basin, a most interesting social, political, and economic experiment was begun. Here was a people united by bonds of religion and persecution, led by Brigham Young, a man they believed to be a prophet of God, the authoritative spokesman for Deity, who wore the "mantle" of their beloved Prophet Joseph Smith. Separated by a thousand miles from their former enemies, they had the possibility of working out their own temporal salvation, and there was no one to challenge their new prophet's leadership. This gave him great secular as well as religious power.

From 1847 to 1858 Brigham Young was to exercise his greatest secular power. He had a vision of a self-governing theocracy, the "State of Deseret," bounded "on the north by the British, the south by the Mexican dominions, and east and west by the Rocky and Cascade Mountains" (J. F. Smith, 1946, p. 476), and controlled through the priesthood of the church. Such a provisional state was actually established in the absence of federal action and governed the people until 1851, at which time Congress created the Territory of Utah with a slate of federally appointed officers, including Brigham Young as governor. Unfortunately a destructive antagonism developed between the Mormons and the non-Mormons, including apostates. Their enemies reported the Mormons to be seditious and Brigham Young the dictator over a duped and enslaved people. They could not conceive of a people almost slavishly following, of their own free will, what seemed to be the dictatorial demands of a leader.

While secular territorial officers were elected, they were largely bishops and stake presidents, giving the church's General Authorities substantial political influence that amounted to secular power. Even the judicial function on the local level was church dominated, Bishop's Courts having been established and functioning in secular affairs prior to the territorial government. Even after territorial courts with appointed, largely Gentile, judges were created, the Saints were admonished to refrain from using them, using Bishop's courts in their stead. Brigham Young, commenting on these Bishop's Courts, said: "There is not a righteous person in this community who will have difficulties that cannot be settled by arbitrators, the Bishop's Courts, the High Council . . . far better than to contend with each other in lawsuits" (Neff, pp. 187–97).

The people's mistrust of Gentile government officials was clearly seen in the attitude of the Latter-day Saints toward their appointed officials, an attitude that is understandable but one which must have also produced a reciprocal antagonism on the part of "outsiders."

Upon an apparently false and unsubstantiated report from some of these appointed federal officials that court records had been destroyed, President Buchanan in 1857 sent an army of 2,500 men to put down the Mormon "rebellion." The Mormons met the "invasion" with bloodless delaying tactics, keeping the troops outside the Territory for the winter, during which time a compromise was effected and a newly appointed Gentile Governor was allowed to enter the Territory peacefully in the spring, followed by the army. From this time official domination of secular government by church leaders was at an end, future power being exercised unofficially and indirectly by moral suasion. However, there was little peace. The unofficial power of church leaders antagonized the appointed Gentile territorial officers, and they in turn acted as if called on a mission to destroy the power of Brigham Young and his successor, John Taylor, as well as the entire church hierarchy. The Mormons claimed, at that point in time, the right to follow the laws of God even when they were in conflict with those of the land, and thus they were accused of sedition. One church leader, upon being sentenced for illegal cohabitation, said (J. F. Smith, 1946, p. 599):

> Your honor, I regret very much that the laws of my country should come into conflict with the laws of God; but whenever they do, I shall invariably choose the latter . . . . The Constitution of the United States expressly says that Congress shall make no law respecting an establishment of religion or prohibiting the free exercise thereof . . . . The law of 1862 and the Edmunds Law were expressly designed to operate against marriage as practiced and believed in by the Latter-day Saints. They are therefore unconstitutional and of course they cannot command the respect that a constitutional law would.

There appear to have been several points of conflict. One was the great secular power (political and economic) still wielded by the church leaders, indirect though it may have been. Another was the peculiar practice of polygamy. The first was objected to by the federal appointees who saw their authority somewhat diminished, as well as by resentful Gentiles and apostates who refused to be governed by a theocracy. The second, polygamy itself, was attacked by religious leaders throughout the country as being barbarian, immoral, and anti-Christian. The government officials used the emotional polygamy issue to help break the secular power of the church. The attack on the church found its way into Congress, where repeated efforts to obtain autonomous statehood were thwarted, where anti-polygamy laws were enacted, and where the rights of citizenship were denied the Saints.

Government persecution and prosecution reached a peak in the 1880s when Mormons were finally disfranchised, church property was escheated (except for houses of worship and cemeteries), the Perpetual Emigration Fund (organized to finance immigration of converts) was dissolved, the church disincorporated, female suffrage abolished, and church leaders driven underground. Federal officers ranged throughout the Territory arresting Mormon male polygamists wherever they could be found.

Finally in 1890, the new church president, Wilford Woodruff, issued a manifesto, sustained by the people at Conference,[2] forbidding the practice of the unique marriage custom, with the understanding that Mormons would also give up their separate political People's Party. Finally, in 1896, Utah was allowed to enter the union as a state. While these actions did not end hostilities between Mormon and Gentile, they marked the beginning of more amicable relations, making such eventually possible.

Economic Development during the Territorial Period[3]

The first decade of pioneer existence was one of fulfilling Brigham Young's vision of a great empire through the orderly and systematic colonization of more than 150 settlements, from Fort Limhi on the Salmon River in Idaho to San Bernardino in California, and from Carson Valley at the eastern base of the Sierra Nevadas to the Green River in southwestern Wyoming. It also involved the formation and rationalization of economic institutions. The efforts were temporarily halted with the "war" of 1857–58, and many of the outposts were drawn back.

---

[2]The church almost from its inception has held semiannual "General Conferences" to which the church membership has been invited for instruction, inspiration, and church business.

[3]The best sources in the subject matter covered in this section are the numerous publications of Leonard J. Arrington, the present church historian, many of which were written before he assumed that position (see "references" at end of chapter).

The colonization took place through "calls" generally issued by the church leaders in the church's *Deseret News* or at General Conferences. The popular literature of the day and later periods maintained that a secret police forced the people to accept their "calls," but fear could not have been responsible for the herculean efforts of these people. Their response, while not perfect, was so good that only love for and faith in their leaders, the church, and the Gospel could have induced them to respond to these "calls."

With the end of the Civil War, Mormon colonization throughout the West proceeded again, eventually moving into Canada and Mexico. It was made necessary and possible by the aggressive worldwide missionary program, converting people not only to the Gospel but to the need to "gather to Zion," then considered Utah and the surrounding states and territories, to "build up the Kingdom." The Perpetual Emigration Fund helped finance the immigration of thousands of converts, largely from the working classes of Europe, dissatisfied and discontented with their economic and social conditions as well as with religious restrictions found in most countries.

While the geography of the new Zion was forbidding, it was an area that no one else particularly wanted in the early years; it could and would be made to "blossom as the rose" under the hands of the Children of God, preparing a perfected kingdom — to be delivered to the "Savior at His Second Coming." But to do so they would have to be independent of the world — Babylon. Each family would have to be as self-sufficient as possible, as would each community and the Mormon commonwealth itself, through cooperative efforts. In a message exhorting the people to economic independence, Brigham Young urged (Neff, 1940, p. 278):

> Produce what you consume; draw from the native elements the necessities of life; permit no vitiated taste to lead you into indulgence of expensive luxuries which can only be obtained by involving yourself in debt; let home industry produce every article of home consumption.

Home industry became a theme of the Saints and was to remain such long after the railroads crossed the Territory. In fact, strong elements of the principle persist in the church today, both in the Church Welfare Program as well as in the homes of members in which sewing, canning, and home storage are a part of the everyday personal life of a large proportion of modern Latter-day Saints. While reliance was largely on self and the Mormon society, some government assistance was sought from the territorial and federal governments.

By 1860, the Saints had had both successes and failures in their attempts to implement the home industry practices of the church. Express mail, carrying companies, grain mills, and sawmills had been successfully established. Homespun woolens were the usual fare until the 1860s when a pioneer woolen mill was successfully established. The tanning industry made a strong but eventually abortive effort to survive. Agriculture was firmly established. The story was not the same for iron and sugar. It was some years before these were successfully produced, but eventually they became major Utah industries.

The field of commerce was neglected in the early years. To church leaders, with an attitude reminiscent of the Catholic fathers of the Middle Ages, it seemed immoral that a middleman should be able to take advantage of the laws of supply and demand in the reaping of "excessive" profits. Such was continually preached against. The result was that early commerce was largely dominated by Gentiles and apostates who became increasingly evident and powerful after the coming of the railroad in 1869. Eventually, however, the church, through the cooperative movement, did enter the field. It also participated in the establishment of several financial institutions. Once this happened, church members could enter business with clear consciences.

Precious-metal mining was frowned upon by the church in the early years. There was fear that the search for silver and gold would lure men away from the search for truth and that church members might become subject to the gross immorality usually associated with such mining camps. It was not until the 1880s with the discovery of silver by Mormon "Uncle" Jesse Knight (as the result of personal revelation) that such activity found any degree of acceptability.

While the Saints were discouraged from such mining, there were no restrictions on making profits from the sale of agricultural surpluses to the mining camps and the teamstering that resulted. In fact in the 1860s and '70s Utah became the granary of the intermountain mining country, including eastern Nevada, Idaho, Montana, Colorado, and Utah.

When the economic laws of supply and demand operated to produce high prices, church leaders became concerned. Mormon farmers, because of the highly competitive nature of agriculture keeping agricultural prices down, especially at harvest time, were not able to enjoy fully the fruits of price inflation, while the less competitive, largely Gentile commercial houses and transportation agencies were able to do so. In the 1860s prices began to soar, and church leaders called a series of price conventions in which the Saints agreed upon observing a list of accepted prices. These attempts were followed by the church's creation of the Utah

Produce Company, a type of producers' cooperative, buying up all produce at "fair" prices and handling the resale, the benefits accruing to the producers.

In the early pioneer years, property rights were not looked upon as absolute. Theologically, the earth was the Lord's; man was only a steward. The church, as the official spokesman of God, was presumed to have directing power over the distribution and use of the land. Aside from the short period in which attempts were made to establish the Law of Consecration and the later, more extended but short-lived efforts to establish the United Orders, the Saints retained possession of their property, but it was expected that they should be controlled in its use. Land settlement was under the direction of the Church. In 1847 Brigham Young set the policy: "No man should buy or sell land, every man should have his land measured off to him for city and farming purposes, what he could till. He might till as he pleased, but he should be industrious and take care of it" (Arrington, May 1951, pp. 339–52). In several instances property was taken away from people who were not using it or not properly using it. The water and timber were considered community property, as were mineral deposits and grazing lands. Property rights were further restricted in the regulation of business income, with a committee appointed at one time to "regulate the price of grinding and all things worthy of note" (Arrington, May 1951, pp. 339–52).

Aside from the basically Gentile domination of commerce and teamstering, the Saints were the controlling economic force in the Territory until the coming of the railroads in 1869. That industry was, in itself, an important one, but it also made mining profitable. By 1871 some 32 mining districts had been formed in Utah Territory. With mining came the smeltering and refining industries. The great bulk of miners, railroad workers, and refinery and smelter workers were imported Gentiles. Likewise, capital requirements were met by importation of Gentile monied interests. The Saints feared these intrusions, seeing another Ohio, Missouri, or Illinois. These fears were not unfounded, for strong efforts were made to destroy Mormon religious, political, social, and economic power.

The cooperative and the United Order movements, beginning in 1869 and continuing into the 1880s, were attempts to consolidate Mormon economic power, to increase self-sufficiency, and to reduce reliance on outsiders. When John Taylor, third president of the church, established the Zion's Board of Trade in 1878 (Arrington, Winter 1950–51, p. 20), its purposes were to:

(1) Assist members in buying cheap and selling dear in external trade

(2) Assist home industry

(3) Help to prevent hurtful competition

(4) Help to keep supply in closer balance with demand

(5) Help to increase demand when supply was in excess

(6) Assist in minimizing middleman functions

(7) Assist in the speedy resolution of business disputes

(8) Help to develop adequate transportation

(9) Foster capital and protect labor, uniting them as friends

(10) Stimulate manufacturing

(11) Assemble and disseminate essential economic data

(12) Teach that the "watchword will be 'organization'; 'Union is strength, division [is] weakness' "

The antipolygamy crusades of the 1880s eventually brought the demise of these boards and the cooperative system. By statehood in 1896, Utah was well on its way to becoming as capitalistic as any other state or territory.

Historical Implications for Labor

From the unique Mormon history may be drawn the following points which would affect the relationship of the church and the development of labor unions in Utah:

(1) There was great reliance of the faithful church members on the leadership of church authorities in secular as well as strictly religious affairs. As church members faced unionizing efforts, the question facing them was how much weight they should give to what they considered to be secular, sometimes anti-union, sentiment of church leaders and publications.

(2) While the church had a strongly authoritarian structure, there were democratic checks giving some opportunity to church members to influence official attitudes. Strongly anti-union sen-

timent, especially that not strongly founded in gospel principles, could be moderated somewhat by LDS union members who remained faithful to the church.

(3) The principle of arbitration of disputes by councils of church leaders, starting at the local level, was established early in church and Utah history. Union members in the church were not unaware of the possibility of this principle being used in adjusting industrial disputes.

(4) The Latter-day Saints historically had had unhappy experience with what could happen when mob psychology took over groups of people. Union action which involved appeals to mob psychology, such as mass picketing, would be suspect to church members.

(5) There developed early a mistrust of Gentiles and apostates. Both were frequently found to be seeking the destruction of "the kingdom." This same fear would tend to be carried over to outside union leaders and unions led by apostates.

(6) The philosophical and geographical isolation of the Saints gave the opportunity to develop a uniqueness in attitude toward union affairs as well as other secular activities.

(7) The importance of cooperation and its success in overcoming the problems the Latter-day Saints historically had faced would predispose them to rely on cooperation in resolving problems in the workshop. Union efforts at cooperation would find a fruitful field among Latter-day Saints.

(8) The church had used its religious power secularly since its inception. While this use had created problems, it probably resolved more problems. It was to be expected that the church would continue to exercise its secular influence when it felt it necessary to preserve the kingdom. This applied to unions as well as other secular institutions.

(9) The Saints had been strongly admonished to avoid physical conflict, to resolve problems peacefully. Resistance against U.S. troops in 1858 and what was considered unconstitutional action by federal officials in breaking the secular power of the

church in the late 1800s amounted to passive resistance in the form of civil disobedience, a technique made famous in more modern times by Mohandas K. Gandhi in India and Martin Luther King, Jr., in the southern United States. Passive resistance by workers to unrighteous domination of employers would be preferable to armed or physical conflict. Unfortunately, passive resistance and civil disobedience could sometimes break into violence when the established powers chose to force the issue.

(10) The Saints had historically relied upon divine revelation and inspiration for guidance in secular pursuits, each member being entitled to such. Mormon businessmen often based business decisions on personal revelation or inspiration. Inspiration which might guide workers to form or join unions, or which might guide LDS union leaders, would be less known.

(11) There were mixed feelings toward government. The Saints were told that they should obey the law and that governments were instituted of God, and yet their experience with government action limiting their freedom of religion and used in attempts to destroy or weaken their political and economic power made them somewhat wary of government, especially federal officials.

(12) The principle of contract by mutual consent, with both parties having somewhat equal power, gave precedence to the establishment of collective bargaining to deal with industrial conflict.

(13) There had been a history of philosophical, and at times institutionalized, egalitarianism which would redistribute income, taking it from the rich and giving it to the poor. While the role of government in achieving such was questioned, nongovernmental action would be much more acceptable, if it was accomplished by acceptable means. This of course was one of the roles or attempts of unions: to produce a more equitable distribution of wealth.

(14) The fact was the church itself, through its own commercial establishments, and church leaders, who were either involved in church business operations or were businessmen on their own account, gave them the pyschology of employers. As such, they were bound to come into conflict with their employees over differences of opinion dealing with working conditions and terms of employment. The extension of democracy into the workplace was likely to increase the possibility of such conflicts. Unions representing or attempting to represent these workers would therefore come into conflict with church leaders on questions involving the workplace. Church leaders, who were accustomed to being looked upon as authoritative, would tend to see this conflict as symptomatic of rebellion against their "duly constituted" authority, exacerbating the conflict.

References

Arrington, Leonard J. *Great Basin Kingdom*. Cambridge, Massachusetts: Harvard University Press. 1958.

————. "Property among the Mormons." *Rural Society* (May 1951).

————. "Zion's Board of Trade: A Third United Order." *Western Humanities Review* (Winter 1950–51), vol. 5, no. 1.

Bancroft, H. H. *History of Utah*. San Francisco: The History Company. 1890.

Doctrine and Covenants. 121:39. Salt Lake City: Church of Jesus Christ of Latter-day Saints. Numerous editions.

Neff, Andrew Love. *History of Utah, 1847–1869*. Salt Lake City: Deseret News Press. 1940.

Roberts, B. H. *A Comprehensive History of the Church of Jesus Christ of Latter-day Saints*. Salt Lake City: Deseret News Press. 1930.

Smith, Joseph. *History of the Church*. Six volumes. Salt Lake City: Church of Jesus Christ of Latter-day Saints. Several editions.

Smith, Joseph Fielding. *Essentials in Church History*. Salt Lake City: Deseret Book Company. 1946.

3

Deseret's Pioneer Mormon Guilds 1846 to 1874

Lloyd G. Reynolds in his popular *Labor Economics and Labor Relations* (1954), in discussing the development of unions, avers that unionism, contrary to some beliefs, did not first develop among the exploited or the industrial workers but among the "skilled and prosperous workers" (p. 43). The Utah experience in some measure points to the validity of this conclusion as well as to an evolution from guilds — in which masters, journeymen, and apprentices most likely associated — into unions of journeymen and apprentices. It serves as an interesting case history in the development of unionism within a geographical area, although assuredly in a unique one.

The Mormon Pioneers

The Mormon pioneers were a peculiar people, engaged in an unusual experiment. They were a religiously motivated people, tried and tested by persecution and mobbings, with almost an absolute faith in the leadership of Brigham Young and other leaders of the Church of Jesus Christ of Latter-day Saints; a people who, when called to leave family and home, would travel to the ends of the earth as missionaries, as colonizers, or as gold miners; a people "called" to make the "desert blossom as the rose," to establish a "commonwealth," perfecting it for

31

delivery into the hands of Deity; and a "royal priesthood" composed of almost all of the adult male members of the church.

The pioneers of the first few years of Utah's history were an agrarian people with a sprinkling of professionals, merchants, and craftsmen. In 1850 there were just fourteen manufacturing establishments employing 51 people, from a population of eleven thousand. In that same year there were 3,125 gainfully employed persons over fifteen years of age. Of this number, 1,649 were in agriculture, while there were 828 persons engaged in commerce, trade, manufactures, mechanic arts, and mining. Twenty-six residents listed themselves in the professions, and 620 indicated other types of employment. The heritage of the first pioneers was mostly from industrialized New England and other northern states, although there were some Southerners and a few of foreign birth, with increasing numbers from highly industrialized England and, later, agricultural Scandinavia. Literacy was high; the figure for the 1850 census was 99.75 percent. Utah was near California and Oregon in its level of wages and the cost of living (Neff, 1940, pp. 116–17).

The Guild Inheritance from Nauvoo

The first pioneers brought with them from Nauvoo not only a strong religious faith but also some experience with budding unionism. A number of craft guilds — the tailors, smiths, boot and harness makers, coopers, wagon makers (Halford, 1945–46, p. 41), printers,[1] and actors (Maughan, 1949, p. 27) — had previously been established in Nauvoo, from whence the Mormon pioneers had been driven. Flanders (1964, p. 167) reports that a guild of boot- and shoemakers was established in Nauvoo in 1843. However, the guild was not well received by many of the residents who feared that it was established to create a monopoly in shoemaking, forcing prices higher. The shoemakers guild replied in the *Nauvoo Neighbor* that its members were attempting to bring the high prices down, so that foot wear made in Nauvoo could compete with eastern factories, through the establishment of a producers cooperative with increased buying power in the purchase of raw materials. The boot- and shoemakers were willing to barter and hoped to bring employment to two hundred of their craft. Their dedication to union is shown in the following Glasgow spinners' lyrics that "the working man's only protection . . . is Union . . . / Union walls are high and grand / Union walls

---

[1] Diary of Charles Lambert, Church Historian's Office, Salt Lake City, Utah.

are nobly manned / Union walls are made to stand / against the strongest Foe."

The next year the members of the 18th Ward[2] in Nauvoo established a spinners and consumers cooperative. Joseph Smith, the leader of the Mormons, reported that the cooperative was a good idea and would be the source of employment for mechanics as well as consumer items at a low cost (Flanders, 1964, p. 167).

The Deseret Dramatic Association

On February 20, 1852, just four and a half years after the pioneers first arrived in the Salt Lake Valley, a group of Saints met at the home of William Clayton (M),[3] at the request of Brigham Young, to form an association to promote theater in Salt Lake City (Maughan, 1949, p. 27). (Biographical accounts of several pioneers refer to some organizations of theater workers as early as 1850.) While the association may not have been intended to become a union, and indeed may never have actually become such, it did lead the way, becoming the precursor of such organizations as the Actors Guild, the Stage Employees Union, and the Musicians Union.

William Pitt (M), a musician, was the temporary chairman, with A. M. Musser (M) as secretary, and with the following charter members, all of them Mormons (Maughan, p. 27):

R. T. Burton	J. F. Hutchinson
R. L. Campbell	Edward Martin
H. B. Clawson	James Smithies
William Clayton	H. K. Whitney
James Ferguson	O. K. Whitney
William Glover	

Of this group, Horace K. Whitney and Jacob F. Hutchinson were also charter members of the Deseret Typographical Association organized on

[2]In the Church of Jesus Christ of Latter-day Saints, each congregation is drawn from a specific geographical area known as a "ward." In Salt Lake City and other towns and cities, there are enough members — three hundred to a thousand — for a ward every few blocks. In areas with scattered Mormon population, a ward may encompass hundreds of square miles.

[3]Throughout the remainder of this book, names of persons associated with worker associations and unions will be designated as: (M), a Mormon; (N), a non-Mormon; or (U), religion unknown. Designation is made from an examination of genealogical records, obituaries, and church census records.

January 13, 1855. Robert L.Campbell also was associated with both the typographers in 1855 and the schoolteachers in the 1860s and '70s. In addition, Edward Martin was the leader of the painters and glaziers in the July 4, 1861, parade. Thus at least four of the organizers of this association were involved in other pioneer efforts at developing guilds and unions. In addition, many became active in the church's economic experiments of the 1870s.

On March 2, 1855, the name the "Deseret Dramatic Association" was adopted, and while a committee was appointed to draw up bylaws, such were later deemed unneeded. James Bond (M), H. P. Richards (M), and Francis Fletcher (M) were added as members (Maughan, p. 27). Bond had played a key role in the fledgling printers association in 1853, delivering an address to that association at its annual picnic.

The first recorded concerted action of the Deseret Dramatic Association, aside from staging productions, was the petitioning for the use of the LDS Tabernacle for performances, the old "Bowery" being considered inadequate. When the request was turned down, Brigham Young met with the group on March 15, 1852, for preliminary discussions on the construction of an amusement hall. T. O. Angell, an architect, was appointed to draw the plans. The Social Hall was the eventual result of this and subsequent conferences, a much finer facility than the association had planned (Maughan, pp. 29, 30).

Membership in the association grew. On March 9, thirteen members were added; by early summer there were 28 new members, including George D. Watt (M) who was also to play a significant role in the Deseret Typographical Association in 1855 and 1856. By January 7, 1853, the membership had increased to 83 persons, and several rules concerning members had been adopted: Names of proposed new members had to be presented a week in advance; no member of the association was to participate in a performing activity outside the association without its consent (Maughan, p. 31); an earlier rule of 1852 forbade any performance "under the influence of intoxicating drinks" (p. 32) — members were to be suspended for violating this rule; fines were imposed for violation of the rules and regulations such as unexcused absences, improper appearance or conduct, need for undue prompting, unnecessary conversation or noise behind scenes, and loss or mutilation of books or parts (*Journal History*, July 19, 1852).[4]

----

[4]The *Journal History* is mostly a collection of newspaper articles and diaries maintained by the Church Historian's Office, Salt Lake City.

In 1855, the following were the officers of the association, once again, all members of the church (Maughan, pp. 40, 41):

Office	Name
President	James W. Cummings
Secretary	Asa Calkin
Treasurer	H. B. Clawson
Stage manager	Leo Hawkins
Critic	John Lyon
Doorkeeper	William C. Staines
Costumer	Claude Clive
Hairdresser	William Hennefer
Scene shifter	William Derr

Of this group of nine leaders, at least three were to be associated with other guild or union organizations: John Lyon of the typographers, Claude Clive of the tailors, and William Derr of the comb makers. Of the 22 performing members, at least three were associated with the typographers: James Ferguson (M), Horace K. Whitney (M), and Henry Maiben (M) (Maughan, pp. 33, 34).

On February 18, 1856, the following officers were named, none of which appear to have been otherwise associated in guild organizations, although Clawson, a son-in-law of Brigham Young, was to become a leader in the cooperative movement, heading the church's ZCMI (Maughan, p. 34) — all were Mormons:

Office	Name
President	J. W. Cummings
Treasurer	H. B. Clawson
Stage manager	David Candland
Secretary	T. W. Ellerbeck

Of the additional members (Maughan, p. 34), at least seven were associated with later guilds and unions. In addition to Hutchinson, Whitney, Derr, Maiben, Clive, and Lyon (already mentioned), was added David McKenzie (M), who was the leader of the engravers in the 1861 Fourth of July parade. All of these guild leaders have been identified as church members.

The association evidently went into decline in 1855--56, possibly due to the economic recession of those years (Maughan, p. 35). It also had no recorded activity in 1859 and 1860. On March 9, 1861, a meeting was held in Brigham Young's office to reconstitute the association and to get his "mind on the reorganization" (p. 47). That year marked the end of performances at Social Hall as well as a significant change in the operations of the association, and on July 1, 1861, construction was begun on the Salt Lake Theatre under the direction of Brigham Young.

A salary system was apparently established as the result of a meeting on April 30, 1864, near the height of the Civil War inflation. This is the first recorded labor dispute in Utah history. Association members were in the unpaid employ of Brigham Young, who conducted the meeting at which several members indicated financial problems, requiring pay for services or they would have to leave (Maughan, p. 52). Annie Adams Kiskadden (M), mother of the famous frontier actress Maude Adams, later reported about the meeting (pp. 119–21):

> Traveling stars and companies received salaries. The orchestra, after much muttering, decided they should receive a salary. They put it up to the managers, who put it up to Brigham Young. . . . Brigham spoke and said we were only doing our share for the uplift of the community, as were elders and missionaries . . . [except that] our work, he said, was being done at home. We were asked to state our demands individually, but there was a deep silence. No one made demands on Brigham Young. . . . The chief agitators were silent. . . . Finally, David Evans in the orchestra, and a shoemaker by trade, pulled his crippled frame up on crutches and hit out straight from the shoulder. He said we were all forced to earn our daily bread outside the theatre and yet were giving half our lives to it. He told Brigham that the theatre was making oodles of money and he could not see why the entertainers should not share in the profits. . . . [T]he intimation was plain. It was "no pay, no work." Brigham tried every means and every plan to settle the matter without putting the home-talent players on salary, but none of the plans suited the actors and grumbling grew louder, with the final result that a salary list was drawn up. No one could say that the salaries were magnificently large, but it comforted us to know that we were worth something.

Henry McEwan (M), who played a key role in the Deseret Typographical Association and who was the first president of Deseret Typographical Union Local 115 in 1868, was a member of the Deseret

Dramatic Association in the 1860s. Also active in both associations was John B. Kelly (M) (Maughan, pp. 122–23).

While the confrontation with Brigham Young (often referred to as the "Lion of the Lord") in 1864 must not have been too pleasant, he still maintained a personal warm relationship with the Salt Lake Theatre company. He sponsored a ball for the association on April 28, 1865, and invited its members, the orchestra, and others connected with the theater to his home for a supper on July 4, 1866 (Maughan, p. 125).

The association, so far as is presently known, died away between 1869 and 1874. If it lasted as long as 1874, it was probably the victim of the depression then in progress, as were many other unions and worker organizations throughout the Territory and country. It also may have been a victim of "Retrenchment" and the new economic experiment of Brigham Young, the United Order movement, beginning in 1874.

The Deseret Typographers

The first known permanent craft guild in Utah, and the first known one to evolve into a full-fledged labor union, was established at least by February 24, 1852, when Brigham Young attended and opened the first annual printers' festival with prayer (*Journal History*, February 24, 1852). This was the same year the National Typographical Union, America's first permanent national union, was formed. Apparently the Printers Guild was the successor to a similar organization of printers in Nauvoo. It was a unique craft guild, motivated at its outset more strongly by religious ideals than by economic goals. But considering the reform of much of the worker movement previous to and contemporary with that period, it was not quite so strange as it might seem today. Nevertheless, it was undoubtedly the only guild in the world to open its meeting with the song "Come All Ye Sons of Zion."

Annual festivals were held in 1853 and 1854, both of them having strong religious overtones, typified through nonalcoholic toasts to various features unique to Mormondom such as the "First Presidency," to economic progress with "Deseret Manufacturers," and to the trade or occupation, "The Printers of Utah" (*Journal History*, January 22, 1853, and March 16, 1854).

On January 13, 1855, the more formalized Typographical Association of Deseret was organized. To be a member of this association, one must also have been a member of the church in good standing; association members could be expelled for immoral conduct — after an impartial trial and a two-thirds vote. Involved in the association were such prominent men as George Q. Cannon (M), later a member of the First Presidency of the church; William W. Phelps (M), famed Mormon printer and poet; Horace K. Whitney (M), prominent LDS musician; and Phineas H. Young (M), Brigham Young's brother and a church leader in his own right. Phineas Young became the first president of the association (*Journal History*, January 13, 1855). Other General Authorities played roles in or with the association over the next few years — Ezra Taft Benson, Jedediah M. Grant, Erastus Snow, Albert Carrington, Orson Pratt, Amasa Lyman, and Wilford Woodruff. In 1856, the requirement of church membership was evidently dropped, and the name was changed to the Deseret Typographical and Press Association (*Journal History*, October 4, 1853, November 1, 1855, and February 8, 1856).

In 1861, the Deseret Typographical Association marched in the Fourth of July parade in Salt Lake City, with Henry McEwan (M) in the lead, and with a scroll inscription "The Printers of Deseret" (*Deseret News*, July 4, 1861). In 1868, the Deseret Typographical Association Local 115 was chartered by the National Typographical Association, America's first permanent national union. Henry McEwan was the president of the local. Of the ten charter members and initial officers of the local,[5] at least eight were "endowed" members of the church — two not having been identified as to church affiliation. ("Endowed" members of the church are those who at the time of this special ordinance are living in accordance with certain standards of personal conduct. While the precise application may vary slightly over the years, at present generally the individuals must be living in accordance with the health law of the church [the Word of Wisdom], are making their appropriate financial contributions [a tithe of gross income], are morally clean [free from adultery and fornication], and support the leadership of the church as "prophets of God." Their local bishop interviews them and issues a "recommend,"[6] and the regional leader [stake[7] president] countersigns after an interview.)

This group of ten association members, eight of whom are known to have been Mormons, was not so illustrious — in terms of church prominence, at least — as the charter members of the association, none of them ever rising to the ranks of the General Authorities, and possibly none even becoming bishops or stake presidents.

---

[5]Charter, Deseret Typographical Union Local 115 (copy in author's files).

[6]A "recommend" is a written certification that the church member conforms to the standards listed above.

[7]In the Church of Jesus Christ of Latter-day Saints, a "stake" is made up of several "wards."

In 1871 the local sponsored a strike against the Salt Lake *Tribune* for firing two members of the local, the first known formal strike in Utah's history (Salt Lake *Tribune*, November 7, 1871, p. 3). In 1872, the local sent a delegate, endowed Mormon Robert Gibson Sleater, to the national convention of the International Typographical Union, into which the national union had evolved. He was elected a national vice president and was to rise to prominence within the International Typographical Union, the Utah union movement, and even the American Federation of Labor. (The details of this will be expanded upon in chapter 8.)

The Principle of Arbitration

Early in the history of Utah and the church, it was recognized that disputes would arise between workers and their employers and that some means of peaceful solution was essential. In 1852, the legislative assembly established a system whereby the mechanics of each county would elect twelve "Select men as Referees" to resolve disputes brought to them by mutual consent. While the decision of the arbitration board was to be final, it was not intended to take the place of the judicial power of the Territory (Neff, 1940, p. 195). Unfortunately history has not yet recorded the experience under this territorial act. It may well have lapsed into disuse with the political turmoil of the ensuing years.

However, while the Territory of Utah established an arbitration system by law, the church system of arbitration functioned independently and concurrently, and actually antedated the secular system, finding its roots earlier in the ecclesiastical operations of the church. A favorable non-Mormon treatment of this system was given in 1886 by D. D. Lum, an apologist for the Knights of Labor. According to Lum, the church organization set up in 1834 to handle disputes among church members was essentially a system of arbitration, with various levels of appeal. Should a dispute arise, the church members, by mutual consent, would take their dispute to the "home teachers" (consisting of two male holders of the "priesthood" who were assigned to visit several homes in a ward or basic ecclesiastical unit for the purpose of strengthening the church membership of the family unit; the same system prevails in modern times). Appeal could then be made to the bishop and his counselors. The next step was an appeal to the stake high council and stake presidency, a council composed of about fifteen men. Final appeal could be made to the First Presidency (top leadership) of the church (Lum, 1886, pp. 24–33).

Other Organizations by Crafts or Trades

The unique mutual interests of workers other than the typographers and theater employees were recognized rather early. At the Fourth of July parade of 1861, groups of workers participated by marching according to their trades (*Journal History*, July 5, 1861). Fortunately for the labor historian, the event was recorded in some detail by the *Deseret News*. The parade had three interwoven and recurring themes. First, there were strong religious overtones with such banners as: "Zion's Bulwark" (Youth), "Mothers in Israel, teach us how to be great," "purity bringeth peace," "Virtue adorns Zion," "Kingdom of God or nothing," "In God is our trust," and so forth. The second general theme was patriotic, with such slogans or signs as "Columbia," "Utah, the Nation's Hope," "Liberty, union and virtue," "Good for the Constitution," and with platoons of soldiers, sailors, cadets, and midshipmen, as well as a group of typographers, singing patriotic songs. The third general theme was economic, with the marching of workmen, organized by craft or trade, each led by a prominent member of that trade. The craft workers carried banners, most of which were of religious, patriotic, or economic implications. These groups were:[8]

Trade	*Leader*	
Agriculturists	Reuben Miller	(M)
	Jacob Miller	(M)
	John Scott	(M)
Artists	William V. Morris	(M)
Bakers and confectioners	William L. Binder	(M)
Basket makers	Daniel Cammomile	(M)
Blacksmiths	Jonathan Pugmire	(M)
Bookbinders and paper rulers	J. B. Kelly	(M)
Boot- and shoemakers	Edward Snelgrove	(M)
Bridge builders	Henry Groo (Grow)	(M)
Broom makers	Moses Wade	(M)
Butchers	Charles B. Taylor	(M)
Cabinetmakers, carvers, turners, and upholsterers	William Bell	(M)

---

[8]Alternative spellings found during research are added in parentheses.

Trade	Leader	
Carpenters and joiners	Miles Romney	(M)
Chemists	A. C. Pyper	(M)
Civil engineers	General J. W. Fox	(M)
Coopers	Abel Lamb	(M)
Comb makers	William Derr	(M)
Deseret School Teachers Association	(No leader mentioned)	
Dyers	John Evans	(M)
Edge toolmakers	Robert Dart	(U)
Engravers	David McKenzie	(M)
Foundrymen	Z. Derrick	(M)
Gun- and locksmiths	James Hague	(M)
Hairdressers	John Squires	(M)
Hatters	Lyman Leonard	(M)
Horticulturists	E. Sawyers	(M)
Jewelers	Charles Kidgell	(N)
Lumbermen and sawyers	Edmund Ellsworth	(M)
Masons, plasterers, brick and adobe makers	J. H. Rumell	(M)
Match makers	Alexander Neibaur	(M)
Millers	John Neff	(M)
Millwrights	F. Kesler	(M)
Painters and glaziers	Edward Martin	(M)
Paper makers	T. Howard	(M)
Potters	John Eardly	(M)
Quarrymen	Adam Sharp	(M)
Rope makers	William A. McMaster	(M)
Saddle and harness makers	Francis Platt	(M)
Silversmiths	John Rodgers	(N) (Later, M)
Stock raisers	B. Stringham	(M)
Stonecutters	Charles Lambert	(M)
Tailors	Claude Clive	(M)

Trade	Leader	
Tanners and curriers	James Robson	(M)
Tin- and coppersmiths	Dustin Amy	(M)
Tobacco manufacturers	Benjamin Hampton	(M)
Typographical association	Henry McEwan	(M)
Watch and clock makers	O. Ursenbach	(M)
Weavers	Thomas Lyon	(M)
Wheelwrights	Samuel Bringhurst	(M)
Whitesmiths	(No leader mentioned)	
Wool carders	Theodore Curtis	(M)

At least twenty of these trades had organized into unions across the nation by 1860, many of these in the decade of the 1850s: foundrymen, gun- and locksmiths, wheelwrights, cabinet makers and carvers, stonecutters, masons and plasterers, tanners and curriers, saddle and harness makers, weavers, tailors, hatters, bakers and confectioners, butchers, comb makers, basket makers, tobacco manufacturers, silversmiths, quarrymen, typographers, and bookbinders. Most of the others were to organize into unions within two decades. As already stated, a number of these crafts had previously been organized in Nauvoo — tailors, smiths, boot- and shoemakers, saddle and harness makers, coopers, wagon makers, actors, and printers, as well as spinners, indicating a substantial period of craft organization for some. Three of the leaders, Martin, Clive, and Derr, had been associated in the dramatic association, and two, McEwan and Kelly, were in the typographical association. A substantial number of men involved with the various guilds are known to have also become involved in the church's United Orders in the mid-1870s (all were Mormons):

Trade	Leader
Bakers and confectioners	William L. Binder
Boot- and shoemakers	Edward Snelgrove
Bridge builders	Henry Groo (Grow)
Chemists	A. C. Pyper
Engravers	David McKenzie
Horticulturists	Reuben Miller
Millwrights	F. Kesler
Rope makers	William A. McMaster

Trade	Leader
Saddle and harness makers	Francis Platt
Stonecutters	Charles Lambert
Theater workers	H. B. Clawson
	J. W. Ellerbeck
	A. M. Musser
	William C. Staines
Typographers	George Q. Cannon
	Albert Carrington
	John B. Kelly
	George A. Smith
	Erastus Snow
	Daniel H. Wells
	Wilford Woodruff
	Brigham Young

Several of the tradesmen carried banners, which would seem to be even stronger evidence that formal organization was approaching unionization — if not already achieved.

The printers or typographical association carried a banner proclaiming "Printers of Deseret." While this appellation may not be too conclusive of union organization, the fact that it was led by a former Scotsman, Henry McEwan (M), who was to be a charter member and the first president of the Deseret Typographical Association Local 115 in 1868, indicates some movement in that direction. In addition, his father had been active in a workers' Mutual Benefit Association in Great Britain.

The blacksmiths, led by Jonathan Pugmire (M), formerly of Carlisle, England, marched under the banner: "The Sons of Vulcan." The United Sons of Vulcan, a national union, was organized as a local in a Pittsburg iron mill in 1858 and adopted a constitution and bylaws in 1861. A more general constitution was adopted in 1862. It would appear that the Utah Territory may have been a leader in the organization of this craft.

The tin- and coppersmiths, led by Dustin Amy (M), carried a banner: "True to the Constitution and Union." Whether the word "union" referred to the union of states or to labor unions is not known, but the smith trades were among the earlier trade unions nationally, and among the earlier known unions of Utah.

The carpenters and joiners broadcast a typical union slogan: "Union is Strength." The inclusion of the two trades — carpenters and joiners — is indicative of at least a philosophical association with the Amalgamated Carpenters and Joiners, an English-based union formally established about 1860 but not coming to the United States for another decade. It is interesting to note that the leader of the Mormon guild, Miles Romney (M), formerly of Dalton, England, had recently returned from an LDS mission to England. Just as capital goods and the idea of cooperatives were brought home by returning missionaries, it is possible that a "union" was also imported. Romney's son, Miles Park Romney (M), was to become the leader of the Builders Union in St. George, Utah, in the next decade.

The coopers, led by Abel Lamb (M), formerly of Rowe, Massachusetts, claimed that "United in These Bands We Stand." This trade had been organized round the country since the early 1800s. The painters and glaziers, led by Edward Martin (M), formerly of Preston, England, had emblazoned "United Painters," a common terminology within the labor movement.

The boot- and shoemakers, led by Edward Snelgrove (M), formerly of St. Mary's, England, had two banners indicating a strong group cohesiveness and possible union organization. One banner read "May the True Sons of St. Crispin ever feel an interest in the *soles* of all mankind" (italics mine). A local union, called the Knights of St. Crispin, was organized in Milford, Massachusetts, in 1864, being credited as the first local of this national union, with the first lodge established in 1867 in Milwaukee. At least the idea if not the actual organization in Utah seems to antedate that of the rest of the country. The use of the adjective "true" may have been an attempt to differentiate the Utah shoemakers from those elsewhere. Snelgrove was to become a leader in the United Order of Boot and Shoemakers in 1874.

At least one of the leaders, Charles Lambert (M), the leader of the stonecutters and a convert from England, had had union experience in England, having been a member of a "Mechanics Institute" and an "Operative Society" in his native land. He had also participated in at least one strike.[9] Lambert was a director of the 7th Ward United Order in 1874.

Of the fifty listed trades leaders in this parade, at least 47 were members of the church. Of the remaining three, at least one joined the

[9]Diary of Charles Lambert, Church Historian's Office, Salt Lake City.

church three years later. A substantial number of these were endowed members, and most of the others soon were. All of the individual leaders discussed above were Latter-day Saints.

In the Provo 24th of July[10] parade of 1863 (*Journal History*, July 24, 1863), the following trades were represented:

Trade	Name	
Carpenters, joiners, and millwrights	Thomas Allman	(M)
Machinists and blacksmiths	George Brown	(M)
Tanners, curriers, and shoemakers	Samuel Clark	(M)

Two McEwans, related to Henry McEwan who had marched at the head of the typographers in the 1861 Fourth of July parade in Salt Lake City, were also prominent in connection with the Provo parade: Joseph (M) who led a group of 24 young men, and John (M) who was the reporter. Joseph was to become associated with the typographers.

Workers were organized again according to guilds or trade associations, if not yet unions, in the Salt Lake Fourth of July parade of 1865 (*Deseret News*, July 5, 1865). While the leaders were not listed, the crafts were enumerated:

> ... embracing representatives of the Trade, Professions, Societies, Associations, etc., of our city ... bearing beautiful banners with appropriate mottos, and carrying characteristics of their vocations. ... Among many things worthy of note we were pleased to see the Agriculturists and Horticulturists ... the Blacksmiths hard at work. ... The Carders, Spinners and Weavers were graced with the presence of several young ladies from President Young's Cotton Factory. ... The Gun and Locksmiths and the Carriage-Makers bore some evidence of their handy work; the Butchers were busy wielding a cleaver. ... The Telegraphic School ... the Deseret Dramatic Association, the Deseret Musical Association (*Journal History*, July 4, 1865).

No mention was made of the typographers, and many other trades marching in the 1861 parades were not mentioned by name in connection with the 1865 parade.

---

[10] A date celebrated by Mormons in commemoration of the first Saints to arrive in the valley on July 24, 1847.

The *Journal History* records for July 5, 1869:

> The Mechanics Union carried a magnificent banner, painted by Dan. Weggeland, Esq., on which were designs representing the principal branches of manufacture and trades in the city, over which appear the/words: "Home Manufacture; All kinds of pay taken." . . . The Engineers presented some beautiful designs of their handicraft, among which we noticed a miniature locomotive and miniature reapers and mowers. The next in order were Tinners, Gunsmiths, Wagon Makers, Tanners and Curriers, Harness Makers and Bakers, all with banners and representations of their respective trades. The Book Binders and Paper Makers made a very good display. The Deseret Typographical No. 115, comprising the printers attached to the different offices of this city, were next in line in handsome car representing a printing office, with typos busily engaged at the case and pressmen printing circulating handbills for the afternoon and evening performance at the Theatre. . . . Also represented were the Photographers, Butchers on horseback, Delivery Stable men in carriages, Roper Makers, Shipwrights with the sailing boat "Deseret Queen."

The use of the term "home manufacture" is interesting in view of the fact that it was a term frequently used by labor unions throughout the country in the preceding decades as they sought to discourage competition from outside workmen. The use of the term "mechanics union" indicates the likelihood of some formal union organization.

Of the group of fifty trades in the 1861 parade, ten were represented again in 1869, although the new Mechanics Union probably included many of the crafts individually listed in the 1861 parade. In addition to the mechanics, there were five other new crafts or trades designated: engineers, wagon makers, pressmen, shipwrights, and photographers.

Labor Strife

Brigham Young looked upon Mormon capitalists as honorable men and counseled worker-converts to "work for the capitalists and work honestly and faithfully and they will pay you faithfully" (*Journal of Discourses*, 11:297). However as already indicated, the 1860s were trying years for Utah workers. Prices and wages were both high, the high wages being looked on as a primary cause of high prices. Nationally, prices more than doubled during this period, helping to push up the Utah price level. It was feared that high prices and wages made Deseret an attractive market to outside capital and labor, attracting them, and would hinder making Mormondom economically self-sufficient. A *Deseret News* editorial of August 3, 1864, referred to the high prices of that year, infering that a strike was imminent.

The upshot was a convention called by the church leadership to do something about prices. At this meeting, worker representatives were allowed to express themselves, and from it came a system of price regulation which apparently calmed the troubled waters. Probably more important in controlling wages was the national collapse of prices. On February 1 of the following year, the newspaper reported that a sufficiency of breadstuffs protected laborers and mechanics from injustice and that conditions of work were improving (*Deseret News*, February 1, 1865). It may well have been the intervention of the church to lower wages that in the case of the typographers, at least, provoked them into formal association with a national union, the National Typographical Union, in 1868, and induced the Deseret Dramatic Association to disband. Also as reported later, in 1869, church leaders took strong action to induce "mechanics" to accept a lowering of wages. The fact that workers were admonished again to refrain from strikes would indicate that unionism, or at least collective action, was making gains.

In 1866 high wages were still a common complaint. William W. Riter, a recently returned missionary, in a letter sent to his former field of missionary labor, wrote that carpenters were earning from $5.00 to $10.00 a day depending on their abilities (*Journal History*, September 17, 1866). It was felt that high wages made it difficult for Utah's production to compete with goods from other states and territories. This assumed inability to compete meant that the people would purchase goods from Gentile importers rather than Mormon craftsmen, thus retarding the balanced economic development of Mormondom. (Trade was largely in the hands of non-Mormons, and the problem was aggravated by a shortage of domestic goods in exchange.) Deseret was still apparently far from being economically independent from the rest of the country. By 1869 there was so much concern that the School of the Prophets (an organization which looked after the secular interests of Zion) took action to induce the mechanics to agree to a lowering of their wages. Brigham Young and other church leaders took an active interest in this movement (*Journal History*, July 3, 1869; *Deseret News*, June 22, 1869).

On May 27, 1868, the *News* recognized the conflict between capital and labor, appealing for a Christian approach to its resolution:

Throughout the world there is a struggle for power and supremacy between capital and labor. Capital seeks to have labor helplessly in its power, tied hand and foot, so to speak, and entirely subservient to its will. And labor, to find an equality, resorts to every means in its power to successfully combat capital. . . . A result of this is class combinations. Capitalists unite together to make terms for the laborer. Workmen form societies and demand terms from the employer. . . . The gospel has to remove the cause of every existing wrong, to heal up the wounds of society, to introduce correct feeling, brotherly love. . . . We are looking for a day . . . when the Order of Enoch shall be established . . . for Capital must deal by labor, as it would wish to be done by . . . and labor must learn to act in the same manner.

However, this balanced approach to the labor question was not to last. The friction between the church and labor unions was to grow as church members joined with outsiders, as the church became more and more persecuted, as the church as an employer came face to face with union demands, and as closed shops, sometimes excluding church members, became more and more prevalent.

During this pioneering period, when public works were constructed, workers were obtained by requisitioning men through their respective bishops; official assignments were frequently made from the pulpit in Sunday meetings (Neff, 1940, p. 62). The same held true for the construction of church buildings. This meant that the church played an important role in directing the work force, often bringing church leaders face to face with unions and union leaders who believed workers should be paid well for their work.

Deseret School Teachers

An organization denoted as the Deseret School Teachers Association marched at the end of the worker section of the Fourth of July parade in 1861. Unlike the other groups of workers, no leader was mentioned. The *Journal History* is silent on this group until 1872. On October 4, 1872, the Territorial Teachers convention met in the University Building, effecting a "permanent organization" known as the Deseret Teachers Association (*Journal History*, October 4, 1872, p. 3). Evidently the earlier association had become defunct. The duly elected officers, at least six of the seven being members of the church, were:

Office	Name	
President	Warren N. Dusenberry	(M)
Vice president	Robert L. Campbell	(M)
Vice president	John R. Park	(M)
Corresponding secretary	O. H. Riggs	(M)
Recording secretary	Wilson H. Dusenberry	(M)
Assistant recording secretary	R. B. Tripp	(U)
Treasurer	Karl G. Maeser	(M)

The *Deseret News* reacted favorably to this organization, urging that county associations be organized throughout the Territory (*Journal History*, October 10, 1872). Two years later in 1873, the *Journal History* (October 6, p. 3) records another convention, with Dr. Park presiding and conducting an election which resulted in the following officers, all of whom were Mormons:

Office	Name	
President	O. H. Riggs	(M)
Vice president	John R. Park	(M)
Vice president	W. N. Dusenberry	(M)
Corresponding secretary	Joseph L. Rawlins	(M)
Recording secretary	Wilson H. Dusenberry	(M)
Assistant recording secretary	J. Z. Stewart	(M)
Treasurer	Karl G. Maeser	(M)

At this meeting a resolution was passed encouraging an educational system dedicated to be a "moral influence in aid of establishing a proper system of free schools in the Territory" (*Journal History*, October 6, 1874, p. 3). Some discussion was engaged in concerning this particular resolution, although there was no report on the exact nature of that discussion. Calling for "free" education was a progressive step for that day. The *Journal History* is silent on this particular organization after a brief entry a few days later. The association may have become a victim of the depression of the 1870s. As of this writing, there is no record of concerted, traditional trade union activity at the time, but there was established a tradition of group cohesiveness, similar to that of the guilds, that could evolve into either a professionally oriented association or a trade union.

Of the nine different men, at least eight were members of the church; at least one of them, Campbell, had participated in two guilds, the Deseret Dramatic Association and the Deseret Typographical Association.

The Break in Church Encouragement

While Deseret's pioneer guilds of 1846–68 were dominated by members of the church, and through them strongly influenced by the church leaders — at times through the membership and activity of General Authorities or members of their families — there was no institutionalized control by the official church organization. They were quasi-independent and evidently came to admit non-Mormons to membership. With Mormon dominance they ran little risk, it was thought, of running contrary to church policy. However, with the economic stress of the wartime inflation and the church-sponsored policy of wage controls (including reductions), guild leadership and membership began to give indications of independence of judgment and action. In the eyes of the church leaders, this independence constituted rebellion against duly constituted authority and resulted in the withdrawal of church sponsorship and encouragement, if not its approval. These guilds could no longer be depended upon to build up an economic kingdom dedicated to the Lord.

Nor were Mormon workmen alone. Mormon businesses were likewise exercising independence of judgment, increasing their "worldly business practices." They could not be relied upon to maintain low prices — not when higher prices were so attractive and possible. The coming of the railroad, increasing the competition from goods produced outside Deseret, would likewise interfere with the development of a self-sufficient economic kingdom. And Mormon consumers were becoming more and more reliant on non-Mormon–produced goods and services. If the goal of the kingdom, with unique political, economic, social, and religious characteristics, was to be retained, a different course of action was necessary, a course with tighter ecclesiastical control.

A new danger was also coming upon the Saints: a Gentile "invasion" spawned by the coming of the railroads and the discovery of precious metals. There was no holding it back. If the Saints were to be protected from the sins of the world, a new, closely knit, more tightly controlled, unique economic system would need to be developed, a system in which Mormon workers were to play a different role from those in the guilds. But before that story is told, we need to take a detailed look at the Printers of Deseret, Utah's first documented permanent union.

References

Arrington, Leonard J. *Great Basin Kingdom*. Cambridge, Massachusetts: Harvard University Press. 1958.

Deseret News, Salt Lake City, July 4, 1861; August 3, 1864; February 1, 1865; July 5, 1865; May 27, 1868; June 22, 1869.

Flanders, Robert Bruce. "Nauvoo Kingdom on the Mississippi." Madison: University of Wisconsin. 1964. Doctoral dissertation.

Halford, Reta Latimer. "Nauvoo — The City Beautiful: A Historical, Social, and Economic Study." *Proceedings of the Academy of Sciences, Arts and Letters* (1945–46), XXIII.

International Typographical Union (I.T.U.) Convention *Proceedings*. 1872.

Journal History. Salt Lake City, February 24, July 19, 1852; January 22, October 4, 1853; March 16, 1854; January 13, November 1, 1855; February 8, 1856; July 5, 1859; July 5, 1861; July 24, 1863; July 4, 1865; September 17, 1866; July 3, 1869; October 4 and 10, 1872; October 6, 1874.

Journal of Discourses. 11:297. Liverpool. 1854–86. Several editions.

Lum, D. D. "Social Problems of To-Day; or the Mormon Question in Its Economic Aspects . . . ." Point Jervis, New York. 1886.

Maughan, Ila Fisher. "History of Staging and Business Methods of the Deseret Dramatic Association, 1852–1869." Salt Lake City: University of Utah. 1949. Master's thesis.

Neff, Andrew Love. *History of Utah*, 1847–1869. Salt Lake City: Deseret News Press. 1940.

Reynolds, Lloyd G. *Labor Economics and Labor Relations*. Second edition. New York: Prentice-Hall, Inc. 1954.

Salt Lake *Tribune*, November 7, 1871.

COURTESY UTAH STATE HISTORICAL SOCIETY

Labor organizations were often in evidence in parades during the early years in the Salt Lake Valley.

4

The Printers
of Deseret
1852 to 1885

The printers in Nauvoo, along with other crafts, had been organized, meeting at the home of Apostle John Taylor (Halford, 1945–46, p. 41). Following the Nauvoo expulsion of the Saints in 1846, the economy of Zion was in a state of flux, but by 1852 it had settled down enough to organize workers and producers into guilds. One of the earliest of these groups to organize in Deseret was the printers.

First Annual Printers' Festival — 1852

As previously introduced, on February 24, 1852, the first annual printers' festival was opened with prayer by the church president, Brigham Young, and with the opening song, "Come All Ye Sons of Zion." The festival took place in the schoolhouse of the 14th Ward — "the first Typographical Feast celebrated in the Vallies [sic] of the Mountains" (Deseret News, March 6, 1852). After the prayer and the song, the foreman of the Deseret News printing shop, Ariah Coats Brower (M), a former resident of Nauvoo, delivered an address which read in part (Deseret News, March 6, 1852):

> It is a pleasure, on this occasion that I present a few remarks on behalf of the Fraternity of Printers, and more particularly that portion of our brotherhood assembled before

53

us — who, with our illustrious guests, have an interest in the great and glorious work of building up the Kingdom of God on earth. . . . The word of the Lord, when he deigned to converse with apostate man, was confined to the few copies [of the Bible] that could be transcribed with the pen, which were occasionally read to the people; and consequently the scriptures were very scarce and valuable, and out of reach of any, except the rich. . . . But it pleased the Lord, in his own due time, to disperse the midnight gloom . . . and it was . . . by the inspiration of his spirit that the first inventors of our art . . . were led to make their discoveries. . . . And when the art began to develop itself, so mysterious was it to the world, that Faust was accused of having dealings with the devil. . . . A copy of the first Bibles printed was deposited in one of the old churches of England, and chained to the wall, to prevent the people from taking it away. . . . Immediately upon the discovery of printing an impetus seems to have been given to all branches of science. . . . Numerous are the improvements and discoveries made of late years; and those of our noble art stand among the most prominent. . . . We have an interest in the up-building and establishment of the Kingdom of God. . . . Having this interest, we feel it our duty and privilege to employ our talents and abilities in the service of our God, and for the benefit of the human family. . . . May the richest blessings of heaven and earth always be upon them [church leaders]; may they ever enjoy the light of the Spirit of Truth and Wisdom, that by their skillful direction, we may be enabled to employ our time, talents, profession, substance, and lives, in a proper manner. And may we all receive a reward in the Celestial Kingdom of our God.

President Heber C. Kimball, counselor to the church president, pronounced the blessing on the food. Numerous "nonalcoholic toasts" were offered, including (*Deseret News*, March 6, 1852):

To the Kingdom of God	To the *Deseret News*
To the First Presidency	To the Beehive State
To the Twelve Apostles	To Home Manufacture
To the Seventies	To Our Mountain Home
To the Fair Daughters of Israel	To Our Martyred Seer

To the Press

To the Body Typography

To the Printers of Deseret

To the World

To the Spirit, the Pen, and the Press

Phineas H. Young (M), brother of Brigham Young, offered the concluding toast. A song, "The Mountain State," was written for the occasion, reading in part (*Deseret News*, March 6, 1852):

> We have come to the mountains
> Where the silv'ry, sparkling fountains
> Flow luxuriant from the bounties
>   Of Fair Freedom's Mountain State.
> We're a band of brethren,
> We are Zion's freemen,
> We are joined in union,
>   And we fear no tyrant's fate.

In the toasts and the song, we see a loyalty to both church and the profession; in the toasts "the body typography" is mentioned, and in the song reference is made to being "joined in union."

After the dinner, President Kimball delivered an address which recounted the persecution of the Saints, observing that he could see nothing "inappropriate or unbecoming this occasion," closing his remarks by "expressing his feelings of regard for the Fraternity" (*Deseret News*, March 6, 1852). The printers, along with the clerks, marched in the 24th of July parade of that year (*Deseret News*, July 24, 1852).

Second Annual Festival of the Printers of Deseret — 1853

On February 15, 1853, the second annual festival of the Printers of Deseret was held in the 14th Ward. John Young (M) blessed the food, and after dinner Phineas Young (M) opened the dance with prayer. Both men were brothers of the church president. James Bond (M), a 23-year-old convert of 1845, addressed his "Brethren, Friends and Fellow Associates" (*Deseret News*, January 22, 1853):

> ... Again we have met ... to surround the festive board ... savored with that spirit which emanates from the fountain of all truth, and strengthened with those ties of Union and Brotherhood. ... As a Fraternity, The Printers of Deseret would humbly hope, to retain that confidence and maintain

that position in society and community that they now have the honor to enjoy. . . . Although by profession, Mechanics, and at present devoting our humble energies to the working type and press, yet we would rather be considered as artisans in the business of Salvation. . . . Thus may we hope to acquit ourselves as skillful workmen, under our great head and Master Jesus Christ, directed by his Foremen on earth. . . . Printing as an Art speaks loudly for itself. . . and shows itself among the sciences as one calculated in its nature to educate the mind, and ennoble the soul. . . . Our humble efforts shall be devoted to the welfare of our fellowman. We will dispense nothing but truth; and though now in infancy in our establishment and literature; yet soon shall we see the time when the eyes of nations will be drawn, and the attention of Kings and potentates be directed to the refulgent brightness of those social, moral, political, and eternal truths that issue from the Press of Deseret.

As with his father-in-law, A. C. Brower, Bond shows a devotion to both church and the profession. His loyalty to the church is further shown by his acceptance of a mission call to England the following year; his professional loyalty is recognized by his reference to the "fraternity," "the printers of Zion," and to "Union and Brotherhood." Elder Phineas Young (M) dismissed the exercises with the benediction.

Third Annual Printers' Festival — 1854

On March 7, 1854, the third annual printers' festival was held at the United States Hotel, owned by J. C. Little, prominent Mormon pioneer. The bar was closed at the request of Brower, still head of the printers. The name of the printers organization had been changed to the Typographical Society of Deseret, using much the same terminology as the National Typographical Union but giving it a distinctly Mormon flavor with the word "Deseret." Dancing started at 2:00 p.m. and continued until 3:00 a.m. The address for the occasion was delivered by a member of the fraternity, Elder James McKnight (M), and reads in part (*Deseret News*, March 16, 1854):

Our annual festivities have brought us again together as the Typographical Fraternity of Deseret. . . . Associated in our profession with arts, sciences, literature, philosophy, religion, politics, government, improvements, inventions, and the general progressive spirit of the age. . . . We hold the Press to be the great harbinger of progression; the mightiest engine for the diffusion of universal knowledge, ever introduced to the world. . . . Men, by no means ignorant of the influence of the Press, have prostituted its power to the basest purposes — making it the instrument of pollution and death. . . . But our prerogative, as servants of the Most High God, is to correct the abuse . . . prepare a people for the Millenium [*sic*]; for Christ at his coming. . . . It is not without some degree of satisfaction that we notice the favorable expression of journalists in various parts of England and America. . . . We are glad to know there are yet among the editorial corps, men who are fearless to advocate the cause of the oppressed, and do justice to the innocent. . . . The Pacific Railroad is an enterprise in which we recognize a fellow champion and coworker with the Press, to promote the commonwealth. . . . May its completion be speedily accomplished. . . . Some who were present with us at our last reunion, are not here today. Elders James Bond and Matthias Cowley are on foreign missions. Our beloved Editor . . . now lies upon the bed of sickness. . . . The *Deseret News*, which thro' part of the past summer was discontinued by lack of paper, was commenced again in October; and on the first of January '54, was changed to a weekly. We have now again been compelled to publish semi-monthly . . . under the supervision of our worthy fellow associate, Elder A. C. Brower, the mechanical department will be sustained by a master of his Art.

The toasts offered for the occasion were (*Deseret News*, March 16, 1854):

To the First Presidency	To the Deseret Manufacturers
To the Twelve Apostles	To the Pacific Railroad
To the Press	To Israel's Elders
To Mormonism	To Zion's Daughters
To the Printers of Utah — publishers of truth; setting things in order; imposing their works upon the world; proving the follies of ages; correcting false traditions; working off the rust of darkness, superstition, and crime	To Deseret — A state in embryo; only waiting for delivery from territorial dependency

In these as in earlier toasts, a dual loyalty — to church and profession — is manifest. However, the occasion seems to have been less tied to religion and the church, being more secular than the two previous occasions.

Elder J. G. Chambers (M) gave an "excellent imitation of a learned religious discourse of modern times." In the words of the reporter of the occasion, "Paulos" (*Deseret News*, March 16, 1854), "We shall not soon forget this occasion; and trust that each annual return of our festivities may be more happy, and more welcome — until the day of universal joy and peace ushers in a jubilee to the world."

First Annual Festival of the Typographical Association of Deseret — 1855

On January 13, 1855, at its first annual festival, the constitution and bylaws of the more formalized Typographical Association of Deseret were adopted and the association formed, with the following charter members ("Constitution and By-laws," January 13, 1855), all Mormons:

Joseph Bull	William W. Phelps
William M. Cowley	Brigham Hamilton Young
George Hales	George Q. Cannon
James McKnight	Henry A. Ferguson
Matthew F. Wilkie	John B. Kelly
John G. Chambers	Horace K. Whitney
Jacob F. Hutchinson	Phineas H. Young
John S. Davis	

Section 2 of Article II of the constitution says: "Professors of the Typographical Art, permanently residing in Great Salt Lake City, and of good standing in the Church of Jesus Christ of Latter-day Saints, may become Active members." Section 5 of the same article provides that while other than active church members might participate in discussion, only active members could vote. Section 8 provides that members could be impeached and expelled for immoral conduct by a two-thirds vote, after "affording every reasonable facility for a fair and impartial trial." Apparently it was an organization with membership initially closed to all but active members of the church and with a group of charter members distinguished by their past, contemporary, and future church positions. All of these fifteen charter members have been identified as church members.

Meetings of the Deseret Typographical Association

On July 3, 1855, a meeting of the Deseret Typographical Association was held (*Journal History*, July 3, 1895). With President Phineas Young (M) absent, Elder James McKnight (M), new foreman of the printing shop at the *Deseret News*, was in the chair, and the opening prayer was offered by W. W. Phelps (M), who had played a leading role in the publication and literary efforts of the church in its Ohio, Missouri, and Nauvoo days. Elder George D. Watt, an English convert and church reporter, introduced the subject of the Deseret alphabet, an "invention of the Regents of the University of Deseret with the assistance of the First Presidency," which it was hoped would lead the way toward the institution of a single, Adamic language, uniting Saints from all countries in a single mode of communication. The clerk of the meeting was John G. Chambers (M). This is the first reported meeting of this newly named association. However, the *Journal History* of the church comments that it was a "regular meeting," an indication that previous meetings had possibly been held.

Monthly meetings were held and reported in the press at least through November. Phineas Young (M) presided at most meetings, but when he was absent James McKnight (M) presided. George D. Watt (M) continued to play a key role, instructing in and promoting the Deseret alphabet. A library was promoted and donations to it encouraged and accepted. Henry McEwan (M), who was to play a key role thirteen years later in the organization and governance of a true typographers trade union, was an active member, serving on a committee to draft the bylaws for the association and, interestingly, "general regulations for the Typographic Art in this Territory" (*Journal History*, August 2, 1855), a step that was to become common within the trade union movement.

In the October meeting, the members were addressed by the Honorable Ezra Taft Benson, a member of the Quorum of the Twelve,[1] as well as the "Honorable" Samuel W. Richards (M), prominent missionary and civic leader (*Journal History*, October 4, 1855). In

---

[1]The body of the church leadership next in authority to the presidency of the church, assuming church leadership upon the death of the church president. Its members are sustained by church membership as apostles and prophets and hold considerable authority by virtue of their positions.

November, Erastus Snow, of the Quorum of the Twelve, "accepted the appointment tendered him" (*Journal History*, November 1, 1855), although no explanation is made of what the appointment was.

Second Annual Festival of the Deseret Typographical Association

On February 8, 1856, the second annual festival of the association was held, this time in Social Hall. Phineas H. Young (M), still president of the association, opened with prayer. President Heber C. Kimball of the First Presidency of the LDS church again blessed the food. In attendance were such notables as President Jedediah M. Grant, also of the First Presidency; Elders Ezra Taft Benson and Erastus Snow of the Quorum of the Twelve; as well as Daniel H. Wells (M), who later that year succeeded President Grant in the First Presidency; Albert Carrington (M), editor of the church's *Deseret News* and later an apostle; and Judge Elias Smith (M). The annual address was delivered by Elder John S. Davis (M) of Wales, a member of the association. He referred to a committee established to form a new constitution and bylaws, recommending a new name, "Deseret News Press Association." This name, while not adopted, would have tied the association more closely to a single employer, the *Deseret News*, which it probably already was in reality. Davis looked forward to the coming of the "electric telegraph, with lightning speed," as well as "a 'Daily Mountain Express,' published in this city, which of course will require steam to work it." While a reference is made to "the fatherly kindness of our beloved President Brigham Young," outward religious expressions are noted by their paucity (*Journal History*, February 8, 1856). However, several songs, composed especially for the occasion, were tied to the profession of typography as well as the church (*Journal History*, February 8, 1856):

"Our Mountain Home"

(Sung to tune of "Come All Ye Sons of God")

By W. W. Phelps (M)

Come all ye "royal" sons,
    Who "work" with just precision,
'Tis time to "prove" the world,
    And take the grand "revision"
Of realms, and men, and kings, and thrones,

That all may learn the truth, and come
To build the wastes of Zion—
                    Our mountain home.

The ancient "sheets" in gold,
    Like prophets full of spirit,
Have open'd to our view,
    That Jacob may inherit
The Gentiles—deserts, hills and dales,
The earth—the fame—that saints may come
And build the wastes of Zion—
                    Our mountian home.

While nations "blur" with war,
    And Europe girds on tackle,
We'll "set our sticks" for peace,
    And let the Christians "mackle"—
Our kings and priests, with light and love,
"Lock up our forms," and "preface" room
To build the wastes of Zion—
                    Our mountain home.

The "volume" of our fame,
    Is "bound" in "golden letters";
Our wives and children "lead"—
    "The Mormons 'break' all fetters";
From north to south, from east to west,
We're preaching—"let the kingdom come,"
To build the wastes of Zion—
                    Our mountain home.

The Father cries—"My son,
    "The 'font' of blood is seething,
"The 'star' of empire shines—
    "The man-child is a-teething";
The "errors," "points" and "stops" of all
Must be " corrected" now—'tis doom—
To build the wastes of Zion—
                    Our mountain home.

While wrangling nations jar,
    The mighty men are coming,
With "shooting sticks" in hand
    (Like bees to swarm are humming),

To "cast" the "sinners" all in "hell,"
And "clear" the way—and "sweep" the room,
To build the wastes of Zion—
                    Our mountain home.

Song from the Press
By Henry Maiben (M)

For the press,
For the press,
We will give a short address,
    Using rhyme,
    Using rhyme,
As it suits the time,
Since we have met here tonight
To put ev'ry care to flight,
    And enjoy,
    And enjoy,
Mirth without alloy.
    We would say,
    We would say,
To the gentlemen who play,
    Music sweet,
    Music sweet,
Always is a treat,
And it adds much to our bliss
On occasions such as this,
    Tune up then,
    Tune up then,
Like true merry men.
    Those who dance,
    Those who dance,
Should now make use of the chance,
    To display,
    To display
Their taste in that way,
To the music as they go
"On the light fantastic toe."
    "Balance all,
    "Balance all"
Is their welcome call.

We who sing
We who sing,
Humbly forth our talents bring,
    And unite,
    And unite
With those friends who write
To make pleasure general
At this *Printers Festival*;
    While the Press,
    While the Press
Wish us all success.

"The Printer's Song"
By John S. Davis (M)
(Peculiar metre. Tune — "Duke of Marlbre")

I am ready
For some copy;
My Minion case is rather low,
    But Nonp'reil is quite full.

(Chorus)
Let us sing and merry be,
'Tis the Art's festivity;
Then sing of Printing,
Keep up the feasting,
And be merry all the night,
'Til morning light will show.

This for beading—
'Tis all standing;
And leaded matter is the kind
    That I delight to set.

No Italics;
Type with three-nicks.
I'll set six thousand ems to-day,
    Unless I'm out of sorts.

Awful spelling,
And bad pointing:
I never thought it was so bad,
    Till I began to set.

On what galley
Shall I empty?
I ought to have an extra price
For setting such a scrawl.

Curse that devil—
See his squabble:
I'll have to set it o'er again,
And he must clear the pi.

I'll charge double
For this stickful:
Let devils mind their p's and q's,
And journeymen their pay.

CAPS are wanting
For this heading:
I guess SMALL CAPS will do as well,
And look much neater too.

I'll have borders,
With neat corners;
And fine brass rules of different kinds,
To make my work look well.

Now 'tis waiting
For imposing:
On the stone I'll find a chase,
To lock it up with quoins.

What's the matter
With this plainer?
We'll want new mallets pretty soon,
And shooting-sticks to match.

Also side-sticks,
And some foot-sticks;
And gutter, riglets, and so forth,
Are furniture we want.

Next is pulling
Proof, and reading;
Mark the errors I have made.
And then correct them all.

"Education"
For "excursion,"
And "lumps" for "lamps," and few such like,
    Are all the errors made.

Now 'tis better
To wet paper:
The form is ready for the press,
    But wants to be revis'd.

Devil, color —
Ink the roller:
The tympan, frisket, points, and all,
    Are ready for to work.

Now, be careful,
Sharp, and watchful,
Lest monks or friars spoil the sheets,
    When I look for the bites.

Every token
I will reckon,
So that the number may be right,
    Before I lift the form.

After washing
It and rinsing
In the trough, we lay it up
    For distribution now.

Such is Printing,
And my rhyming;
And some may think I've been too long,
    For they see nothing done.

"The Deseret Press"
By W. G. Mills (M)
(Tune — "To the West")

Ho! A song to the Press — to the Deseret Press,
  With its broad sheeted banners of wisdom unfurl'd
To that herald of truth we will wish all success
  Till its principles spread and control the whole world.

In the midst of the mountains, whose crowns pierce the sky,
  Like temples communing with heav'n, it is set
As a beacon of light, that the world may descry
  That life and salvation flow from Deseret.

(Chorus)

Then a song for the Press — for the Deseret Press,
  With its broad sheets as banners of wisdom unfurled;
That great herald of truth we will wish all success,
  Till its doctrines and sheets shall envelope the world.

Oh, the Press. Oh, the Press. 'Tis the mightiest gift
  That Heaven to mortals has ever bestow'd;
'Tis the handmaid of truth, with whose pow'r it will lift
  Our darken'd and poor human nature to God.
An epoch was formed when its hist'ry began —
  Then Satan, 'twas said, to its being gave birth —
It does more to enlighten and civilize man
  Than all the philosophy known upon earth.

Then a song for the Press, & c.

Oh, the Press. Oh, the Press. In the hands of the wise
  Is a terror to tyrants tho' ever so great;
By its aid the acquiring and virtuous will rise,
  And liberty triumph in kingdom and state
As the notes of the songster would die on the breeze.
  So the thoughts of the wise, if not by the Press caught;
As the sunbeams are stamped on the flow'rets and trees,
  So the Press to the world is the record of thought.

Then a song for the Press, & c.

What tho' some from the Press lies and error impart,
  And the tastes of mankind vitiate and degrade?
It but proves the great power that belongs to the art;
  And we know there is sunlight where'er there is shade.
Oh, the Press is the track of the great march of mind
  That treads like a god to enlighten this ball;
'Tis a monarch that faithfully governs mankind,
  Yet stoops from his throne as the servant of all.

Then long life to the Press, & c.

"Song of the Deseret Press"
By John Lyon (M)
(Tune — "The Steam Arm")

Let them sing of invention, discovery, and trade,
And mechanical arts, of every grade —
Yet, there's none of them all, be it quietly said,
When compared — the Press throws them all in the
    shade:

(Chorus)
    Li tu ral ur al ur al a.

Its sword is a *stick*, laid with zinc and lead,
Arranged in lines, by compositors, bred
To wield the power of an editor's head,
Who writes all day, and composes in bed.

The click of the type is its infant voice,
And the "devil's-tail" presses hard its choice,
Then it bounds away with a mental noise —
Till far-off lands are made to rejoice.

The *deaf* can hear its intelligent sound,
As it speaks to the eye in signs profound,
And cares not a fig what opposing ground
Its votaries may take, if in error found.

There's not a thought in the world of art
That selfish men would hide, or impart,
But what you will find engraved on its chart
To please, or pierce you thro' like a dart.

Should drunken senators kick up a squall,
And rogues fall out, and each other maul,
No matter on whom its notice may fall,
With an elephant's voice, it tells it all.

It bursts on the mind like a sunbeam, afar —
And lectures the peasant, and statesman, and czar,
On morals, and vices, and famine, and war,
And laughs at the world, and people, ajar.

It turns up the grist of the miller's mind,
The farmer's, on pasture, and dairy combin'd,
And where he is like the best market to find;
And damns the forestaller, who the poor would grind.

It shines alike in the dark prison cell,
As in palaces, where the noble dwell;
It knows of Heaven, and Earth, and Hell,
And has the same truth for all to tell.

It speaks of a child raised in travel, and pain,
Whom old Uncle Sam cast out in disdain;
And how this same lad, grown to manhood, would fain
Prove his right to be linked to his family again.

But, where you will ask, are those stirring views
To be found without flatt'ry, fraud, or abuse?
Where men find their level, and devils their dues?
Then read, my dear friends, the *Deseret News.*

The "unity" of this profession is exhibited in a round of unknown origin (*Journal History*, February 8, 1856):

How good and how pleasant when brethren agree,
Bound closely together in firm unity;
How sweet and how pleasant when Christ is our theme,
His love above all else is supreme;
Sweet — sweet 'tis to sing in harmony —
Pure harmony — the praises of our king.

The Deseret Typographical and Press Association

On February 22, 1856, the Deseret Typographical Association met in the courtroom of the Council House for the purpose of presenting the new constitution and reorganizing the association under a new name. With this organization, a major step toward secularization was taken. The new constitution lost its close ties with the church, perhaps purposely avoiding the implications of the name proposed at the festival — the Deseret News Press Association. The new name chosen was Deseret Typographical and Press Association. Its objects were the encouragement of arts and sciences, the development of language, and the dissemination of truth in general." It was governed by a board of twelve directors, with a president and two counselors, following a church pattern of organization. Members were to be nominated by the board and elected by two-thirds of the members present at a regular meeting. "To all shall pertain the freedom of speech, the privilege of voting, and eligibility to office." There was no requirement that guild members be members of the church. Officers were to be chosen annually by a majority vote, although there had been strong support in the meeting for decision by plurality. Dues were $0.50 a quarter for each member except those on missions, an exemption existing with Salt Lake Typographical Union Local 115 as late as the 1920s. Meetings were to be held the first Tuesday of each month. A library was to be maintained (*Journal History*, February 22, 1856). The inclusion of the words "and Press" represents a recognition of the pressmen as a separate but related profession.

Elders Ezra Taft Benson (M) and Amasa Lyman (M) of the Quorum of the Twelve, along with Claudius V. Spencer (M), were elected members, and the following slate of officers was "re-elected." Whether all of them had been officers of the previous association is not certain, but Phineas Young, McKnight, and Chambers had definitely been officers:

Office	*Name*	
President	Phineas H. Young	(M)
First counselor	James McKnight	(M)
Second counselor	John S. Davis	(M)
Clerk	John G. Chambers	(M)
Assistant clerk	William G. Mills	(M)
Reporter	George D. Watt	(M)
Assistant reporter	Wilford Woodruff	(M)
Librarian	John B. Kelly	(M)
Treasurer	Brigham H. Young	(M)
First attendant	George Hales	(M)
Second attendant	Benjamin Allen	(M)
Third attendant	John M. Bollwinkel	(M)

All previous members were retained. The meeting was adjourned, the next to be held in March, notice to be given through the *Deseret News*. The benediction was offered by W. W. Phelps (M).

The new association retained its Mormon leadership, all the thirteen officers being members of the church. However, with the festival and the new constitution and bylaws, the association apparently took an additional step or two toward secularization.

Participation in the Fourth of July Parade of 1861

The history of the typographers becomes obscured until 1861, although the association was toasted at a picnic of the Saints in Philadelphia in 1857 and again in Salt Lake City in 1859 (*Journal History*, August 8, 1857; July 15 and 16, 1859). In 1861 typographical association members, led by Henry McEwan (M), marched in the Fourth of July parade. The words "and Press" had been dropped, at least in the newspaper report. However, the typographers had a press and fixtures in a wagon, along with a compositor "working at the case." In a second wagon, "pressmen" were "striking off" patriotic songs and distributing them among the people as they passed. Their "magnificent" banner, represented the "goddess of liberty, standing by the side of the press, and on her left a bust of Benjamin Franklin, to whose brow she was extending a wreath of glory." On the banner were the scroll inscriptions: "The Printers of Deseret" and "The pen is mightier than the sword." Following this was a third wagon under the direction of J. B. Kelly (M), librarian of the typographical association in 1856, with the bookbinders and paper rulers (*Journal History*, July 5, 1861). Evidently there were four occupational groupings of printers: typographers, pressmen, bookbinders, and paper rulers.

There was no mention of the typographical association in the subsequent Fourth of July parades until 1869, when they marched under a new name (*Journal History*, July 5, 1869).

Organization of the Deseret Typographical Union
Local 115

On August 17, 1868, the Deseret Typographical Union was chartered as Local 115 by the National Typographical Union (Scorup, 1935, pp. 7–8). None of the charter members had been charter members of the earlier Deseret Typographical Association, although at least the president, Henry McEwan (M), had been a prominent member of the association, and was its leader in the parade of 1861. William M. Cowley (M), a member in 1869, was a charter member of the Typographical Association of Deseret in 1855. R. G. Sleater (M) was to become the founder of the Utah labor movement. The charter members were (Scorup, 1935):

John E. Evans	(M)	William Fuller	(M)
Henry McEwan	(M)	Robert G. Sleater	(M)
Theo A. Smith	(M)	Robert Aveson	(M)
Walter Davis	(U)	Joseph T. McEwan	(M)

The initial officers of this local were ("Notice," January 5, 1869):

Office	Name	
President	Henry McEwan	(M)
Vice president	John Priestley	(M)
Secretary	John E. Evans	(M)
Treasurer	Samuel Roberts	(M)
Corresponding secretary	William Fuller	(M)
Janitor	Henry W. Attley	(M)

In addition to the officers, the following were members of the local in 1869 ("Notice," January 5, 1869):

James A. Thompson	Robert G. Sleater
Theodore A. Smith	Robert Aveson
Thomas G. Odell	Robert Wilson
Richard Matthews	Truman C. Brown
Lyman G. Littlefield	William H. Scott
Scipio A. Kenner	Thomas McIntyre
Aaron Pratt	Henry C. Lawhorn
Adam Aulbach	William M. Cowley
William L. Price	Joab S. Roberts

Two charter members, Walter Davis (U) and Joseph T. McEwan (M), had evidently dropped out of membership.

The constitution of Local 115 ("Notice," January 5, 1869) provides that:

> The objects of the Union shall be the maintenance of a fair rate of wages, the encouragement of good workmen, and to use every means which may tend to the elevation of printers in the social scale of life, and providing a fund for sickness or burial of its members. . . . Those who shall compose the Union are . . . practical printers known to be competent and of good character, who shall sign the Constitution and comply with the rules and regulations made by this Union . . . [also] practical printers, who have retired from the business, and who have conferred benefits upon the craft here or elsewhere; also members of this Union who may become employers, and not working at

the profession, and have paid all dues and fines; and those immediately connected with the business and favorable to the
principles of the Union may be elected honorary members by a
two-thirds vote.

All of the union's officers and at least six of its eight charter members
were members of the church and had received their "endowments."
However, contrary to the membership of the earlier associations, none
would rise to prominence in the church hierarchy.

References are made to other meetings and parties of the
typographers as late as 1869 (*Journal History*, April 9, 1869) when Deseret Typographical Union Local 115 took its place in the Fourth of
July parade (*Deseret News*, July 5, 1869). With this organization, the
typographers took another significant step toward secularization, even
though they retained the name Deseret, and Mormons were to continue
to dominate the local for almost two decades. Why this step was taken in
1868 is not known. However, there had been considerable agitation over
the inflation of prices and wages associated with the Civil War, and
association members might well have felt the need for the support that a
national organization could provide. In addition, the church leaders had
not yet begun to resist unionization. The church was just beginning its
retreat from worldly associations that would come in full force the next
year. There was probably no strong reason not to associate with the
national body. But once this happened, the die was cast. The local would
eventually lose its distinctly Mormon orientation.

Typographers and the United Orders

Four men involved with the typographers in the early years became
involved in a leadership capacity in the United Orders in the mid-1870s:
George Q. Cannon (M), assistant vice president of the General Order in
Salt Lake City (1874); John B. Kelly (M), director of the 7th Ward
United Order in Salt Lake City (1874); William Price (M), director of the
Central Board of the United Orders, Utah County (1874); Wilford
Woodruff (M), assistant vice president of the General Order in Salt Lake
City (1874).

Of this group, only Price was associated with the typographers as
late as 1869, having maintained his membership in Local 115. Kelly was
associated with the printers as head of the bookbinders and paper rulers
in the 1861 parade, while Woodruff was assistant reporter of the Deseret
Typographical and Press Association in 1856; George Q. Cannon along

The *Deseret News* was first published shortly after the arrival of the Mormon pioneers in the Salt Lake Valley, with Willard Richards as editor and manager. The *Deseret Evening News* commenced in the fall of 1869, with George Q. Cannon as editor and manager. This pen sketch depicts the first issue of the *Deseret Evening News*, showing the great interest of the citizens in the new issue.

COURTESY UTAH STATE HISTORICAL SOCIETY

with John B. Kelly were charter members of the Typographical Association of Deseret in 1855. Two, Cannon and Woodruff, became General Authorities, Wilford Woodruff becoming president of the church.

The 1870s

The first three years of the 1870s were prosperous ones for the typographers. Economic prosperity prevailed in the Territory, and Local 115 grew. Table 4 presents a composite of membership activity for the decade. It can be seen that membership peaked at 32 in 1872, declining to sixteen by the end of the decade, the decline mostly due to the depression beginning in 1873.

Table 4

Membership Activity of Typographers Local 115 for Selected Years (1870–79)[a]

Status of Member	1870	1871	1872	1873	1875	1876	1879
Initiated	7	1	11	23	2	8	
Admitted by card	6	3	7	16	1	4	
Rejected	3			1		1	
Withdrew by card	7		14	18	9	6	3
Deceased				1		1	
Expelled	1		4		1	3	1
Suspended		7	2				
Reinstated	1		6				
Members in good standing	19	17	32	15	21	22	16

[a] The years 1874, 1877, 1878 were omitted because there were no reports for those years.

Source: International Typographical Union convention reports, 1870-79.

R. G. Sleater (M) was president of the local in 1871 and led a strike against the new anti-Mormon Salt Lake *Tribune* for expelling two union members (*Typographical Journal*, 1871; and Salt Lake *Tribune*, November 7, 1871). He also was its representative at the International Typographers Union convention in 1872, when he was elected as one of two international vice presidents (I.T.U. convention reports, 1872). William Fuller (M) represented the local on the I.T.U. executive committee in 1871, as did Henry McEwan (M) in 1872 (I.T.U. convention reports, 1871, 1872).

In 1873, 23 persons were initiated into the local, while sixteen were admitted by card, having been members of I.T.U. locals elsewhere. However, eighteen persons withdrew by card, still in the good graces of the union, indicating a heavy turnover usually associated with hard times. This was the heaviest reported turnover of the decade. E. D. Young (U) represented the local on the I.T.U. executive committee in 1873 and 1874 (I.T.U. convention reports, 1873, 1874).

From 1871 to 1873, the only years of the decade for which salary figures are available, typographers received $24.00 a week (1871), increasing to $30.00 (1872), and decreasing once more to $24.00 (1873), making Salt Lake City, along with Washington, D. C., the top-paying city in the nation (I.T.U. convention reports, 1871, 1872, 1873). Little wonder that there was such an influx of printers into Zion in 1873.

In 1879, the first year since 1869 for which Local 115 leadership and membership are known extensively, we find the following leaders (I.T.U. convention reports, 1879):

Office	Name	
President	Henry McEwan	(M)
Vice president	S. B. Phillips	(U)
Recording secretary	J. E. Basch (Bosch)	(N)
Corresponding secretary	R. G. Taysum	(M)
Financial secretary	J. E. Evans	(M)
Treasurer	R. T. McEwan	(M)
Seargeant at arms	T. J. Donkin	(M)
Executive committee	S. B. Phillips	(U)
	R. G. Sleater	(M)
	R. C. McEwan	(M)
	John Priestley	(M)
	William Grimsdell	(M)

Of the eleven different officers and executive committee members, at least nine were members of the church, one was not a member, and the church affiliation of the other is unknown.

Of the charter members and officers, Robert Aveson (M) had dropped out of union membership, although he remained active in the profession, much of the time with the *Deseret News*. Theo A. Smith (U) had left the local, having moved to Ogden, Utah, and becoming associated with the fledgling newspaper industry there. He was to become president of typographers Local 236 in Ogden. Walter Davis (U) evidently left the profession, becoming a railroad worker. J. S. Roberts (M) was not a member of the local at the time, spending several years in England, possibly on a mission, but was to reassociate himself temporarily with Local 115 in the 1880s. The other charter members were still associated with the local in some way, although William Fuller was expelled in 1879 (I.T.U. convention reports, 1879).

The name McEwan is prominent, with four McEwans associated with Local 115. Henry, R. T. , and J. T. were sons of Henry McEwan, all originally from Glasgow, Scotland, and endowed members of the church. R. C. McEwan (M), son of R. T. McEwan, was to become associated with the printing profession and typographers Local 236 in Ogden, eventually being expelled by that local. J. T. was a partner with R. G. Sleater in his Provo publishing ventures in the mid-1870s. Henry, employed much of the time by the *Deseret News*, was to continue to dominate Local 115 through the 1880s, and R. T. was to hold important positions in that local through the same decade. This was a unique printer family — one with, as yet, an untold story.

While the 1874–78 period had evidently been a difficult one for the typographers, largely because of the depression, the local had begun to recover enough by 1879 to pay for the listing of their leadership and membership in the I.T.U. convention report of that year.

1880 to 1886

The decade of the 1880s, while not completely with a bright outlook, was to prove to be on the whole a good one for Local 115, at least in numbers. However, it was also the period of time in which the local lost its unique Mormon-oriented name, Deseret Typographical Union, and was to become controlled by non-Mormons who were often either unsympathetic with or antagonistic toward the church. It was a decade in which the local was to become secularized.

Indicative of the continued Mormon domination of the local is the list of officers and executive committee members taken from the I.T.U. convention reports for the years 1880–85:

1880:

Office	Name	
President	Henry McEwan	(M)
Vice President	J. H. Ackerman	(N)

Office	*Name*	
Financial secretary	J. E. Evans	(M)
Recording secretary	J. E. Bosch	(N)
Corresponding secretary	R. G. Taysum	(M)
Treasurer	R. T. McEwan	(M)
Sergeant at arms	T. J. Donkin	(M)
Executive committee	R. T. McEwan	(M)
	J. E. Evans	(M)
	R. G. Sleater	(M)

1881:

President	Henry McEwan	(M)
Vice president	J. H. Ackerman	(N)
Financial and corre- sponding secretary	R. T. McEwan	(M)
Secretary-treasurer	J. E. Bosch	(N)
Janitor	T. J. Donkin	(M)
Executive committee	R. G. Sleater	(M)
	R. T. McEwan	(M)
	J. E. Evans	(M)

1882:

President	R. G. Sleater	(M)
Vice president	J. H. Ackerman	(N)
Financial and corre- sponding secretary	R. T. McEwan	(M)
Secretary-treasurer	J. E. Bosch	(N)
Executive committee	Henry McEwan	(M)
	R. S. Andrews	(M)
	R. T. McEwan	(M)

1883:

President	R. G. Sleater	(M)
Vice president	J. H. Ackerman	(N)
Financial and corre- sponding secretary	R. T. McEwan	(M)
Secretary-treasurer	W. F. Grimsdell, Jr.	(M)

Office	Name	
Janitor	T. J. Donkin	(M)
Executive committee	Henry McEwan	(M)
	John Priestley	(M)
	W. F. Grimsdell, Jr.	(M)

1884:

President	Henry McEwan	(M)
Vice president	W. F. Grimsdell, Jr.	(M)
Financial and corresponding secretary	Henry Sconberg	(M)
Recording secretary and treasurer	Thomas Crawford	(U)
Executive committee	W. F. Grimsdell, Jr.	(M)
	R. G. Sleater	(M)
	J. F. Webley	(U)

1885:

President	Henry McEwan	(M)
Vice president	John Priestley	(M)
Financial and corresponding secretary	R. C. McEwan	(M)
Recording secretary and treasurer	J. F. Webley	(U)
Executive committee	R. C. McEwan	(M)
	William Zeidler	(U)
	Henry Sconberg	(M)

Even as late as 1885, of the six different officers and executive committee members, at least four were church members, while the religious affiliation of two is unknown.

The addition of non-Mormons between 1880 and 1885 may have led to the group's complete secularization. In 1880, three new members were admitted to the union, and there were three each for the next two years. In 1883 thirteen new members were admitted; five in 1884, and nineteen in 1885. Among the five in 1884 was S. Stenhouse (U). T.B.H. Stenhouse was an outspoken apostate whose genealogy has been hard to trace but who was well chronicled by newspaper accounts in the 1870s (see chapter 8). S. Stenhouse may well have been his son. However, not all of the new additions were non-Mormons. One of the new members was William Cowley (M) who had been associated in the Typographical Association of Deseret in 1855 and was associated, along with Samuel Roberts (M), in Local 115 in 1869.

In 1886 the local, now dominated by non-Mormons, was to lose it unique appellation, Deseret Local 115, becoming known as Salt Lake Local 115. By 1890, the secularization of the local had proceeded to the point that its leadership could challenge the open shop policy of the church's *Deseret News* — the challenge was to lead to a complete rupture between the church and the union movement. This phase is discussed in detail in chapter 9.

Table 5 presents the membership activity of the local for the first half of the decade, rising from a low of fourteen in 1880 to a high of 35 in 1885.

Table 5

Membership Activities of Typographical Local 115
(1880–85)

Status of Member	1880	1881	1882	1883	1884	1885
Initiated		3	1	5	4	9
Admitted by card	2	3	5	9	2	12
Rejected						
Withdrew by card		2	1	9		4
Deceased						
Expelled	3		1		1	
Suspended			2			
Reinstated	1					4
Members in good standing						
Members	14	16	17	18	25	35
Number of non-unions or "rats"	5					
Non-union females						

Source: International Typographical Union convention reports, 1880–85.

References

"Constitution and By-Laws of the Typographical Association of Deseret." Salt Lake City, January 13, 1855.

Deseret News, Salt Lake City, March 6, July 24, 1852; January 22, 1853: March 8, 1854; July 5, 1869.

Halford, Reta Latimer. "Nauvoo — The City Beautiful: A Historical, Social, and Economic Study," *Proceedings of the Academy of Sciences, Arts and Letters* (1945–46), XXIII.

International Typographical Union (I.T.U.) convention reports. 1871-74, 1879-85.

Journal History. Salt Lake City. July 3, August 2, October 4, November 1, 1855; February 8 and 22, 1856; August 8, 1857; July 15 and 16, 1859; July 5, 1861; February 1 and 14, 1862; April 9, July 5, 1869.

"Notice of Deseret Typographical Union, Local 115." Salt Lake City. January 5, 1869.

Salt Lake *Tribune*, November 7, 1871.

Scorup, Dee. "A History of Organized Labor in Utah." Salt Lake City: University of Utah. 1935. Master's thesis.

Typographical Journal. 1871.

5

Zion's Workmen
1867 to 1886

From the Nauvoo period to 1868, church policy toward workers in Zion was apparently that of encouraging the organization of worker associations in the various trades. These associations would be controlled or influenced by holders of the priesthood who, because of their loyalty to the church, would (it was hoped) subject themselves and their membership to priesthood authority. While some of the associations briefly flirted with closed membership, open only to "good" church members, they eventually admitted non-Mormons. Because of the overwhelming numbers of men who held the LDS priesthood, their activities could, it was also hoped, be held in check and they would be subservient to Zionic hopes. However, the inflationary pressures of the Civil War were so great that association members and their leaders began to exercise considerable independence, even to the point of challenging Brigham Young and other church authorities.

Beginning in 1867, the church, over the next fifteen years, developed three successive but interrelated programs for dealing with economic problems of Zion, including the problems of worker-employer relationships: (1) cooperatives, (2) United Orders, and (3) Zion's Boards of Trade. Since all members of the United Orders were automatically members of the church, no reference to church membership will be made in this chapter. Known leaders of the United Orders who were also involved in other worker activity are listed in Appendix B, part I.

The Cooperative Movement

The church's first answer to the growing independence of Mormon workmen, businesses, and consumers was the cooperative movement. While the movement was essentially economic, it had strong religious, social, and political overtones. The interlocking directorates of the various cooperatives, controlled by the priesthood through its leadership, could maintain a unique Mormon politico-socio-economic system, with a limited amount of intercourse with the Gentile world. There were four major elements to this movement: (1) the Schools of the Prophets, (2) retrenchment, (3) consumer cooperatives, and (4) cooperative-sponsored local production units. One of the most visible church leaders was Apostle George Q. Cannon, counselor in the First Presidency, who had played a role the previous decade in the typographical association. A. M. Musser, who had been involved in several associations, was a frequent companion to Cannon.

Schools of the Prophets

Priesthood direction for the church's cooperative movement came through the Schools of the Prophets. Originally organized in Kirtland, Ohio, for the purpose of educating the priesthood, the new school, organized in Salt Lake City in December 1867, established branches throughout Mormondom, with some five thousand priesthood leaders involved. It was concerned mostly with the political and economic affairs of the Kingdom of Zion. The purpose of the schools was to prepare an earthly kingdom, ready for delivery to the Master. Meetings were closed, admission being by cards that had been issued by ecclesiastical leaders. In dealing with political and economic problems facing Zion, especially with the coming of the railroads and an anticipated increase in the influx of Gentile influence, the schools exercised both secular and ecclesiastical sanctions to help implement their policies. The secular sanctions included boycotts, while the ecclesiastical sanctions went so far as to withdraw fellowship, a step short of excommunication. The schools remained in operation for several years, their functions finally absorbed by the United Orders.

According to Arrington (1958, pp. 245–51), the schools developed seven major objectives:

(1) Minimize the influx of those antagonistic to the goals of the Kingdom

(2) Establish local cooperatives and industries to provide work to Mormon workmen and make the Mormon community as economically independent as possible

(3) Reduce wages to keep the prices of locally produced goods competitive, improving the export potential of the community

(4) Establish a network of railroads to transport locally produced goods and improve internal communication

(5) Establish a church-owned and -controlled wholesale house to control imports, distributing to the network of locally owned consumer cooperatives

(6) Protect the land rights of the Saints, in the face of antagonistic federal officials

(7) Encourage the immigration of Mormon workmen through the Perpetual Emigration Fund

It may be noted that three of the seven major objectives applied directly to the Saints as workmen.

Retrenchment

Intrinsic to the success of a cooperative movement was a spiritual regeneration that would convert the Saints to the need to make the necessary sacrifices to become Zion's Workmen. This regeneration would take place through retrenchment, a forsaking of the "ways of the world." According to Arrington, this retrenchment — spiritual, social, political, and economic — began in November 1869 with Brigham Young's family. Calling his numerous wives and daughters together, he declared (Arrington, 1958, p. 252; words in brackets are Arrington's, quoted from Gates, 1911, pp. 8–9):

> All Israel [the Mormon people] are looking for my family and watching the example set by my wives and children. For this reason I desire to organize my own family first into a society for the promotion of habits of order, thrift, industry, and charity, and, above all things, I desire them to retrench from their extravagance in dress, in eating, and even in speech. . . . The time has come when the sisters must agree to give up their follies of dress and cultivate a modest apparel, a meek deportment, and to set an example before the people of the world worthy of imitation. . . . I want you to set your own fashions. Let your apparel be neat and comely, and the workmanship of your own

hands; wear the good cloth manufactured in our mills, and cease to build up the merchant who sends your money out of the Territory for fine clothes made in the East.

Under the leadership of Sister Eliza R. Snow Young, a wife of Brigham Young, the "Young Ladies Department of the Cooperative Retrenchment Association" was formed, spreading throughout Zion, with members agreeing to the following (Arrington, 1958, p. 253; quoted from Gates, 1911, pp. 10–12):

Resolved, that inasmuch as the Saints have been commanded to gather out from Babylon and not take part in her sins, that they may receive not of her plagues, we feel that we should not condescend to imitate the pride, folly and fashions of the world. . . . Resolved [that] as fast as it shall be expedient, we shall adopt the wearing of homemade articles and exercise our united influence in rendering them fashionable.

Retrenchment was provided both for the young ladies in the "Young Ladies' Mutual Improvement Association" and for married women in the "Retrenchment Departments" within the "Relief Societies" of the church. Retrenchment associations were to remain throughout the cooperative movement until the organization of the United Orders in 1874.

Consumer Cooperatives

At the October General Conference of the church in 1868, church leaders began the promotion of consumer cooperatives. Conference sermons were followed by meetings in LDS wards conducted by priesthood leaders, first starting in Salt Lake City and then extending throughout Mormondom.

Arrington summarizes the messages of the priesthood leaders as they presented the idea of consumer cooperatives to the church membership (pp. 297–98):

. . . (1) The Latter-day Saints should not trade with "outsiders." (2) A cooperative wholesale house or "Parent Institution" should be established in Salt Lake City, which would purchase all goods imported into the Territory for sale. (3) Cooperative retailing establishments should be established in each ward and settlement, and these should patronize the parent wholesale house in Salt Lake City, and also control the trade within their respective communities. (4) The retail stores should use their profits in establishing local shops and factories which could supply the people's wants.

While locally owned and directed cooperatives had been previously established in two Utah towns, Brigham City and Lehi, due in some measure to the influence or the example of cooperatives established in England during the preceding decades, according to Arrington the cooperative movement began with the organization of the Zion's Cooperative Mercantile Institution on October 24, 1868, with the approval by the central Salt Lake–based School of the Prophets of its preamble, constitution, and bylaws. Cooperative retail stores were organized in more than a hundred communities in the next few months, with purchases of non-Mormon-produced goods made through the parent organization in Salt Lake City. The local cooperatives were under the control of the local Schools of the Prophets.

While church members were stockholders in these cooperatives, the earnings were to be tithed before the distribution of dividends. Officers, with the exception of the secretary and treasurer, were not paid, and prices were to be controlled, being set at the "lowest feasible level." In general, the stores were previously privately owned, with cooperating stores sporting a sign "Holiness unto the Lord," below which was "Zion's Cooperative Mercantile Institution." Employees were paid partly in cash and partly in orders on the retail stores.

H. B. Clawson (a son-in-law of President Young), who was associated with the firm of Eldredge and Clawson and who had been involved in the leadership of the Dramatic Association in the early 1850s, was appointed as general superintendent, while William Clayton, who had likewise been involved, was appointed chief clerk.

The cooperative movement prospered until the depression of 1873. The depressed economy of that year, along with poor management (which frequently has attended the cooperative movement whether in or out of the church), resulted in the abandonment of many of the local cooperatives. Some became legally incorporated as private, profit-oriented businesses, while some failed and others were merged into the United Orders.

Production Units

If an economic Zion was to be established and Zion's Workmen involved in the building of the Kingdom, under priesthood direction, production units must be established. "Home manufacture," the clarion cry of much of the union movement of that part of the century, became the motto. Apostle George Q. Cannon pointed to the need for locally or Mormon-controlled economic enterprise (Arrington, 1958, p. 247; quoted form *Deseret News,* August 12, 1868):

> The railroad will not be an unmixed benefit to us unless we prepare for it. It will not put an abundance of money in circulation unless we lay the foundation of branches of business that will bring it to us. It is a mistake to suppose that the railroad, in and of itself, is going to make our country great and our people wealthy. While there is demand for labor upon its construction, and we have that labor to supply, money will flow unto us; but when this demand ceases, and we have no products that we transport at a profit for which money can be had in return, we will be in a worse position than if we had no railroad; for the ease with which the country can then be drained, at speculators' own prices, of breadstuffs and such articles as we now produce will be a detriment to us. . . . We must take the necessary steps to create new industries. . . . Our manufacturers, mechanics and merchants should endeavor to shape their various branches of business so as to be prepared for the coming change. Home manufacture must be extensively and persistently pursued.

The production units were to be the beneficiaries of the consumer cooperatives in several ways:

(1) The creation of larger, more efficient retail outlets would release Mormon capitalists and workers to the organization of such units.

(2) The surplus earnings of the cooperatives were to be used to finance their establishment.

(3) Their products were to have ready outlets; production in excess of local needs could be readily sold through the ZCMI wholesale house in Salt Lake City, if necessary, with markets throughout Mormondom as well as outside it.

Encouraged by the Schools of the Prophets, numerous manufacturing concerns were established throughout the Mormon commonwealth, including those producing wagons and carriages, agricultural machinery, woolen and silken goods, blankets, ink, matches, and men's clothing. In addition, cooperative butcher shops, dairies, carding machines, gristmills, sawmills, tanneries, boot and shoe shops,

The Eagle Emporium was the first home of Zion's Cooperative Mercantile Institution (ZCMI).

molasses mills, and furniture shops were established (Arrington, 1958, p. 309).

These production units met with varying success. However, with the depression commencing in 1873, an increasing number failed or were on the verge of failure when the local United Orders frequently took over their assets.

Low Wage Policy

If Mormon-produced goods were to have a competitive edge in local as well as regional and national markets, they must be competitive in price. The principal element of price was the cost of labor due to the labor-intensive nature of most production. The School of the Prophets therefore initiated a campaign to depress the wage level. Arrington informs us (p. 248):

> At an important meeting of the school in July 1869, at which members of the First Presidency, several members of the Council of Twelve Apostles, and a full membership of the school were present, a decision was reached to elect a committeeman from each trade. The committeeman was expected to submit to his trade the proposition that wages be reduced "in order that Utah might be able to compete with the manufacture of the states." The goal was to reduce wages by as much as one-third to one-half. The reactions of the tradespeople to this proposition are not chronicled, but it seems doubtful that the school was successful in reducing wages substantially or permanently. There seems, however, to have been a willingness on the part of many Mormon mechanics and artisans to make sacrifices for the cause of building up Zion. It is interesting to note that wage reduction was the first announced policy of the church, which the Godbeites undertook to criticize in print.

The low-wage policy not only provided the apostate Godbeites with a point of attack to be exploited in its challenge to the church's leaders, it also was antagonistic to one of the primary goals of the labor movement. Trade unions, being democratically oriented institutions, were primarily interested in the economic advancement of their memberships. While trade unionists could benefit as consumers through low prices, the more direct route to economic improvement was through higher, not lower, wages. Besides, low wages did not necessarily result in compensatorily low prices. While the Mormon cooperatives may have been well intentioned in their stated objective of low prices, the monopoly power they possessed could easily result in higher than necessary prices. Local priesthood leaders, who controlled the local cooperatives and manufacturing concerns, were usually also the dominant furnishers of capital. While the distribution of the profits of some cooperatives was on the Rochdale principle of distribution on the basis of patronage, in others it was based on the amount of capital furnished. Thus the system provided the opportunity for the exploitation of labor, whether or not it actually occurred, and it is suspected that it at least sometimes did.

When it happened, workers might well feel that they were taken advantage of. So long as they saw their sacrifices were for the "building up of Zion" there was no serious problem. Many were content to be Zion's workmen. But once they became convinced, or probably even suspected, that their low wages made possible fine homes and fancy clothing for the capitalist leaders and their families, they would rebel. Of course the "feelings" about "exploitation" were crucial and depended to some extent upon the level of conversion. The spiritually weak were most ready to impugn the system as one of exploitation, while the devout would require substantial evidence before they became critical.

The low-wage policy, with the possibilities of being both misunderstood and misused, helped to create a breach between workers and the church, a breach which was taken full advantage of by the apostate Godbeites. It also provided a point of attack by non-Mormon trade unions innocent of any antagonism toward the church as a religious institution, but who only saw the church policy as driving down wages, injuring them. A public protest by workers in 1874 (discussed later) was primarily over this issue (Salt Lake *Tribune*, March 24, 1874). And while these trade unionists may have been innocent of any desire to attack the church as such, their protest — coupled with the attacks of the Godbeites and their organ, the *Tribune* — placed them in the camp of the enemies of the church . . . at least in the minds of church authorities, Mormon capitalists, and devout church members, extrasensitive during that period to attacks on the church, its doctrines, practices, and leaders.

Not only was there a point of real conflict, the church cooperative movement also automatically, although perhaps innocently, helped intensify the conflict. Many devout Mormon workmen, who might have mediated differences, became involved in the cooperatives, removing their influence from nonchurch-directed or secular worker organizations.

The United Order Movement

In the mind or vision of Brigham Young, the cooperative movement was not really enough. There was insufficient involvement of the Saints. To prepare a perfected economic Kingdom would require even greater community involvement and dedication. He saw in the successful and prosperous communitywide Brigham City (Utah) Cooperative an example of the next level of the Lord's economic system, which would prepare the Saints for eventually living the Law of Consecration given through his predecessor, Joseph Smith. This law would require the consecration of all that one possessed to the "building of the Kingdom." But the church membership had not been able to live the earlier law and could not unless they were prepared for it.

The economic collapse of 1873–74 provided both the incentive and the opportunity for the replication of the Brigham City Cooperative or something approaching it throughout the church. St. George, Utah, the winter home of the aging prophet, was the most likely place to initiate the new system — the United Order. The preamble of the charter of the United Order of St. George saw it as the primary means of resolving the conflicts between capital and labor, which were resulting in a new wave of industrial warfare throughout the nation. It also saw the consequent specialization of labor resulting in greater productivity, which would in turn result in an improved standard of living.

Arrington (pp. 327–28) quotes at length from Edward Allen (1936, pp. 136, 137):

> Realizing the signs and spirit of the times and from the results of our past experience, the necessity of a closer union and combination of our labor for the promotion of our common welfare:
>
> And whereas: — we have learned of the struggle between capital and labor — resulting in strikes of the workmen, with their consequent distress; and also the oppression of monied monopolies.
>
> And whereas: — there is a growing distrust and faithlessness among men in the political and business relations of life, as well as a spirit for extravagant speculation and over-reaching the legitimate bounds of the credit system; resulting in financial panic and bankruptcy, paralyzing industry, thereby making many of the necessities and conveniences of life precarious and uncertain.

And whereas: — our past experience has proven that, to be the friends of God we must become friends and helpers of each other, in a common bond and brotherhood.

And whereas: — to accomplish such a desirable end and to become truly prosperous, we must be self-sustaining, encouraging home manufacturing, producing cotton, and other raw materials; and not only supply our own wants with manufactured goods, but also have some to spare for exportation, and by these means create a fund for a sure basis upon which to do all our business.

And whereas: — we believe that by a proper classification of our labors and energies, with a due regard to the laws of life and health, we will not only increase in earthly possessions, at a more rapid rate, but will also have more leisure time to devote to the cultivation and training of our minds and those of our children in the arts and sciences.

And whereas: — at the present time, we rely too much upon importation for a large share of our clothing and other necessities; and also bring from abroad many articles of luxury of but little value, for which we pay our money, most of which articles could be dispensed with.

And whereas: — we believe that the beauty of our garments should be the workmanship of our own hands, and that we should practice more diligently economy, temperance, frugality, and the simple grandeur of manners that belong to the pure in heart.

And whereas: — we are desirous of avoiding the difficulties above alluded to, and feeling the necessity of becoming a self-sustaining community, fully realizing that we live in perilous times, socially, morally, politically, and commercially.

Therefore, be it resolved: — That we, the undersigned, being residents of the places set opposite our respective names, do hereby, of our own free will and choice, and without mental reservation, or purpose of evasion, and also without any undue influence, constraining or coercion having been used by any party whatever, to direct and guide us in this action, — mutually agree, each with the others, and with our associates and successors, to enter into and form a co-partnership for the purposes and subject to the provisions as herein set forth.

In the spring of 1874, as Brigham Young and other General Authorities moved north through Mormondom in their return to Salt Lake City they organized United Orders in community after community. Within a year, United Orders were established in almost every Mormon community in Utah, Nevada, and Arizona. According to Arrington, the United Orders had three primary objectives (p. 330):

(1) The economic unity necessary for the fight against "depression, unfriendly merchants, and poverty"

(2) The reduction of imports

(3) The pooling of surplus capital with which "to initiate new industries, develop new resources, and establish new colonies"

To these may be added a fourth, the retardation and prevention, if possible, of a market-oriented money exchange economy.

Evidently the church membership accepted the new system with open arms. It came at the depths of a depression and offered new hope. It was received especially well by the working men in the church. This acceptance is not surprising. Throughout the country, and during the nineteenth and at least the first third of the twentieth centuries, whenever recession came, workers turned from trade unionism to broad social experimentation as the most appropriate solution of their economic plight. Trade unionism, which primarily sought economic benefits through increased wages, was abortive in depression. Workers would not support a program which could not produce results, and during a depression the demand for higher wages fell on unsympathetic ears. An employer could not pay higher wages, or even maintain existing wages. Moreover, a strike to enforce demands would only result in unemployment in the face of the substantial ranks of unemployed workers who would be willing to take the place of strikers. Thus Mormon workers, the devout and the not so devout, accepted the United Orders. The devout were probably the more likely to go through the rebaptism ceremony characteristic of the United Order period.

Arrington identifies four types of United Orders (pp. 330-34): first, the "St. George-type Orders" in which persons in the community contributed "all of their economic property to the Order and received differential wages and dividends, depending upon ... [the value of] . . . their labor and the property contributed." Gains were achieved through the rationalization of agriculture and the increased specialization of labor. This type of Order was shortlived. Most were dissolved within a year or two of their founding, the death of Brigham Young in 1877 accelerating the dissolution. The St. George Order itself collapsed in 1878.

Second, the "Brigham City–type Order," with "increased community ownership and operation of cooperative enterprise" but not a "consecration of all of one's property or labor." By the early 1880s, these Orders fell on difficult times, even the previously successful Brigham City experiment having its problems because of the administrative nightmare of trying to coordinate some forty cooperative enterprises.

Third, the "Orderville [Utah] type of communal Orders," where there was no private property. People shared roughly "equally in the common product and lived and ate as a well-regulated family." Some of these Orders, in relatively isolated areas, lasted until the mid-1880s, and in fewer cases until the late 1880s, when antipolygamy raids and economic change drove them out of business.

Fourth, the "specialty-type Orders," located mostly in the larger urban centers of Salt Lake City, Ogden, Provo, and Logan. In these Orders, a ward had a given product or closely related products to produce on a cooperative basis, with all members of the ward expected to participate in the financing of the enterprise. Arrington lists the following specialty Orders (p. 333):

City or Town	Place	Product or Facility
Salt Lake City	8th Ward	Hats
	19th Ward	Soap
	11th Ward	Tailored merchandise
	20th Ward	Boots and shoes
Logan	1st Ward	Foundry and machine shop, producing sawmills, planing machines, agricultural tools and implements
	2nd Ward	Planing mill and woodworking shop
	3rd Ward	Dairy

To these may be added (*Deseret News*, June 4, 10, and 11, 1874):

City or Town	Place	Product or Facility
Bountiful		Bricks
Salt Lake City	8th Ward	Horticulture
Salt Lake City	(Ward unnamed)	Leather goods

These United Orders cut down the number of potential Mormon members of conventional unions and had the specific effect of drawing Mormons, both members and leaders, from whatever unions remained after 1873. Thus most of those strictly worker organizations that may have survived the depression beginning that year probably came under the control of non-Mormons or the less devout members of the church, typographers excepted.

After the death of Brigham Young in 1877, few United Orders remained, most of these evidently being the specialty and communal types. In 1878 there was a soap factory reportedly making good products (*Journal History*, April 17, 1878, p. 2), as well as a United Order foundry, wagon and machine company (*Journal History*, February 26, 1878, p. 6). In Logan in 1877–86, there was a United Order foundry (*Journal History*, October 8, 1877, p. 4; March 6, 1879, p. 3; May 15, 1886, p. 10), as well as a United Order manufacturing and building company in 1881–84 (*Journal History*, January 31, 1881, p. 4; February 11, 1882, p. 2; February 9, 1884, p. 8). By 1886 the remaining United Orders had either collapsed, been converted into conventional cooperatives, or become strictly private enterprises.

Leather Goods

On May 1, 1874, 119 men of the Salt Lake City 20th Ward met to form a United Order composed of "various trades and professions." What these trades and professions were is not known, but it was intended that superintendents or foremen would be elected at subsequent meetings (*Journal History*, May 1, 1874). On June 10, 1874, "a meeting of persons interested in the manufacture of leather, and of boots and shoes, harness, etc., was held at the City Hall" (*Journal History*, June 10, 1874). Presiding Bishop Edward Hunter acted as chairman, assisted by the ubiquitous A. M. Musser as clerk. In attendance were four tanners and curriers, nine saddle and harness makers, and 35 boot- and shoemakers. G. C. Riser, Edward Snelgrove, and Charles Crow constituted a committee to

. . . wait on the butchers, hide and skin dealers, to ascertain whether they were willing to co-operate with the leather makers and workers in endeavoring to establish a home industry in that line on a broader basis than theretofore (*Journal History*, June 10, 1874).

This was evidently a citywide cooperative effort, for at least four wards — 11th, 12th, 16th, and 17th — were represented by Riser, Snelgrove, Crow, and Hunter. On November 20, 1874, the 20th Ward United Order met "to establish a first-class manufactory of boots and shoes. The capital stock was placed at $80,000 in shares of $5.00 each, all of which were immediately taken" (*Journal History, November 20, 1874*).

On November 22, the Salt Lake *Herald* (Mormon controlled) called for the establishment of a tannery to produce the leather needed for the leather goods industry. "The extensive manufacture of boots and shoes here will therefore render a leather tannery a necessity. . . . Let us have a tannery at once" (*Journal History*, November 22, 1874). Two days later, the *Deseret News* discussed the advantages of producing leather goods locally (*Journal History*, November 24, 1874):

> The boot and shoe makers here have not, it is true, much advantage over the eastern makers in the matter of freight, but they have other advantages. . . . The imported articles sold here are not purchased directly from manufacturers, but from middle men or jobbers, and therefore a home manufacturer has the advantage of the Jobbers' profits and expenses, and the matter of high rents, etc., of eastern establishments. . . . The plan of a United Order organization taking hold of one particular branch of business and making that a specialty and a success appears to be much better than "having too many irons in the fire." It is much easier to commence in a single line of manufacture and make that one thing successful by a grand concentration of capital and practical ability, and after that particular branch is in good and satisfactory working order to make that the initial point, and then take up another, and another. Business, like everything in nature, to be healthy and sound must have a gradual and natural growth.

John Sharp was named president, with W. C. Dunbar and W. L. N. Allen as vice presidents, D. O. Calder as treasurer, and B. H. Schettler as secretary. George Romney, brother of Miles Romney who had headed the carpenters and joiners in 1861, was a member of the executive committee.

The St. George Builders Union

On June 6, 1877, the members of the St. George United Order organized, under articles of agreement, the St. George Builders Union — representing the carpenters, joiners, cabinetmakers, turners, wagon makers, coopers, painters, masons, stonecutters, plasterers, quarrymen, brick and adobe makers, lime burners, and tending laborers — formed to "promote our interests and those of the community" (*Journal History*, June 6, 1877). Wages were to be fixed or controlled by the union, similar to attempts of secular unions. The disposition of any surplus of union receipts was to be made as directed by the union and the priesthood, no member having any claim to them ("Manuscript History of St. George," 1877).

Similar to the typographical association in 1855, it was a closed union, only church members in good standing being allowed membership. All members were required to sign the articles of agreement and could be expelled by a two-thirds vote for "acts detrimental or prejudicial to the interests of the union." The presiding officer (superintendent) was assisted by foremen over each department of work. All were elected to office by the union membership and were to hold office so long as they were willing to serve or until rejected by a two-thirds vote. The superintendent and foremen were to be "passed upon, or sustained in their positions by the vote of the members, each of whom shall be entitled to one vote."

Each member agreed to allow the union officers to negotiate all contracts for work and to be controlled by the officers in his labor. Meetings were to be held as called, except that one was scheduled for June 1 of each year for the purpose of "sustaining" the leaders (a practice in which church members are periodically given the opportunity to vote by a show of hands to sustain or oppose each leader). Any five members could require the superintendent to call a meeting. The workday was held at ten hours. Wages were to be credited for overtime — but evidently not at premium rates. Intoxicating beverages were not to be consumed on the job (*Journal History*, June 10, 1877).

Most of the leaders in this organization were men who had been prominent in the construction of the church tabernacle and temple in St. George (Miller, 1946, p. 151). Bishop Miles P. Romney (the son of Miles

Romney, the general superintendent of construction on these church buildings [Lundwall, 1949, p. 88] and leader of the carpenters and joiners in 1861) was the first to sign the agreement and was elected the first superintendent of the union (*Journal History*, June 10, 1877).

It is not known how long the St. George Builders Union remained in existence, but the *Deseret News* reported on April 18,'1878, that the union had the contract for erecting a two-story building on a cotton farm ten miles east of St. George. It is known that the local church leaders were actively interested in this development, for without their leadership the union could not have been formed by the United Order. At a stake conference on July 8, 1877, Henry Eyring, a counselor to the stake president, reported on the progress of the mechanics in uniting and felt that the farmers should do likewise in the near future (*Deseret News*, July 8, 1877). The farmers did unite on July 20, 1877 (*Deseret News*, July 20, 1877). The union may well have been organized to deal on a more favorable basis with the Gentile silver mining camp of Silver Reef near by. The Silver Reef population was largely Gentile, for the LDS church leaders strongly discouraged mining of precious metals by members at this time. However, enough Mormons lived in Silver Reef at the time to warrant holding church services in rented quarters.

Zion's Boards of Trade

As already indicated, by the time of Brigham Young's death in 1877, most of the previously established United Orders had ceased to exist. Upon Young's death, John Taylor headed the church. According to Arrington (1958), Taylor saw the United Order as "a step in the right direction" but recognized the need for "a new type of economic planning" exemplified in Zion's Central Board of Trade. This board's members were: President Taylor; Bishop Edward Hunter and William Jennings, vice presidents; and fifty priesthood leaders from throughout the church. The board of trade concept was patterned after a board created in Cache Valley (Utah) in 1872, which was seen by founder Moses Thatcher as a means of "regulating the commerce of producers and consumers and introducing a more healthy and stable condition of supply and demand" (Arrington, 1958, p. 342).

In October 1878, the concept was presented to and accepted by those attending the General Conference of the church. Once again, the General Authorities were sent out, this time to organize local boards of trade. According to Arrington, the declared objectives were (pp. 343–44):

(1) To maintain a commercial exchange

(2) To seek remunerative markets for the produce of the "brethren" and help to bring them as cheaply as possible what they would have to buy

(3) To aid in organizing and sustaining such home industries as would tend to the independence and self-sustenance of the people

(4) To attempt to prevent the Saints from overstocking the market and introducing and sustaining among themselves "hurtful conditions"

(5) To promote uniformity in the customs and usages of producers, manufacturers, and merchants

(6) To acquire and disseminate valuable agricultural, commercial, and manufacturing information

(7) To bring "home producer and manufacturer" into close business relations with the consumer, preventing intermediate parties from exacting margins for transacting business which, with a little forethought and care, the people, through the Boards of Trade, could do as well for themselves

(8) To help the producer fix living prices on the "fruits of his own toil"

(9) To foster capital and protect labor, "uniting them as friends rather than dividing them as enemies"

(10) To facilitate the speedy adjustment of business disputes

(11) To arrange for transportation

(12) Generally, to secure to its members the benefits of cooperation in the furtherance of their legitimate pursuits, and "to unite and harmonize the business relations of the stake Boards of Trade."

There was little difference between these stated objectives and those of the cooperatives and the United Orders. However, the tight controls on personal freedoms, characteristic of some of the United Orders, were eliminated. The system was much more adaptable to the more prosperous years of the 1880s. ZCMI was seen as a key institution within this new movement, being well represented on the Central Board.

The implications of these objectives for Zion's Workmen are clear. Demand for the labors of the workmen was to be stimulated, keeping them employed. They were to be protected from outside competition.

Market gluts, which would result in unemployment, were to be minimized. Cutthroat competition, which would tend to drive wages down, was to be controlled. Competition among workers was eliminated by "promoting uniformity in the customs and usages of producers." Prices were to be kept at a low level through reduced reliance on middlemen, making workmen's wages go farther. A living wage for workers was to be fixed. Cooperation between labor and capital was to be promoted, quickly adjusting labor disputes. Few Mormon workers would challenge these as laudable objectives, which if fully implemented would promote the economic interests of the workers. Certainly they were not to be "thrown to the wolves" of a capitalistic, competitive world. They were to be protected through the priesthood organization and the church.

Some nineteen industry groups were recognized, and the boards were given the responsibility to promote "home industry" in these fields. The *Deseret News* (April 20, 1881) saw the system as "the grandest opportunity for the building up of a self-sustaining, industrial and powerful system of cooperative effort. . . . What is needed? Union of capital and labor, mutual interest between consumer and producer" (Arrington, 1958, p. 345).

Substantial attention and capital were given to the development of the iron, sugar, and wagon and agricultural implements industries, the first being unsuccessful and the other two registering success. Considerable effort was also devoted to improving transportation throughout the state. Rather than adding to church business interests, the movement was evidently more interested in developing privately owned industry.

Zion's Boards of Trade made a limited impact. The early years found them at the tail end of a depression, and with the increasing prosperity of the 1880s interest in the support of them waned. The death blow was dealt with the increased fervor of the national campaign against Mormon political power in Utah, the unique and uncapitalistic Mormon economic system, and, most importantly, the peculiarly Mormon practice of polygamy. Church President John Taylor was forced into hiding to avoid imprisonment; numerous ecclesiastical leaders (including Cannon) and members were imprisoned; church commercial properties were escheated; and devout Mormons were denied the right to vote. With such political turmoil, the protective Mormon economic system was doomed to failure. But even without the turmoil, it was probably doomed. It was the heyday of uncontrolled capitalism, a development with which Mormons would have to accommodate if they were to survive. Such accommodation was made, but Mormon workmen were left without the protec-

100   :   DESERET'S SONS OF TOIL

tion previously afforded them. They were at the mercy of the new, almost omnipotent capitalists.

It is interesting to note that during the decade of the 1880s, and the less restrictive economic program of Zion's Boards of Trade, Utah unionism was reborn. This church program was not competitive with trade unionism in the sense of drawing away devout church members into a church economic system. Unfortunately for the historian, except for the typographers, little is yet known of the membership of these new worker organizations of the 1880s. Therefore, except for a few, the fate of church members vis-a-vis unionism has not yet been definitely established. But irrespective of their spiritual fate, Zion's Workmen were probably in an economic limbo.

References

Allen, Edward Jones. "The Second United Order among the Mormons." New York: Columbia University Press. 1936.

Arrington, Leonard J. *Great Basin Kingdom.* Cambridge, Massachusetts: Harvard University Press. 1958.

Deseret News, Salt Lake City, June 4, 10, and 11, November 24, 1874: July 8 and 20, 1877; April 18, 1878; April 20, 1881.

Gates, Susan Young, *History of the Young Ladies Mutual Improvement Association of the Church.* Salt Lake City: *Deseret News.* 1911.

Journal History. Salt Lake City. May 1, June 10, November 20, 22, and 24, 1874; June 6 and 10, October 8, 1877; February 26, April 17, 1878; March 6, 1879; January 31, 1881; February 11, 1882, February 9, 1884; May 15, 1886.

Lundwall, N. B. *Temples of the Most High.* Salt Lake City: Bookcraft. 1949.

"Manuscript History of St. George." Salt Lake City: Church Historian's Office. March 27, 1877.

Miller, Albert E. *Immortal Pioneers, Founders of the City of St. George, Utah.* St. George. 1946.

Salt Lake *Tribune*, Salt Lake City, March 24, 1874.

6

Utah's Fledgling
Labor Unions
1868 to 1888

The pioneer, embrionic Utah trade unionism of 1852–69 had been dominated by Mormon craftsmen, with only a smattering of non-Mormons. Of the fifty known leaders of guilds or unions in 1861, 48 (or 96 percent) were known to have been members of the church at the time of their worker leadership activity, while another soon became a church member. The church leadership had played a significant role in the formation of several craft associations — the Deseret Dramatic Association, the Deseret Typographical Association, and the Deseret School Teachers Association. Deseret Typographical Union Local 115, Utah's first documented labor union associated with a national body, was dominated by church members; at least eight of ten charter members and all of the initial officers were members of the church. Use of the word "Deseret" (a peculiar Mormon term designating the honey bee, thus connoting "industry"), carried over from the earlier associations, indicates a lingering attachment of the typographers to the church, at least to its culture.

Beginning of Worker Independence

As already shown during the inflation associated with the latter part of the Civil War, there had been great upward pressure on wages. The members of the Deseret Dramatic Association, as well as representatives from the various crafts, had experienced confrontation with several church leaders over wages — church leaders feeling that wages were too high, attracting non-Mormons into the Territory, diluting Mormon influence, and inhibiting the growth of domestic industry or "home manufactures." It may well have been these confrontations that convinced President Young that his hope for economic direction through control of the craft guilds could not hold up, that perhaps his confidence in them had been misplaced. On the other hand, the confrontations could well have convinced some craftsmen, even Mormons, that they would need to exercise independence, at least in secular affairs, from ecclesiastical authority. Evidence of this independence may be seen in the chartering of Deseret Typographical Union Local 115 as an affiliate of the National Typographical Union in 1868.

With this organization, at least, the guild may be said to have been transformed into a full-fledged union, demonstrating the evolutionary characteristics of many unions of the period. The business unionism of the later decades of the nineteenth century often found its roots in the local reform unionism and guilds of the first half of that century. However, as unionization proceeded, it was found necessary to become affiliated with national organizations. As markets expanded, workers came into competition with each other. Unrestricted competition drove wages down and often emasculated the crafts as they were broken into components for greater efficiency. The functions could then be taken over in large measure by semiskilled workers or machinery. To protect their crafts and their perquisites, local trade unions united into national unions. This the printers of Deseret accomplished in 1868.

For Zion's craft organizations this trend proved troublesome, for the religious motivation and influence characteristic of earlier years would now suffer as the local unions merged their interests with those of the national unions. Religious leaders would less and less be able to affect the decisions and actions of the unions, understandably creating some apprehension on the part of church leaders, who were somewhat protective of their influence and whose vision was still one of a theocratic Zion. Such new outside affiliations represented a breakdown of Zionic hopes, even though such separateness was to be the wave of the future not only for workers but also for professional and business groups. This particular affiliation of the printers indicates that the religiously motivated and influenced printers guild was not adequately representing the interests of its members, at least in their view. It must be remembered that this association took place before the intrusion of Gentile unionism and was dominated, if not monopolized, by Latter-day Saints.

The growing independence of Deseret's workmen from Church control or influence can also be seen in the defiance of and breaking away from the Church and its leaders of a substantial number of church leaders and members beginning in 1870 in what has become known as the Godbeite movement, heresy, or apostacy. In addition to the intellectual, business, and church leaders involved (including Apostle Amasa Lyman), a number of working men and their leaders were also associated in this movement. At the first General Conference of the Church of Zion, the rallying organization of the movement at the time (April 1870) of the fourteen men seated on the stand, three were or became involved in the budding union movement: Joseph Silvers represented the Amalgamated Carpenters and Joiners in 1896 and could well have been so associated in 1870; Joseph H. Randall was to become associated with Local No. 236 of the International Typographical Association in Ogden at least in the 1890s; Edward Martin, leader of one of the ill-fated handcart companies in the 1860s, was a member of the Deseret Dramatic Association in the 1850s and led the painters and glaziers in the 1861 Fourth of July parade. In addition to these leaders, missionaries of the Church of Zion included three other men associated in the labor movement: T.C. Armstrong, a leader of the Jordan Assembly No. 3543 and District Assembly No. 205 of the Knights of Labor in 1887 and an officer in the typographical union Local 115 in the 1890s (both of these organizations were to take strong anti-church positions); another missionary was Robert Nichols, who participated in the protest meeting of 1874, being a member of the Resolutions Committee as well as secretary of the "permanent" organization created at that meeting (there were some anti-church overtones at this meeting with attacks on the low wage policy being implemented by church leaders during that period). The third missionary was Samuel Carlisle, a returned missionary in 1867 who strongly defended Brigham Young, who represented the stonecutters at the 1874 protest meeting, attacking the low wage policy of Brigham Young, and who in 1890 wrote a strong letter to the Salt Lake *Tribune* attacking Robert G. Sleater and the Workingmen's Party which was allied with the church-sponsored People's Party. These relationships could not help but leave the impression with church leaders that unionism was antagonistic to Mormonism.

Diminished Union Activity

In 1869 another Fourth of July parade featured the guilds and unions (*Deseret News*, July 4, 1869) It was apparently a much diminished labor oriented parade, with only twelve separate trades groups or crafts represented — engineers, gunsmiths, wagon makers, tanners and curriers, harness makers, bakers, photographers, butchers, stablemen, rope makers, mechanics, and the typographical Local 115, the only trade group known to be affiliated with a national or international union. This compared with the fifty trades represented in the 1861 parade. This observation must be qualified somewhat by the possibility that the mechanics may have included the construction crafts as well as such crafts as blacksmiths, wheelwrights, and the like. But even if these trades were so represented, the 1869 parade still had far fewer trades represented. Unfortunately for historians, the leaders of these trades groups were not listed, thus their relationship to the church is unknown.

While the worker movement may have been diminished, it was not dead. The typographers were evidently quite active. They called Utah's first documented strike — against the *Tribune* for expelling two workers (Salt Lake *Tribune*, November 7, 1871). They sent Robert G. Sleater as a delegate to the International Typographical Union convention in Richmond, Virginia, in 1872, where he was to distinguish himself by becoming one of two vice presidents (I.T.U. convention report, 1872). The typographers were also able to form a local in the Tintic silver mining area that same year (Salt Lake *Tribune*, August 27, 1872). In 1872, a new Salt Lake City craft, the plasterers, met to form a union (Salt Lake *Tribune*, May 27, 1872), and later that year the mechanics were considering the formation of a union (Salt Lake *Tribune*, December 31, 1872). This latter newspaper report would seem to indicate that the mechanics union which had marched in the 1869 parade had become defunct.

In 1872 the Salt Lake *Tribune* (May 27, 1872) saw what unionization there was as "an indication of the growing independence of our workingmen and as evidence of the widening breach between the Church and State." The very fact that the anti-Mormon *Tribune* was championing the labor movement as an instrument for driving a wedge between the people and the church helped to create a wedge, making the church leadership and devout church membership skeptical of trade unionism. But in addition, it indicates that some sort of breach may already have occurred.

The Depression of 1873–79

The winter of 1873 was a bad one economically — in the Territory as well as in the nation — initiating a depression that was to last until

1879. Unemployment was rampant, and there was downward pressure on wages. Evidently employers, despite unemployment, were seeking even greater power to reduce costs by driving wages down, for they advertised for additional craftsmen to move to the Salt Lake Valley. On March 24, 1874, a group of two hundred workmen assembled in Independence Hall in Salt Lake City to protest a statement in the *Herald* (a Mormon-controlled newspaper) that "there is employment in this city for outside mechanics." The chairman of the meeting was James Stevens (M), a carpenter, with Edward Tyson (U), who represented the plasterers, as secretary (Salt Lake *Tribune*, March 24, 1874).

A resolutions committee was named to express the sense of the meeting on the *Herald's* statement, evidently emanating from a Mormon building contractor and self-styled capitalist, Nicholas Groesbeck, who was seeking help at $1.50 a day. Apparently his was an attempt to put into practice the goal of the School of the Prophets to reduce wages by a third to a half (Arrington, 1958, p. 248), a policy strongly attacked by the Godbeites. One man, S.H. Carlisle (M), an apostate Godbeite, of the stone cutters, was extremely vocal in condemning President Young's reported plan to reduce mechanics' wages to $1.50 and laborers' wages to $0.75 per day. A resolution was adopted (Salt Lake *Tribune*, March 24, 1874):

> Resolved, that the article published in the Salt Lake *Daily Herald* of March 19th . . . be read to this meeting by the secretary. . . . Resolved, that it is the sense of this meeting that the statement therein contained is not justified by the facts. . . . Resolved, that we, the workingmen of Salt Lake, in mass meeting assembled, do most emphatically denounce the policy of inviting an outside laboring population into our midst to flood the labor market, as being inimical to their interest and own. . . . Resolved, that it is the expressed sense of this meeting that the labor market has been overstocked for at least two years, and that at no time has the demand been equal to the supply.

Aside from the criticism of the wage-cutting policy of Brigham Young, the meeting demonstrated little animosity toward the church. It was reported in a somewhat garbled account that "Mr. Carlisle wished to know whether he should speak to the *Herald* answer . . . that the question of Mormon or non-Mormon but slightly affected merchants and mechanics" (Salt Lake *Tribune*, March 24, 1874). Although the account was jumbled, the reported reaction — according to the

Tribune — was not: "A few obstrepreous 'no's' at the back of the hall led this speaker to take his seat." Even though the meeting was dominated by non-Mormons, there apparently were leaders and representatives who were not antagonistic toward the church and who did not want those in attendance to get involved in an attack on the church. One of these leaders, James Watson (M), was to become a bishop a few years later.

The first meeting fostered another that, it was hoped, would create a permanent organization. James Stevens (M) was chairman, with Robert Nichols (M),* a carpenter, as secretary; and a committee consisting of two spokesmen from each trade represented was selected. The membership of the committee consisted of the following:

Trade	*Name*	
Bricklayers	William Wilson	(M)
	John Whiting	(N)
Carpenters	James Stevens	(M)
	(Mr.) Longfellow	(U)
Lathers	James Sherlock	(U)
	Thomas Kiernan	(U)
Painters	Joseph Russell	(U)
	O. Stenburg	(U)
Plasterers	James Wyatt	(U)
	Edward Tyson	(U)
Plumbers and gas fitters	Dennis Hogan	(U)
	(Mr.) Moorcook	(U)
Shoemakers	J. W. Fagan	(U)
	Henry A. Cushion	(U)
Stonecutters	S. H. Carlisle	(M)*
	John A. (or Andrew) Woolf	(M)
Tinners	G. W. Bostwick	(M)*
	Anthony Martin	(M)

---

*Godbeite. (See footnote, page 12.)

Other persons prominent in this meeting were James Hunter (M); James Dickson (N), tinner; James Watson (M), stonecutter; and Joseph Salisbury (N), carpenter. It is not known whether any of these worker groups affiliated with national unions, or even if they were organized as formal unions. Of this group, only the tinners had marched in the 1869 parade; however, many of the others may have been represented in the mechanics union. Of this group, only the shoemakers were not in construction work. What happened to this hoped-for permanent organization is not known, but it may have died out, as did most union organizations throughout the country in that decade.

Absent from the 1874 meeting were the typographers. This is not to infer that their organization was defunct, for they evidently retained their national charter from its inception in 1868. They had been independent in the early years of their union, eschewing associations that might have diminished the typographers' options or reflected negatively on them. They were decreasing in size — a 50 percent reduction in membership between 1872 and 1873 (I.T.U. *Proceedings*, 1872, 1873) — thus this meeting in 1874 may have made them wary.

The worker movement in Utah had experienced an immense change since 1860, the earlier movement having been dominated by Mormons. The 1874 meeting, if it was representative of the Utah union movement at that moment in time, was noted by its paucity of church members. Of the 23 major participants known by name, only seven were known members of the church (three Godbeites); there were three nonmembers, while the church affiliations of thirteen are not known. Interestingly, even though this group was protesting attempts to bring outsiders into the Salt Lake Valley, at least four were themselves transients, not being found in any of the city's directories for 1869, 1874, or 1879–80.

Even the typographers had undergone change. Beginning as a Mormon-controlled association and then a Mormon-dominated union, by 1874 its LDS membership had probably been diluted, assuming membership to be open to all members of the craft (there is no reason to assume otherwise). It is questionable whether the more faithful followers of the LDS religion would work for the newly established *Tribune*, a bitterly anti-Mormon newspaper. Therefore at that time, the *Tribune*'s employees were most likely non-Mormons and disaffected members of the church, although some loyal Latter-day Saints may have been employed out of economic necessity. If *Tribune* employees *were* admitted to membership in the local, its character must have been altered materially. One cannot help but wonder what occurred during the typographers' meetings of that period. However, we do know that in 1879, the local leadership was still dominated by Mormons. Of the seven officers of that year, at least six were church members, and at least four had received endowments (I.T.U. *Proceedings*, 1879). The president of the union, Henry McEwan (M), was evidently a devout church member. In addition, the local retained the name "Deseret" until 1886.

Except for the miners (discussed subsequently), there was little documented trade union activity from 1875 to 1879. From a purely historical perspective, the apparent collapse of unionism should have been foreseen. Modern-day students of labor's history could have predicted it, for they know that during prosperity unions flourish. When the economy is prosperous, incomes of workers and profits of business firms increase. Full employment is approached and unemployment diminishes. Worker bargaining power increases. Therefore, when workers demand increased wages and improved working conditions, employers comply more readily with worker demands. If workers are organized and their demands are presented by union representatives, the unions have the appearance of success. At least, that is how workers see it. Workers are then willing to forego some independence, turning it over to the union leaders to do the bargaining for them.

The opposite is true during recession. With profits low, employers cannot afford to give in to union demands (they would as soon lose some workers, anyway). Thus unions are usually not so successful in improving worker benefits. Seeing little value in union membership, workers tend to drop out. This general observation appears to have been valid for the 1874–79 period in Utah.

The United Orders

The church's answer to the depression, as already shown, was an intensification of the cooperative efforts of the late 1860s in the form of the United Orders. Beginning in the spring of 1874, under the active leadership of Brigham Young, the General Authorities moved throughout the church establishing United Orders in most of the Mormon communities. There were several different kinds of Orders, among which were specialty-type Orders built around particular crafts or closely related crafts, such as the boot- and shoemakers, the tailors, and so on (Arrington, 1958, pp. 330–35).

While the specialty Orders were the most competitive to trade unionism, all of them probably resulted in several effects:

(1) They removed some Mormon craftsmen from trade union membership.

(2) They removed some Mormon craft leaders from leadership positions within the trade union movement.

(3) They were part of a separate economy, with reduced interaction with the Gentile or secular economy.

(4) They maintained closer ties between Mormon workers and their employers (Mormons), with a philosophy of greater cooperation and obedience or subservience to employer authority, than was true of members of trade unions.

Thus the mutually modifying influence of unions on the church — and in return, the church on the unions — was essentially eliminated.

Enter Railroaders

Another reason for the shift from Mormon-dominated unionism — in addition to the attempted separate Mormon economic system — was that with the coming of the railroads in 1869 there was a great influx of railroad workmen who transferred to Utah from the unionized east. These probably were largely non-Mormon, even though Mormons had played a dominant role in the construction of railroad tracks through Utah and the approaches to and from the Territory. These were temporary jobs — often to supplement meager agricultural incomes — usually away from home. After the tracks were laid, most Mormon workers likely returned to their homes.

At the national level, the various railroad brotherhoods were among the earlier unions in the country; the Brotherhood of Locomotive Engineers was founded in 1863, the Brotherhood of Conductors in 1868, and the Brotherhood of Firemen in 1873. "Engineers" had marched in the 1869 parade, but to which category they belonged is not certain. The record does not show any union activity among Utah railroaders in the 1870s, except for the visit of P. M. Arthur, of the Brotherhood of Locomotive Engineers, to Salt Lake City in 1874 on an organizing trip for his union. His success is unknown (Salt Lake *Tribune*, August 12, 1874). The reason for this inactivity may have been the national and territorial depression of most of that decade.

However, during the 1880s the Territory's railroaders became organized into the independent railroad brotherhoods as well as the Knights of Labor, most of them refusing to affiliate with the American Federation of Labor (AFL) or the city and state (territorial) federations.

The first-known railroad local in Utah was Perseverance Lodge No. 68, of the Brotherhood of Firemen, organized at Utah's rail center, Ogden, on September 1, 1882 (Pawar, 1968, p. 94), although the engineers had most likely been previously organized. Earlier in the year track layers on the Denver and Rio Grande Railroad had struck for higher wages ($2.50 and $2.75 per day) (Salt Lake *Tribune*, July 19, 1882). The conductors, Wahsatch (Wasatch) Division No. 124, probably associated with the Order of Railway Conductors, organized in Ogden on June 1, 1884 (Pawar, 1968, p. 94). As the Knights of Labor organized District Assembly No. 82 (with headquarters in Denver, Colorado, and covering Union Pacific Railroad workers), some of Utah's railroad workers doubtless were members of that union (Powderly, 1889, p. 638). On August 12, 1884, P. M. Arthur, Grand Chief Engineer of the Brotherhood of Locomotive Engineers, was in Salt Lake City attempting to work out labor-management problems (Salt Lake *Tribune*, August 12, 1884) on the Utah Central Railroad, Wasatch (Wahsatch) Division 222. The engineers held their second annual ball in January 1886, with 175 couples attending (Salt Lake *Tribune*, January 19 and 23, 1886).

Also in that year Utah's railroad workers were involved in the nationwide railroad strike, with significant and perceived effects on Utah's economy (Salt Lake *Tribune*, April 6, 1886). It would seem that the brakemen were also organized well enough to participate as a body in the strike (Salt Lake *Tribune*, May 5, 1885). By 1890, the locomotive firemen and railroad trainmen were organized in Salt Lake City (according to the 1890 Salt Lake City directory). In addition to the conductors and firemen, the Brotherhood of Railway Carmen (car men) Lodge 76 and the Brotherhood of Railroad Trainmen Lodge 68 were organized in Ogden by 1892 (according to the Ogden city directory).

The Miners

Another factor influencing the change from Mormon-dominated unionism was the growth of the mining industry. With the coming of the railroad in 1869, the economic feasibility of developing the rich ore bodies of Utah improved and great numbers of non-Mormon miners entered the Territory, often encouraged by anti-Mormon politicians, clergymen, the military, and business leaders who hoped to dilute Mormon political and economic power which until that time was almost absolute. Of course, many were also interested in exploiting the ore bodies to their own economic advantage. Whatever the motivation, the mining industry boomed — especially mining of precious metals.

Working conditions in the mines were abominable, health and safety standards being almost nonexistent. In addition, the pay was low and uncertain. The result was organizational activities by the miners. In 1871, miners in the Logan area attempted to organize. The attempt was evidently less than successful, due largely, it was said, to the antagonism between non-Mormons and the dominant Mormon community which looked with disfavor on typical mining-town gambling, liquor, violence, and prostitution. The Salt Lake *Tribune* recorded (April 19, 1871, p. 2) that the miners were "determined to be governed by their law of their own making." This friction probably did not differ greatly from that which prevailed wherever settled, conservative, agriculturally oriented communities existed, but in this instance Mormons were dominant and probably sought to impose their standards of morality on a mining community characterized typically by relative lawlessness.

In 1872 the miners in the ore-rich Tintic area in central Utah were organized and, according to the *Tribune* (April 25, 1872, p. 2), were "likely to prove a power for good in Tintic." In view of the anti-Mormon posture of the *Tribune*, this meant that the organized miners would counteract traditional Mormon values and dilute Mormon political power in that section of the Territory.

Not only did the miners organize, they also were often engaged in disputes with their employers over the payment of wages, frequently not receiving wages as agreed upon. Workers were supposed to be paid once a month. However, if anything interfered with the company's income, the firm often refused to pay wages, its hierarchy saying that the workers could not be paid if the company did not have the money to pay them. The result of miner agitation on this issue was a territorial miners' law in 1872 which gave miners legal title to wages earned, whether company income was sufficient or not (Salt Lake *Tribune*, April 11, 1872, p. 3). This law did not necessarily guarantee payment — it only meant that workers could sue to recover wages earned but not paid. Few were in a position to do so.

The mining industry (except for coal mining) was probably dominated by non-Mormons and people who had drawn away from the church. This characteristic, largely developed because of the opposition of Brigham Young to precious metal mining by Mormons, was primarily due to the fear that gold and silver fever would weaken devotion to the "building up of the Kingdom." He felt that greater economic security would be found in the long-run development of agriculture and industry, rather than short-run, highly speculative precious metal mining. Also mining camps were notoriously immoral. The gambling, liquor, violence, and prosititution so characteristic of mining towns were not conducive to spiritual development and could well destroy the faith of the people. Most of Utah's multimillionaires of the 1800s made their wealth in mining — most of them non-Mormons (Arrington, 1958, p. 242). The depression of the 1870s took its toll of mining operations between 1873 and 1878. In the latter year there appears to have been a revival of mining, with miners organizing but apparently more as owners of small claims than as workers. The Salt Lake *Tribune* records (October 25, 1878) the "First Meeting of the Miners" as October 22, 1878, with another organization following three days later.

In 1880 a convention of the Miners Union at Park City was in the discussion stage. The *Tribune* (June 12, 1880) editorialized that "Miners unions are not good things for first class men who understand the business of mining in all its details." The *Tribune* maintained that high wages ($4.00 as compared with $3.00) would keep new mining capital out of the Territory. It also criticized unions for not "discriminating" between "first class workmen" and "clod-hoppers." Finally, it criticized unions for taking away freedom from workers. However, the newspaper's warnings evidently did not forestall union organization.

One of the better documented miner disputes of the period took place in Silver Reef in southern Utah, near St. George. The Silver Reef mining development was booming in the 1870s, and a number of claims had come under the ownership and control of Stormont Mining and Milling Company, an eastern concern. In 1880 the company announced a cut in dividends, but stockholders insisted on wage cuts. In protest, the miners organized a union with about three hundred members, with M. O. Laughlin (U) and later A. H. Lewis (U) as president. When on February 1, 1881, the miners were given notice of a cut in wages — from $4.00 to $3.50 — they went on strike. After a month, approximately sixty men under John Fitzsimmons (U) ordered Colonel W. I. Allen, head of the company's operations at Silver Reef, to leave camp. The exiled company head journeyed to Beaver (Utah) where the federal district court was situated and asked for an investigation.

The authorities acted, and upon the findings of a federal grand jury, indictments were issued against some forty miners, and orders for their arrest were given to U. S. Marshal Arthur Pratt (probably the son of Apostle Orson Pratt). The marshal called on Sheriff A. P. Hardy, of Washington County, to assist with a posse. A force of 25 men, mostly Mormons, was raised, including the county attorney and church leader Anthony W. Ivins. Thirty-six miners were placed under arrest, breaking the strike. The mines reopened with inexperienced workers at less pay (Pendleton, 1930, pp. 99–118; and Salt Lake *Tribune*, March 1, 8, 10, and 13, April 2, May 24, 1881). The seizure of private property was indicative of the radical nature of miner unionism in Utah and elsewhere in the United States. There was frequently little regard for private property, or even personal rights, by these miners.

Somewhat contrary to this union activity in the Gentile mining community of Silver Reef was a coal miners' strike in Pleasant Valley in the southeastern corner of Utah County in central Utah. The miners engaged in a strike in February 1883, 75 to eighty miners walking off the job because workers were being dismissed without explanation. Union leaders were arrested and taken to Provo, but the union demanded their release before ending the strike (Salt Lake *Tribune*, February 28, 1883). A. O. Smoot, the stake president of the area (a branch of the church existed in Pleasant Valley at that time), visited the valley and induced the men to return to work. Several "hostile strikers" were arrested for "intimidating their fellows" (*Latter-day Saints' Millennial Star*, 1883, p. 174; and Salt Lake *Tribune*, February 20, 1883). It is probable that the strikers, in large numbers, were church members over whom Smoot ecclesiastically presided. Only this would account for his influence in settling the strike, for the feeling between Gentiles and Mormons was antagonistic at that time, and it is doubtful that Smoot could have induced other than church members to return to work.

The two interventions by members and leaders of the church — at Silver Reef and in Pleasant Valley — established church members and leaders as a potential strike-breaking force. This would not endear them to staunch unionists, who maintained the sanctity of the right to strike and the immorality of strike breaking.

The non-Mormon monopoly of the precious metal mining of the Territory was to break down in the late 1880s and early '90s. Jesse Knight, a church member, discovered a rich vein of silver in the Tintic area as the result of a dream or "vision." He became a multimillionaire and one of Utah's and the church's great financial benefactors. With him, precious metal mining became more respectable within the church — at least at the entrepreneurial level (Jensen, 1914, p. 770).

With the formation of the Knights of Labor in Utah in the early 1880s, the miners found a home — although temporary — as will be detailed subsequently. This association of miners with the Knights parallels what was taking place nationally.

Trade Union Locals in the Early 1880s

The resurgence of Utah unionism in the 1880s was presaged in the Fourth of July parade of 1880, in which many of the worker organizations — miners and representatives of the trades — participated (Salt Lake *Tribune*, July 4, 1880) as they had in the 1860s. The typographers had continued their existence throughout the 1870s, membership fluctuating during that decade from a high of 32 members in 1872 to a low of fifteen members in the depression year of 1873. Membership in the 1880s fluctuated from a low of fourteen in 1880 to a high of 44 in 1888. Members of the church continued to dominate the leadership ranks of the local during the first half of latter decade, either R. G. Sleater (M) or Henry McEwan (M) being president for seven of the eight years for which the leadership is known. But it was during this decade that the typographers lost their uniquely Mormon name of "Deseret," the local becoming known as Salt Lake City Local 115 in 1886 (I.T.U. convention reports, various years). The control of the local by church members was also lost and the groundwork laid for a confrontation with the church over union security.

The Amalgamated Carpenters and Joiners were organized as of 1880 (Scorup. 1935, p. 10). However, it is possible that they, like the typographers, had had a continued existence since the 1861 parade. The 1861 group had probably not been associated with the English-based Amalgamated Carpenters and Joiners, but the fact that there was a craft group known as the "carpenters and joiners," as distinguished from the more common American terminology of "carpenters," shows at least some informal relationship. It was not until the 1880s that the American-based union of carpenters became known as "carpenters and joiners." (The carpenters, probably with substantial Mormon membership, along with the typographers, were to dominate the Utah labor movement into the early 1930s, helping to establish the basically conservative nature of the state's unionism.)

Twenty-five Western Union telegraphers organized the Overland Circuit of Telegraphers Mutual Union in Ogden on August 1, 1881, with the following officers (Salt Lake *Tribune*, August 2, 1881):

Position	Name	
Chief counselor	E. C. Keeler	(U)
Vice counselor	J. Fletcher	(M)
Secretary	Frank M. Medina	(U)
Treasurer	E. W. Burnum	(U)

They walked off their jobs on July 19, 1883, as part of the nationwide strike for higher wages and shorter hours (Salt Lake *Tribune*, July 20, 1883).

According to the *Tribune*, on July 19, 1882, a hundred track layers on the Denver and Rio Grande Railroad struck for higher wages. The plasterers were organized again by 1884 (*Journal History*, February 9, 1884), and the plumbers of Salt Lake City engaged in a strike in that same year, evidence that they were organized again (*Journal History*, September 6, 1884). Salt Lake Union No. 1, with Arthur L. Thomas (N) as commander and S. H. Snider (U) as clerk, was meeting on Friday evenings in 1884 (Salt Lake *Tribune*, October 10, 1884). Thomas was the appointed territorial secretary and occasionally the acting governor, and was later appointed governor of the Territory of Utah. The nature of Salt Lake Union No. 1 is uncertain. Thomas was intimately involved with a Utah commission that had the responsibility of stamping out polygamy among the Mormons. If Salt Lake Union No. 1 was a part of the union movement, Thomas's leadership no doubt brought negative attention from the Mormon community.

For the first time, brewery workers were organized by 1885, the tinners once again in 1886 (Salt Lake *Tribune*, March 21, 1886), as were the cigar makers again on May 15, 1887. The printers of Ogden were likewise organized as Local 236 of the International Typographical Union in 1887 (Scorup, 1935, pp. 10-11). It appears that some Provo typographers may have also been organized in 1888, although not officially recognized (Salt Lake *Tribune*, January 8, 1888).

References

Arrington, Leonard J. *Great Basin Kingdom*. Cambridge, Massachusetts; Harvard University Press, 1958.

Deseret News, Salt Lake City, July 4, 1869.

International Typographical Union (I.T.U.) Convention *Proceedings. 1872–73, 1879.*

——————— convention reports. Various years.

Jensen, Andrew. *L.D.S. Biographical Encyclopedia*. Volume 2. Salt Lake City. 1914.

Journal History. Salt Lake City. February 9, September 6, 1884.

Latter-day Saints' Millennial Star. XLV. Liverpool, England. 1883.

Ogden City Directory, 1892.

Pawar, Sheelwant Bapurao. "An Environmental Study of the Development of the Utah Labor Movement, 1860–1935." Salt Lake City: University of Utah. 1968. Doctoral dissertation.

Pendleton, Mark H. "Memories of Silver Reef." *Utah Historical Quarterly* (October 1930), vol. III.

Powderly, T. V. *Thirty Years of Labor.* Columbus, Ohio: Excelsior Publishing Co. 1889.

Salt Lake City Directory, 1890.

Salt Lake *Tribune,* April 19, November 7, 1871; April 11 and 25, May 27, August 27, December 31, 1872; March 24, August 12, 1874; October 22 and 25, 1878; June 12, July 4, 1880; March 1, 8, 10, and 13, April 2, May 24, August 2, 1881; July 19, 1882; February 20 and 28, July 20, 1883; February 9, September 6, October 10, 1884; May 5, 1885; January 19 and 23, March 21, April 6, 1886; January 8, 1888.

Scorup, Lee. "A History of Organized Labor in Utah." Salt Lake City: University of Utah. 1935. Master's thesis.

7

The Noble Order of the Knights of Labor 1884 to 1887

Deseret's typographers had become permanently associated with the National Typographical Union (later International Typographical Union) in 1868, their representative participating in that union's national convention in 1872. During the 1870s, sporadic attempts were made to organize workers into labor unions, including a city federation, but we are presently unaware of any permanent success. This is understandable, for during the depression of the 1870s, labor unions were unsuccessful throughout the country, and Utah in the 1870s was no exception.

With the economic recovery of 1879 and 1880, fresh organizing attempts were made. In the Fourth of July parade of 1880, miners and mechanics marched as bodies as they had in the 1860s. In 1881 the telegraphers organized into a local of a national union. In 1881 miners in Silver Reef struck, as did Pleasant Valley miners in 1883. In 1883 telegraphers and tracklayers of Utah struck in support of nationally organized strikes. As the national organization of telegraphers had associated as a district assembly of the Knights of Labor in 1882, they were possibly the first representatives of the Knights in Utah, although not under that name. It is possible, however, that an attempt (successful or not) had been made in 1879 to organize the Knights in Utah, for a Knight, Dyer D. Lum, as shown later, "officially" visited Utah in that year.

117

The National Knights Movement

The Knights constituted a fascinating, colorful labor organization, the first truly national overarching organization of working men in the United States, although there had earlier existed the National Labor Union. Organized in 1869 in Philadelphia, the order grew slowly if at all during the depression years of the 1870s, its district assemblies being limited to Pennsylvania and the New York City area. It was hoped that all workers could be organized into a single union, all occupations being admitted except lawyers, saloon keepers, bankers, and professional gamblers. In keeping with many societies of the time, and to protect workers from anti-union employers, it was a secret oath- and ritual-bound society.

In 1878, a national convention was called for Reading, Pennsylvania, and a national organization formed. The following year, Terence V. Powderly, mayor of Scranton, Pennsylvania, a former machinist and a member of the Order, was elected National Grand Master Workman, the chief administrative officer. Powderly was a devout, lay Catholic moralist who believed the wage system of capitalism to be wrong and in need of replacement by a cooperative system in which workers and management would combine in the ownership of the means of production. He envisaged labor and management sitting down as gentlemen and equals to work out problems. Arbitration rather than strikes and boycotts was preferably to be used to settle impasses. Recognizing the pervading potential for strikes by organized workers primarily interested in their own welfare, local and district assemblies were required by the constitution to receive approval from the national executive board before members could engage in strike or boycott activity. Such approval would come only after all possible effort had been taken to arbitrate the dispute. The problem with the requirement was that the Knights never developed the means of enforcing it, and the organization was plagued with unauthorized or wildcat strikes throughout its turbulent history.

Recognizing the misunderstanding that could come from secrecy, and knowing the fear of the Catholic hierarchy of secret oathbound societies — which had so much of the appearance of the anti-Catholic Masonic orders — Powderly was able to eliminate officially those features of the organization, although vestiges remained — especially in the minds of the public and the clergy.

The first district assembly west of the Mississippi was organized at St. Louis, Missouri, in 1878 when the national organization was formed.

It was followed by the formation of western district assemblies in Des Moines, Iowa, in 1879; Leadville, Colorado, in 1880; Erie, Colorado, in 1881; and San Francisco, California, in 1883. Most local and district assemblies were conglomerate in membership, admitting all but a few occupations. There were a few exceptions, with some local and district assemblies consisting solely of members of a given (or closely related) trade or occupation; for example: telegraphers in 1882, shoemakers in 1884, Union Pacific Railroad workers in 1885, and miners, glassblowers and Jay Gould railroad workers in 1886. However, these "trade" unions were not encouraged by the Order.

Utah's First Knights Affair

Utah's first known Knights activity took place on June 12, 1885, when Fidelity Assembly No. 3286 held a public outing on its "first anniversary" at Grass Creek near Coalville. A parade was led by the Spring Hollow String Band, followed by a day of athletic events and an evening of dancing. Although the local assembly had a Knights number, it may have been a mixed assembly with railroaders from Echo Junction, coal miners from Coalville, and silver miners from Park City and surrounding communities (Salt Lake *Tribune*, June 16, 1885). However, most of those identified were coal miners living in Grass Creek or Coalville. Of the 36 men, at least eighteen (or 50 percent) have been identified as members of the church in 1884, while three have been identified as nonmembers, with the remainder unidentified. Below is a list of those participating in the outing at the first anniversary of Grass Creek Fidelity Assembly No. 3286, Knights of Labor:

Addresses

S. Webster	(M)	J. McPhee	(M)

Participants in Sports Activities

John W. Cain	(N)	W. McRane	(U)
Richard Dexter	(M)	Rasmus Miller	(M)
James (or John) England	(M)	W. Miller	(M)

Thomas Eynon	(M)	John A. Ovard	(M)
Thomas F. Eynon	(M)	J. Robinson	(U)
David Faddis	(M)	S. Sharp	(U)
John (or James) Faddis	(M)	E. L. Simmons	(U)
		J. Smedley	(U)
Robert Faddis	(N)	K. Smith	(U)
William Fowler	(M)	R. Smith	(U)
F. Fowler	(U)	H. Thomas	(U)
A. Gillchrist	(U)	C. Vaughan	(U)
James N. Houston	(M)	S. Webster	(M)
J. Lawrence	(U)	W. Welsh	(U)
John Marshal(l)	(N)	Henry Williams	(M)
R. Marshal(l)	(U)	William Williams	(M)
William McDonald	(M)	Alexander R. (or K.) Wilson	(M)
John McPhee	(M)		
Alexander McPhee	(M)	Ben Young	(U)

Because the local's number is lower than the known numbers of other Utah local assemblies, it was probably the first general local of the Knights as such in Deseret. Since its "first anniversary" was on June 12, 1885, it may be assumed that it was organized a year before, on or near June 12, 1884, although it was not reported as of the October 1884 national convention.

The Ogden Knights

Utah's first publicized unionlike activity under the official name of the Knights of Labor was reported on August 13, 1885, when someone using the pseudonym "Vindex" condemned Ogden's Knights for putting pressure on barbers of the city to raise their prices as "the worst kind of monopoly" (*Deseret News*, September 29, 1886). In May 1886, M. W. Foreman (U) was the secretary of the local assembly when that group passed a resolution condemning the Haymarket violence — in which revolutionaries, ostensibly connected with the Knights but involved with the International Workmen's Association, engaged in bombings — attributed to the Knights in Chicago (Ogden *Daily Herald*, May 6, 1886).

Dr. H. J. Power (U) presided over the second anniversary of Ogden's Local Assembly No. 3533 (probably Utah's second local assembly) on September 29, 1886, and G. G. Warren (U) and Robert Wilson (U) addressed those attending the celebration (*Deseret News*, September 29, 1886; Pawar, 1968, p. 101):

> The pavilion was illuminated with electric lights; was profusely decorated with stars and stripes. In the front of the stand was a beautiful banner on which was inscribed in gold letters the motto "Labor is Noble and Holy." On the stand, besides the officers of the Order, were a goodly representation of the city council of Ogden City and other specially invited guests.

Since this was the second anniversary of the local, it may be assumed that it was organized on or about September 29, 1884.

The Chinese Question

On August 13, 1885, an Ogden lawyer chastized the Knights for boycotting local Chinese business houses (Ogden *Daily Herald*, August 13, 1885). A week later, a letter was published, signed by the "Committee of the Knights of Labor," demanding that the Chinese be boycotted and forced out of town (Ogden *Daily Herald*, August 18, 1885). That same day a public rally attended by some five hundred persons was held in Ogden, with an address by Judge Heed on the "Chinese and the Labor Question," and with Robert Wilson (U), a "prominent" Knight, addressing the sometimes unruly crowd. When General Nathan Kimball (N), Ogden postmaster and Civil War hero, urged that only legal means be used to exclude the Chinese, he was reportedly met with strong disfavor (Pawar, 1968, p. 96).

The emotional moblike action elicited a response by way of an editorial in the *Deseret News* (August 20, 1885) by its rising young editor Charles W. Penrose. His position was that while the Chinese — because of their low morals, uncleanness, and willingness to work at starvation wages — were undesirable, they should not be run out of town.

Since the *Deseret News* was the newspaper of the church, it carried with it the aura of church policy, and therefore this occurrence constituted the first known confrontation of the church with the Knights. A few weeks later the Chinatown section of Rock Springs, Wyoming, where lived a number of Chinese working in the Union Pacific coal mines, was burned and a substantial number of Chinese massacred — reportedly by the Knights (Pawar, 1968, p. 97). While the violence was not repeated in Utah, the boycott against the Chinese was continued, which action did not miss being noted by the *Deseret News* (October 21 and 28, 1885).

Labor Anarchists Visit Utah

The intense concern of Utahns with violent labor union activity, which had begun with the Chinese question in the fall of 1885, was exacerbated by the visit to Utah in October of 1885 of two traveling members of the revolutionary International Workingmen's Association, J. Allen Evans and L. E. Odinga. These men urged workmen to overthrow capitalism by force. The *Deseret News* (October 21, 1885) commented ". . . in this community there is no need for secret organizations. The Saints should leave them alone." Another article in the same issue of the paper said that "The Latter-day Saints see very plainly and deplore the evils that exist in government and society and offer to the world a remedy in the shape of the Gospel . . . . They are not in sympathy with . . . Socialists, Nihilists, Anarchists or Internationalists. No Latter-day Saint can connect himself with them. They are secret organizations . . . condemned by the *Book of Mormon*."

Because it came so soon upon the heels of violent Knights activity in Wyoming, it is perhaps understandable that the community associated the Knights with revolutionary worker organizations. While the *News* distinguished between the Knights and the revolutionaries, its editorials in the spring of 1886 seemed to tie them closer together. In addition, the violent Haymarket riot in Chicago in May made the connection even more tightly held.

Strife on the Railroads

On August 20, 1885, the Salt Lake *Herald* published a telegram from the executive board of the Knights to all local assemblies having members working for Union Pacific and the Jay Could railroads, urging them to boycott the equipment of the Wabash Railroad. J. J. Duckworth (U), reportedly the local Salt Lake head of the Knights, interpreted the telegram to mean the Missouri Pacific rather than the Union Pacific (U.P.), saying that he had received no direct word for the local assembly to be involved. The reporter referred to an interview with a prominent Salt Lake Knight who informed him that the order was seven months old and had 250 to three hundred members in Salt Lake City and about three hundred in Ogden. The Knight also informed the reporter that workers on the Denver and Rio Grande and the Union Pacific railroads were heavily organized. He then went on to disavow the recent dynamiting (in Denver) attributed to the Knights, saying that it was not authorized (Salt Lake *Herald*, August 20, 1885). The Knights indeed had a busy summer and fall in 1885. The interview notwithstanding, the Union Pacific was involved in labor strife with the Knights. Assuming the Knight was correct, the Salt Lake local assembly was organized in February 1885.

The leaders of the church, which had substantial holdings of common stock in the Union Pacific Railroad, could hardly be expected as businessmen (which they were in addition to being ecclesiastical authorities) to fail to respond negatively to the economic sanctions exercised by the Knights against that railroad. In addition, the Union Pacific and the Denver and Rio Grande railroads constituted Utah's primary links with the rest of the nation. In their minds, any tieup of rail traffic by union action was bound to retard Deseret's economic expansion.

The labor strife between the Knights and Jay Gould in the spring of 1886 produced a spate of negative editorials in the local newspapers. However, the *Deseret News* was the most negative and outspoken. On March 10, under the heading "Power and Danger of Secret Societies," the editors pointed to the power shown by the Knights in their boycotting activity in support of the strike against Gould's railroads, suggesting that the power was likely to grow, with "astonishing probabilities":

> The organization called the Knights of Labor is not, at present, so revolutionary in its nature and purposes as many of the secret organizations with which society is afflicted. It is not so radical [or] destructive [or] menacing . . . as they. But it wields enormous power. . . . And its very moderation gives it influence among working people. . . . And herein is the probability of its becoming formidable. . . . It will not take very much pressure to so change the policy and principles . . . as to make it really revolutionary and terrible in its action and power. . . . We look for the greatest trouble with which this nation will be afflicted to come from the secret

> societies. . . . [W]hen outbreaks occur which are impending, it
> would not be at all surprising if societies, organized with more
> pacific motives and designed only to aid the working popula-
> tion by lawful methods, should join in the disturbances.

The editorial then offered advice to the Saints:

> We do not think it wise for any of our people to unite and
> become identified with these secret societies, no matter how
> pacific and apparently harmless may be their present
> programmes and intentions. Our people should unite and
> throw in all their powers together, with a single eye and aim.
> Our forces should not be divided. Everything necessary to
> promote the welfare of the people of God can be found within
> the fold of the Church and kingdom of God. In that should be
> centered all their interests. . . . We do not oppose those
> organizations for the amelioration of the condition of toiling
> mankind. At the same time, we see no need for our friends to
> become identified with them. Our advice would be: Let them go
> their way and we will go ours. We have interests higher and
> more exalting than anything in which they are engaged and it is
> not good policy for Latter-day Saints to be mixed up with other
> societies, organizations, cliques, or cabals of any descrip-
> tion. . . . [K]eep clear from all worldly entanglements.

This article helped to draw the lines. The advice of what was considered
to be the official woice of the church was for Latter-day Saints to "keep
clear" of "all worldly entanglements" — especially the Knights.

On March 20, the Salt Lake *Tribune* editors hoped that the imminent
strike would be averted, saying that if the Knights wanted to run the
railroads, they should buy them. One week later, the editors defended
Powderly, who had attempted to arbitrate the dispute (Salt Lake *Tribune*,
March 28, 1886), and later urged the Knights to put down insubordina-
tion and punish rebellious leaders (Salt Lake *Tribune*, March 31, 1886).
By April 5, the *Tribune* printed: "The strikes are becoming a terror to the
United States."

On March 30, when it prematurely appeared that the Knights had
been victorious in the struggle with Gould, the Salt Lake *Herald* editors
proclaimed: "Labor Is King." They continued, saying:

> . . . The surrender is of such a character as to cause rejoicing
> and jubilation among workingmen. . . . This surrender of
> Gould is the greatest triumph American labor has ever

won. . . . But this victory of the Knights must not be accepted as an unmixed good until it has been seen how the victors use their power. . . . The danger now lies in the abuse of their power by the Knights. . . . If they will recognize that capital has rights, and that a fair acknowledgement of those rights will be best for labor, then their triumph will prove beneficial; otherwise the workingmen will find that their victory has undone them.

On April 16, under "Powderly and Gould — Labor and Capital," the *Deseret News* editor saw Gould as coming out ahead of Powderly by shrewd deception. The editor predicted that the Knights would consequently combine against the capitalist personally and then asked: "And if they do, is not the rich man entitled to the protection of the law?" Disavowing any "great admiration" for the scheming plutocrat, the editor wrote that the strike was

> . . . wrong to begin with, and the violence associated with it deplorable with the beginning of the lawlessness . . . on the side of the Knights. . . . The rights of property are to be held as secure . . . as the rights of life and liberty. . . . Every workman has the right to hold his abilities at a certain figure. But he has not the right to use force to compel any employer to give him that price [or] to hinder his neighbor from laboring at lower wages. . . . The Knights of Labor are engaged in a grand work. The intention of the organization is excellent. But it is able to be turned into an engine of revolution.

On May 4, 1886, the *Deseret News* editors condemned the "anarchists and socialists [who] are brimful of revolution. . . . Their influence is Satanic [and] they fire the hearts of the real workers . . . into deeds of lawlessness." While the church had encouraged the settlement of disputes within the church by a system of arbitration, the strikes in the spring of 1886 were so rife with violence and strife that the editors of the *Deseret News* (May 8, 1886) observed: "Arbitration merely operates as a pail of syrup, without curing. The main hope seems to be in the majesty of the law maintained by enforcement in the courts."

The Knights in Logan

In January 1886 Charles Robertson (U), a Knight and "long-term resident" of Logan (Utah), died. His funeral was conducted by the Logan and Eagle Rock assemblies of the Knights in the Episcopal chapel in

Logan (Salt Lake *Tribune*, January 17, 1886). It was evidently quite an occasion, with the Reverend P. McD. Bleecker and Joseph G. Bywater, foreman of the Union Pacific shops in Logan (evidently neither man was a Knight), participating in the services and the dinner that followed, which was held at the Logan House by the Olive Branch (possibly the women's auxiliary) of the Knights. The *Deseret News* reporter observed: "I was astonished to see some Latter-day Saints in their ranks" (Pawar, 1968, p. 100).

The Salt Lake City Knights

In February 1886, the Knights of Salt Lake City held a "grand concert and ball" (Salt Lake *Tribune*, February 7, 1886) in the Walker Opera House on the eve of Washington's birthday. The concert was given by the Sixth Infantry Band. The choruses were comprised of local people, many of whom had surnames that were prominent in the Mormon community:

Nettie Raleigh	Bell Clayton
Louisa Simmons	Lizzie Latimer
Millie Pack	Bessie Dean
Lutie Whitney	Lutie Thatcher
Annie Simpson	Nettie Latimer
Maggie Crismon	Emma Simmons
Euphelia Latimer	Susie Clawson
Lottie Martin	Nell Hardy
Addie Careless	Tizzie Grosbeck
Jennie Whitney	Mrs. Lou McEwan

Pirates:

R. A. Pyper	J. A. Croft
A. C. N. Howard	D. H. McAllister
H. Kirkman	W. D. Pyper
S. Kirkman	John Gray
K. Anderson	Mr. McKenzie

Policemen:

George L. Savage	G.M. Clark
H. Dinwoodey	J. J. Gallagher

F. D. Richards, Jr.   F. W. Scarff

D. S. Spencer   Ernest Pratt

W. S. Young

In addition, Mr. Young (W. S.?), Robert Gorlinski, and Willard Weihe — who was said to be the "best musical talent of the city" — also performed.

On August 18, 1886, the Knights of Utah and Idaho held a convention at the Clift House in Salt Lake City, hosted by Jordan Assembly No. 3543 in the Salt Lake Area (Salt Lake *Tribune*, August 22, 1886). The Salt Lake convention established Salt Lake City as the temporary district assembly headquarters of the Knights in Utah and Idaho, with the following associated local assemblies, most of them evidently miners or smelterers:

City or town	Number of Delegates
Salt Lake City	3
Park City	3
Blackfoot (Idaho)	2
Bingham	2
Stockton	2
Eureka	1
Alta	1
Sandy	1
Murray	1
Scofield	1

The Master Workman of the Jordan Assembly of Salt Lake addressed those present at the convention, stressing the need for them to address themselves to the questions of free silver, protective tarriffs, and restricted immigration. He also spent considerable time attacking the LDS church — though not by name — charging it with treason against the federal government. The convention then passed a number of resolutions calling for:

(1) Wise national legislation reflecting the will of the people

(2) Free silver legislation, making silver (along with gold) the basis for the money system, stimulating silver production.

(3) Protective tariffs on all foreign products, which would increase domestic prices

(4) Restriction of immigration to a minimum to reduce competition from foreign labor

(5) No statehood for Utah as it would be detrimental to "the best interests of the loyal citizens of the Territory"

(6) Condemnation of socialists and anarchists as the "vilest and most dangerous enemies of law and order"

(7) Amendment to the national's constitution prohibiting bigamists or polygamists, either "practical or theoretical," from membership in local assemblies

(8) Funds for lectures as part of the educational goals of the Order

(9) Sustaining of T. V. Powderly

(10) Refusal to allow "rats" (who worked at below union scale wages) to use the Knights' trademark

Two delegates, H. C. Goodwin (U), a printer from Salt Lake, and David B. Stover (U), a mine owner and worker from Stockton, were elected to the general assembly to be held in Richmond, Virginia, on October 4, 1886. It was the first-known attendance of Utahn's at a national overarching labor organization, although Utah's typographers had been represented at the Typographical Union's national convention in 1872.

Evidently no permanent district assembly had been organized in Utah until that time, but sometime in advance of the 1887 national convention of the Knights, District Assembly No. 205 of Salt Lake City was officially organized (Powderly, 1889, p. 646), being recognized at that convention. It was part of the most successful organizing drive of the Knights, and at the peak of the national union's membership and power.

We are uncertain of the membership figures of the Knights in Salt Lake City. However, on July 24, 1886, the Salt Lake *Herald*, reporting an interview with a Knight, said that there were approximately fifteen hundred members in Salt Lake City alone, and that they met every Thursday night in a hall over Scott's warehouse. This estimate is not in line with the official membership as reported July 1, 1887, when District Assembly No. 205 reported that there were 260 members, all of them in good standing, in that district assembly. It is possible that the Utah membership had collapsed in a year's time, but this does appear to be an inordinately large decline.

Association with the General Assembly

H. C. Goodwin and D. B. Stover, who had been elected in August, attended the Richmond, Virginia, convention (October 4 to 20, 1886), representing locals 3543 (Jordan), 3557, 4006, 4177, 6070, 6161 (Stockton), 6940 (Sandy), 7705 (Eureka), 8355, and probably 3541. Local Assembly No. 3286 of Grass Creek and Local Assembly No. 3533 of Ogden were not represented. The Grass Creek local might well have become defunct, there being no record of local assembly activity beyond 1885. The Ogden local assembly had held an anniversary in September; thus it most likely was still organized, although it was not represented. There was also a local assembly (6854) in Murray during this period.

It would appear that the ten local assembly numbers above correspond with the ten local assemblies mentioned by location in the previous section, although we have not yet been able to assign numbers to all locations. Local No. 3541 was listed as the sponsor of a series of resolutions of the Salt Lake City convention of August. They were among some 355 resolutions offered to the assembly by representatives from around the country. Two resolutions of particular significance to Utah were introduced. The first would have eliminated Latter-day Saints from membership in local and district assemblies.

> Resolution 253 D: Resolved that after the word "broker"
> in the sixth line of Section 3 of Article I of the Constitution for
> Local Assemblies the words "bigamist or polygamist, practical
> or theoretical" be inserted.

At that time, Utah and the church were appealing for statehood, while the Liberal (anti-Mormon) Party was opposed to statehood. The second resolution reads:

> Resolution 253 E: Resolved that we are positively opposed to
> the admission of Utah as a state at this time, as we believe it
> would be a bad and dangerous precedent and highly detrimen-
> tal to the best interest of the loyal citizens of the Territory.

Goodwin moved that the report of the committee on law be "laid on the table," but was ruled out of order by the chairman. Resolution 253 D was referred to the committee on law. The convention report places these two events in this order, but they may have been reversed, the motion to "lay on the table" the committee's report coming after its referral. Resolution 253 E was referred to the next or incoming legislative committee. There is no evidence that either issue came before the special convention of April 7 to 9, 1887, called to consider pending legislation.

We are uncertain of how Utah's two delegates voted on these issues, but on at least one issue they were not united. In the voting in support of a statement on the equality of the races, most likely in its favor, issued by the Master Workman, Terence V. Powderly, Goodwin voted "yes" while Stoker voted "nay."

Utah was evidently not represented at the national convention of the Knights in 1887. District Assembly 205 of Utah was entitled to one seat, which was not filled. The Territory evidently lost the entitlement thereafter, and it was not represented again, at least through 1890. Evidently, District Assembly 205 was the victim of the formation of the Utah Federated Trades and Labor Council in 1888-89, which eventually became affiliated with the American Federation of Labor.

The Knights and Politics

In the political ferment of the summer of 1886, the Salt Lake *Herald* reported that the Knights had taken over the Liberal Party at its convention in Park City in a wild and tumultuous meeting, nine-tenths of whose attenders were "unkempt and unAmerican looking" Knights (Salt Lake *Herald*, July 14, 1886). A few days later the *Herald* (July 18, 1886), backtracking a little, defended the right of the Knights to be involved in politics, saying that involvement was necessary to protect the interests of working men, and a few days later the *Deseret News* (July 20, 1886) saw the split in the Liberal Party (resulting from the takeover by the Knights) as strengthening the position of the People's Party. The Liberal Party of Utah was composed largely of apostate Mormons and anti-Mormon Gentiles determined to break the political and economic power of the church, using the polygamy issue as a major emotional weapon for securing both local and national support. The association of Utah Knights with that political organization must have contributed significantly to the Mormon antagonism toward the Knights.

Mormons vs Knights vs Mormons

In the fall of 1885 Charles W. Penrose and the *Deseret News* had been critical of some Knights' activities and inferred that organizations such as the Knights were secret combinations condemned by the *Book of Mormon*. There appears to have been no serious confrontation over the winter of 1885–86. However, in March 1886, the *News* editors began to criticize the railroad strike activity of the Knights as already detailed, advising Saints not to associate with that organization.

On March 31, 1886, the *Tribune* almost gleefully observed:

The Knights have always refused membership to lawyers, bankers, rum sellers and professional gamblers. They have added later an additional disqualification in refusing admission to their ranks professional bigamists or polygamists. This, it is understood, was done because of the unhappy situation in Utah. . . . But whether it is understood or not, the real reason it is desireable. . . [is that] the Mormons do not render allegiance to any govermnent, order or society but their own. . . . Not only should practical bigamists and polygamists be excluded but the average Mormon as well, for in case of any strike against a church enterprise, they could not be forced to join — the ties that bind them to the Church are above any other ties whatever, and it would stand the order in hand to steer clear of the Mormon system altogether. . . . The exclusion noted is wise, and might well be broadened to cover pretty much all the brethren.

With the settlement of the railroad strike in the spring of 1886, all appears to have been quiet in the relationship of the Knights and the church until the August 18 convention of Salt Lake Knights in which resolutions were passed urging no statehood, which Mormons devoutly wanted, and no admission to the order of polygamists, practical or theoretical (which would probably include all loyal Mormons).

In response, on August 30, 1886, the *News* editors wrote:

A resolution passed by the Knights of Labor in this section, excluding from membership people who believe in the rightfulness of plural marriage, was slightly premature. Of course the resolve was simply and solely intended as an excluder to members of the "Mormon" Church. There may be a few stragglers professing to be members of the Church who have identified themselves with the movement thus far, but doubtless they could almost be counted on the fingers. And even they are probably of doubtful faith and standing. It would have appeared more sensible had the Knights delayed their action in this regard until they saw a small host of "Mormons" rushing towards them with their hair streaming in the wind and their coat tails on a bee line behind them, in a hurry to be admitted. So far as the existence of any danger of their being corrupted by the religious belief of the Latter-day Saints is concerned, if they took the trouble to bar the door at all against that class, they need not have need a tougher instrument for a fastener than a boiled carrot. They might have allowed their pure souls to slumber in security. Doubtless many of the principles of the order are good and its purposes and intents laudable. As to the methods of attaining the objects sought, however, they are far from according with our ideas of propriety. Still we are not oblivious to the fact that the grinding processes of capital are extremely exasperating, and often the inciting cause of disturbances. But, be that as it may, it is not in accordance with the genius of the faith of the Latter-day Saints to be mixed up with the contention and strife constantly being evolved out of the competition between labor and capital. Consequently they will not be likely to put on sackcloth, heap ashes upon their heads and lie awake at nights, because they have received a gratuitous snub at the hands of a labor organization on the ground of their religious belief. Any "Mormon" who would now apply for admission into the order, or one who may be connected with it now and remain in it by its mere suffrance, would be very much left to himself. He would not be specially noted for that independence of spirit, so characteristic of the "Mormon" people. Notwithstanding all this we have no vestige of hostile feeling toward the Knights of Labor. On the contrary we wish them success in every undertaking based on correct and equitable principles.

In September, over the pseudonym "Vindex," the editors were put straight by the announcement that (*Deseret News*, September 11, 1886):

When the proposed amendments came before the local assemblies for consideration, myself and other two, were appointed a committee to draft a protest against the foregoing amendment, which protest, after being approved by our assembly, was forwarded to the delegates who represented District Assembly 82 and by show in the general assembly, and to the credit of the latter body be it said the change in question was promptly quashed. . . . It seems to me that for a local, or even a district assembly to try to do by resolution what the general assembly has specially refused to do, is only deserving of a smile of contempt. For myself I think it is quite time to punish a man when he is guilty of an infraction of the law. . . . The order at large must not be held responsible for the vagaries of a small section thereof. So far as my observation has gone, there are cranks in all organizations (the Church of Jesus

Christ of Latter-day Saints not excepted) who would deprive those of their fellows whose faith and practice failed to touch high water mark of all the amenities of civilized life. . . . Your supposition that the number of Mormons who have identified themselves with the Knights of Labor could be counted on the fingers is erroneous, as I personally know enough of them to require several repetitions of the operation, the standing of many of them in the Church being beyond question. Farther than that there are many members of the Church who are identified with labor organizations other than the ones in question, and I believe that so long as any members of the Church can be found identified with capital and the grinding process adverted to in your article, complete segregation of your membership from the labor movements of the age will be found an impossibility.

This letter, which supports the convention proceedings, would seem to indicate the March 31 statement of the *Tribune*, that the national body of Knights had taken action to exclude Mormons, was in error and the action of the Salt Lake Knights was not final, a negative recommendation being made to District Assembly 82 of Union Pacific employees, which then successfully made that negative recommendation to the national assembly. However, Powderly (1889, pp. 639, 640) makes no mention of the issue.

The *News* editors were somewhat mollified, answering in the same issue:

In this issue appears a communication from one of the Knights of Labor. We like the tone and spirit in which he writes. . . . The declaration of principles of the General Assembly is in many respects admirable, and it is a pleasure to note that when the anti-"Mormon" incongruity was brought to its attention by the more liberal minded Knights of this section, that body promptly quashed what was a most glaring infringement upon what might be termed the Constitution of the order. . . . The excluding clause of the order in reference to those who deal in or are benefitted by the traffic in intoxicating liquors is admirable. . . . The banker and broker being antagonistic to the organization and its objects, it must exclude. . . . And . . . the lawyer . . . is a non-producer. . . . The gambler being a bane to society — can have no lot nor part in it. . . . Our correspondent holds that the News was in error regarding the number of Latter-day Saints connected with the Order. We are not disposed to dispute him, especially as our statement was not assertive but as a matter of belief. It was based upon the fact that the genius of the "Mormons" is to subject all the evils against which the Order was specially organized to contend. . . . Also that it is not in keeping with their profession to mix up with the quarrels and disputes that are agitating the country. But "Vindex" . . . points out an inducement to the working-men to identify themselves with the Knights—the presence . . . of the grinding process of the capitalist. . . . Yet all the forces necessary to correct that and every other ill are held to be embodied in the religious system of the Saints. And whoever grinds his neighbor, whether it be because his capital gives him the power to do it, or if he . . . plays the part of a petty tyrant, [he] acts in conflict with his profession. Such methods are out of harmony with his religion. . . . We also take occasion to repeat that while we deem it inconsistent for the Saints to identify themselves with the Order, we entertain none but kindly feelings toward it, together with desires for its success in every good word and work.

The article fails to counsel the Mormon worker as to what he could do to minimize "the grinding process of the capitalist" when the worker found it necessary to work for him. It was this problem with which the Mormon worker had to wrestle.

Dyer D. Lum

While the church and the Knights were coming into a serious confrontation, one Knight was speaking out strongly in defense of the church. In the summer of 1886, Dyer D. Lum published a pamphlet "Social Problems of Today: Or the Mormon Question in Its Economic Aspects." The pamphlet, published in New York, was "A study of cooperation and arbitration in Mormondom, from the standpoint of a wage-worker." A gentile, Lum strongly supported the church's efforts to develop a cooperative system in the place of capitalism. He showed the historical development and use of the principle of arbitration in resolving disputes among members of the church, pointing to the high moral tone and level of education of the Mormon people and defending their right to practice plural marriage. In the last section of the pamphlet he said (Salt Lake *Herald*, August 15, 1886):

The Mormons have solved the problem [of how to secure a fair day's wage for a fair day's work] for themselves and are offering a passive resistance to oppression. American workmen are banding together [through the Knights of Labor] with similar economic motives to supplant our industrial system by one based on co-operation and arbitration. Will they, like the Mormons in their struggle, feel the weight of oppression? Time will tell. Both are unconsciously marching in the same direction; both have received the same inspiration. . . .The same spirit that is striving in the halls of Congress to devise new and more despotic measures to crush the Mormon industrial system is also plainly visible in the recent decision of the courts in relation to boycotts. The Mormon is free to worship God if he will not endanger profits! We are free to organize if we will be content to remain home and suck our thumbs. . . .Any people who may be proven to rely on the great features of co-operation and arbitration as cardinal factors in their social system are, however, unconsciously our friends and allies.

Lum had published in 1882 another pamphlet "Utah and Its People" in which he had said that he had visited Utah in 1879 in an "official capacity," evidently living among the Mormons for a period of time. This visit might possibly have been as an organizer for the Knights. In that pamphlet he had defended the right of Mormons to practice their religion free of federal controls. He defended Joseph Smith, Brigham Young, and John Taylor (successive church presidents) and showed the economic progress Utah Territory had experienced under the hands of the Mormon people, as well as the religious tolerance practiced, the high morals, and the pervasiveness of democracy, cooperation, and education. He pointed out that education was being given without government support. While disavowing personal attraction to polygamy, he defended its use by the church. On August 15, 1886, the pro-Mormon Salt Lake *Herald* picked up Lum's pamphlet, saying:

Occasionally there is a writer who comes in contact with the Mormon question that has the patience to push his way through the mists of falsehoods created by anti-Mormon prejudices. . . . Few men are willing to befriend an unpopular cause, but few can withstand the sweet, seductive voice of popular applause. . . . Such a man, not long since, wrote a pamphlet on the Mormon question, speaking of it in its economic aspects. The writer doubtless occupies a position of some consideration among the Knights of Labor, since some 20,000 copies of his work have been distributed among that fraternity. . . . [h]e states that: "The whole Mormon system — social, religious, industrial — is essentially based on two fundamental principles: co-operation in business and arbitration in disputes. . . . It could be faced by no more deadly enemy." He shows that these two fundamental features are of no recent development, but have been peculiar to Mormonism from its inception, and have been prime causes of the opposition to wherever it has been established. . . . [T]his writer attributes their subsequent successes to the adherence to the cooperative systems that have been adopted, and which have shielded the people from becoming the victims of the individual rapacity so common to those engaged in trade. . . . In his chapter on Arbitration . . . he gives an accurate description of the operations of the various tribunals of arbitration in the Mormon Church, from the friendly visit of ward teachers to the final appeal to the First Presidency of the Church, points out the advantages that such a system of arbitration affords to a community as compared to the disadvantages of arbitration . . . . He proves that in Utah there is a better distribution of what wealth there is than in other lands. . . . He has given the Mormon question a careful consideration from an economic standpoint. He found certain results; he traced out causes; he points to the great success that has resulted from cooperation of effort in the business affairs of life, and of arbitration in the settlement of difficulties.

In response to the 1886 publication, the *Tribune* kept the political fires hot, editorializing (August 17, 1886):

The *Herald* has found a man at last who claims to be "Knight of Labor" . . . who has thoroughly investigated the rule which governs here, has found out that it is just what he has been looking for . . . . The *Herald* praises the courage of this sagacious and indomitable man, but fails to state how much he was paid for writing and distributing his pamphlet. The man . . . shows just how much he knows about the Mormon system when he tells workingmen that it is based on a co-operation in business and arbitration in disputes.

The *Tribune* article then goes on to picture Utah landowners as "leasees of the Mormon Church . . . paying this year 10 per cent of all they raised in the tithing" and that arbitration "meant the decision of a priestly court [that] set aside the edicts of the real courts and deliberately robbed men."

To the mind of Lum, the similarities of the economic programs of the Knights and the church — namely cooperatives, education, and arbitration — meant that they were unconscious allies. However, there were a number of things that interfered with any conscious alliance: first, while the Knights' national leaders opposed strikes and violence, they were not able to control local assemblies. The only power they had was moral suasion, and that was insufficient to prevent rebellious local groups from engaging in violent action. Therefore violent mob action often ensued where the Knights were involved, something of which church leaders were most fearful. They had seen from their Ohio, Missouri, and Illinois years what mob action could result in.

A second interference was the church's continued general policy of noninvolvement with Gentiles during the early 1880s. The church had no reason to make an exception to this policy for the Knights. A third factor was that both organizations had a high degree of secrecy connected with them. Church temple services and priesthood meetings were not open to the general public — nor were Knights meetings. The very existence of secrecy encouraged distrust on both sides.

A fourth factor was that the Knights, while theoretically involving most everyone, basically represented workers; whereas the church represented church members as workers, consumers, and employers, and was itself an employer. This created an obvious conflict. A fifth possible interference may have been that church leaders considered the producers' cooperatives of the Knights as counterfeits of the Lord's cooperative economic program (then dying), created to deceive the people. Sixth and most important, the Knights apparently attempted to take a position against polygamy during the time the church was fighting against extinction at the hands of its anti-polygamy enemies. While the action may have been rescinded, in the minds of most devout Mormons the Knights were in the camp of the enemy.

Following the September 8, 1886, issue of the *Deseret News*, the conflict between the Knights and the church seemed to subside. The attack by the *Tribune* on Lum, Vindex's conciliatory efforts, and perhaps Lum's pamphlet itself may have combined to at least temporarily calm the fears of church leaders.

While the waters were seemingly calmed, the church leaders undoubtedly remained skeptical of this outside organization with which
church members had become assiciated and over which the church
leaders had no direct and little indirect influence. One student of the Utah
labor scene (Pawar, 1968, p. 104) has concluded that:

> The Knights of Labor uprising in Utah planted the seeds
> of Church opposition to organized labor. It was the first known
> time that the Church came so close to forbidding its members
> from taking part in activities of labor organizations akin to
> "secret combinations" such as the Knights of Labor. The
> Church vehemently denounced all the radical methods to
> achieve goals of labor though at times it was verbally quite
> sympathetic to the cause of labor. . . .As there was no place
> whatsoever for radical philosophies in the theological teachings
> of the Mormon Church, these labor organizations were natur-
> ally looked upon with caution. Afterwards, the Church always
> remained on guard whenever confronted by a labor
> question. . . . Out of this general environment of the late 1880s
> was born a conservative (union) leadership that dominated the
> (Utah) labor movement.

To the observation that the radical methods of some Knights was
what turned the church against unions must be added the more important association of many Knights in the anti-Mormon Liberal Party and
the attacks from within the organization on the practice of polygamy,
which the church was fighting to preserve, as well as opposition to
statehood for Utah, which the church leaders desperately sought.

Nationally and locally, the power of the Knights peaked in 1886.
The nationwide strike and the Haymarket dynamiting in the spring of
that year had turned the public and many unionists against the Knights.
The Knights didn't expire immediately, but both nationally and locally a
new type of overarching unionism was emerging in the form of the
American Federation of Labor and the Utah Federated Trades and
Labor Council, the latter with a Mormon at its head.

District Assembly No. 205

On May 30 and 31, 1887, Jordan Assembly No. 3543 hosted the
organizing convention of District Assembly No. 205 in Salt Lake City,
with five local assemblies represented and the following delegates and
alternates:

Jordan Assembly No. 3543:

Delegate		Alternate	
John H. Campe	(U)	T. C. Armstrong	(M)
William Glassman	(U)	J. T. Lynch	(U)
H. F. Evans	(U)	Lorenzo Cracroft[1]	(M)
James Cracroft	(M)	J. Miller	(U)

Stockton Assembly No. 6162:

Delegate

Captain David B. Stover (U)
Dr. C. W. Mallory (U)

Murray Assembly No. 6854:

Delegate		Alternate	
Robert Gray	(U)	William Smith[2]	(U)
C. H. Raymond	(U)	S. L. Clark	(U)

Sandy Assembly No 6940:

Delegate		Alternate	
Thomas E. Marriot(t)	(M)[3]	James Cushing	(M)
J. R. Drinkwater	(N)	William Hallsteat	(U)

Eureka Assembly No. 7705:

Delegate		Alternate	
James P. Driscoll	(U)	James F. Duffy	(U)
John Duggan	(U)	James Knowles	(U)

[1]Replaced H. F. Evans.
[2]Replaced C. H. Raymond.
[3]While a Mormon, he later claimed to have "resigned" from the church.

Each assembly was entitled to one delegate plus one delegate for every fifty members or fraction thereof. Evidently the following locals that had existed in 1885–86 had either become defunct or did not participate in the convention: Grass Creek No. 3286 and Ogden No. 3533, the Logan Assembly and Nos. 3541, 3557, 4006, 4177, 6070, and 8355.

In addition to officially organizing the district assembly, officers were elected by secret ballot, a district assessment on locals of five cents each member in good standing was made, and a resolution was passed prohibiting locals from "admitting applicants who believe and countenance teachings and practices which are in direct conflict with the law of the United States, especially a theoretical or practical polygamist and bigamist" (District Assembly No. 205 Convention *Proceedings*, 1887). By this action, they meant to reinforce the efforts of the previous year to exclude active, practicing Latter-day Saints. Following is a list of officers:

Office	*Name*	
District Master Workman	T. E. Marriot(t)	(M)
District Workman Foreman	James P. Driscoll	(U)
District Recorder and Financial Secretary	William Glassman	(U)
District Workman Treasurer	James Craycroft (Cracroft)	(M)
Statistician	William Glassman	(U)
Judges of District Courts	Robert Gray	(U)
	C. W. Mallory	(U)
	Lorenzo Craycroft (Cracroft)	(M)
Judge Advocate	J. R. Drinkwater	(N)
Clerk of the District Court	William Smith	(U)

Of the 22 delegates and alternates, only Lorenzo Cracroft (M) is known to have been active in later union efforts. He was to serve as recording secretary of the Utah Federated Trades and Labor Council in 1890 and as its treasurer in 1893, as well as one of the signators on the application of that body for official affiliation with the American Federation of Labor in 1893. This convention was about the Knights' last gasp in Utah.

The mixed nature of the Knights is shown locally by the fact that John T. Lynch and William Glassman placed an ad in the *Proceedings* of District No. 205 representing themselves as real estate brokers. Glassman also placed an ad as general agent for the Home Accident Association of San Francisco; Lynch was also a postmaster. The Cracrofts advertised themselves as painters, and T. C. Armstrong owned a grain store. Mallory is listed as "Dr.," and Marriott was a blacksmith. Campe was a draftsman, Cushing was in construction, and Driscoll was a miner, postmaster, and merchant. Hallsteat (Halsteat) was a furnaceman and Knowles and Stover were miners. (Biographical detail was developed from obituaries, family group sheets, and directories.)

References

Deseret News, Salt Lake City, August 20, October 21 and 28, 1885; March 10, April 16, May 4 and 8, July 20, August 30, September 11 and 29, 1886.

District Assembly No. 205 Convention *Proceedings*. Salt Lake City. May 30, 31, 1887.

Lum, D. D. "Social Problems of To-Day: Or the Mormon Question in Its Economic Aspects . . . . " Port Jervis, New York. 1886.

Ogden *Daily Herald*, August 13, 18 and 20, 1885; May 6, 1886.

Pawar, Sheelwant Bapurao. "An Environmental Study of the Development of the Utah Labor Movement, 1860–1935." Salt Lake City: University of Utah. 1968. Doctoral dissertation.

Powderly, T. V. *Thirty years of Labor.* Columbus, Ohio: Excelsior Publishing Co. 1889.

Salt Lake *Herald*, August 20, 1885; March 30, July 14, 18, and 24, August 15, 1886.

Salt Lake *Tribune*, June 16, 1885; January 17, February 7, March 20, 28, and 31, April 5, August 17 and 22, 1886.

COURTESY INTERNATIONAL TYPOGRAPHICAL UNION

Robert Gibson Sleater has been called "The Father of the Utah Labor Movement."

8

Robert Gibson Sleater
Mormon Pioneer Union Leader
1840 to 1914

Born the son of an Irish father (Robert) and an English mother (Mary Marchant) in Bath, England, in 1840, Robert Gibson Sleater was destined to become the father of the Utah labor movement.[1] He was one of twelve children, of whom only five lived to maturity. His father was a moderately well-to-do merchant who was able to afford a governess and tutor for his children.

As a child, young Robert importuned his father to take him to hear his mother's brother, Abraham Marchant (a Mormon convert and branch or district president), who preached at services. His parents investigated the church and joined, but left it when a daughter eloped with a Mormon missionary. In 1852 his family emigrated to America, settling in Carthage, Illinois, where Joseph and Hyrum Smith had been killed. It was here that Robert took up the printing trade.

In 1861, in the first call of President Lincoln for volunteers to fight in the War between the States, Robert enlisted in Company H of the Sixth

---

[1] The basic source for much of this chapter, unless otherwise indicated, comes from interviews with a granddaughter, Roberta Sleater Baker of Salt Lake City, during October 1973, along with papers in her possession which she had prepared from talking with other family members. She also had Sleater's Union Army discharge papers. Also, some personal and family data were secured from family group sheets in the LDS Genealogical Library in Salt Lake City.

Iowa Volunteers at the age of 21. He served for more than four years in the Western Division under Ulysses S. Grant, fighting in 35 battles, including Shiloh, Corinth, Vicksburg, Missionary Ridge, Black River, Jackson, and Chatanooga. He was promoted to first sergeant for his bravery at Shiloh, and by the end of the war was a second lieutenant. He participated in Sherman's march to the sea and was wounded, carrying a shell fragment in his side until his death.

At the conclusion of the war, he went to visit his Uncle Abraham Marchant who had settled in Peoa, Utah, and was baptized a member of the church in 1866. One Sunday afternoon shortly thereafter, while attending a meeting at the Tabernacle in Salt Lake City, he met Mary Susanne, an independent and spirited daughter of Thomas and Elizabeth Stowe Higgs, handcart pioneers. She had been married at sixteen, but the marriage had not been consummated. Upon cancellation of her first marriage by Brigham Young, Robert and Mary were married in 1867. Sleater shortly thereafter took a trip back to Carthage to see his parents and to take care of some business, returning to his wife and infant son and moving to Peoa where he tried his hand at farming and schoolteaching. He remained there long enough for the birth of his first daughter.

In August 1868, Sleater joined with seven other men to sign the charter of the Deseret Typographical Union, indicating that at some previous time he had become a printer by trade (see chapter 4). His family says that he learned the printing business before joining the army, which was probably in Carthage, Illinois.

In May 1869, he took his wife of two years with him to be endowed and sealed[2] in the Endowment House in Salt Lake City. At this same time, he married and became sealed to a second wife, Eliza (daughter of Henry and Sarah Eyre Hancock). With Mary he was to have eleven children, eight growing to maturity; and with Eliza, he was to have eight children, five of whom lived beyond childhood. In that same year, 1869, he was listed in the Salt Lake City directory as a traveling agent for the *Daily Telegraph*, a Salt Lake newspaper.

Also in 1869, he was associated with a firm called Watt, Sleater and Ajax, General Purchasing Agents in General Merchandise, with offices in Chicago. Sleater's family says that this firm was put out of business by a church-called boycott in which members of the church were instructed

---

[2]In addition to the endowment (explained earlier), the "sealing" ritual is a unique religious ordinance reserved for the more faithful members of the church.

not to patronize the Gentile establishment. However, Sleater's partners, William Ajax and George D. Watt, were also members of the church.

Ajax was a convert to the church from Wales, born in 1835 and baptized in 1853. In 1859 he was released from the presidency of the Monmouthshire Conference in England — the same year that James Bond, one of the early leaders of the Deseret Printers Association of the 1852-53 period, was released from a mission in England. In 1862 Ajax emigrated to Salt Lake City (having worked in England with the church's *Millennial Star*) with his wife to whom he had been married the previous year, being endowed and the marriage sealed in 1864. In 1869 he was in business with Sleater and Watt, fellow Britishers. This business evidently collapsed at a subsequent time (Ajax's obituary says that the partnership had a "brief and turbulent existence"). Upon the business failure, Ajax, broken in money and spirit, moved to Tooele County. In a clay hillside between Slag Town and Vernon, he dug a one-room residence. As the years went by, he enlarged the living quarters by digging more rooms. He kept this up until he reportedly had one of the "most comfortable and hospitable" hostelries in the West, a crude and "commodious castle under the earth." It also reportedly contained the largest store in the county (*Journal History*, October 2, 1899). However, he apparently became inactive in the church upon leaving Salt Lake City; some of his children were not baptized in their youth and most were not endowed (data taken from family group sheets in the LDS Genealogical Library in Salt Lake City).

The other partner, George Darling Watt, an English convert of 1837, was one of the relatively few church members to be endowed in Nauvoo in 1845. He became a prominent member of the church, serving as Brigham Young's secretary or church reporter from about 1847 to 1867. In 1852 he became a member of the Deseret Dramatic Association, serving as its historian in 1861-62. In 1855 and 1856, Watt was associated with the Deseret Typographcial Association, being one of the primary sponsors of the Deseret Alphabet developed by the regents of the University of Deseret, with the assistance of the First Presidency of the church. He was given the responsibility of instructing the members of the association in the Deseret Alphabet and promoting its use (*Journal History*, July 3, August 2, September 6, October 4, and November 1, 1855).

In 1869 Watt played a key role in the attempted development of a silk industry in Deseret, selling mulberry bushes for the culturing of silkworms and importing equipment for processing silk thread. He was also a member of the School of the Prophets, the top-level church organization charged with managing the economic affairs of the kingdom. However, Watt had evidently become associated with T. B. H. Stenhouse, E. L. T. Harrison, and William H. Godbe, who were interested in dealing with the Gentile world, while church policy at that time discouraged such association. In 1869 this group, including Watt, were tried in a church trial, after having been counseled by several General Authorities who reported that the men were "rebellious." Watt apparently repented, at least temporarily, and his fellowship in the church was renewed. However, he was finally excommunicated from the church in a Bishop's Court in Kaysville (Utah) in 1874 (*Journal History*, May 22, June 28, October 4, 1868; February 14, March 4 and 26, June 25, 1870; May 3, 1874).

It seems logical that the firm of Watt, Sleater and Ajax, a group of Mormon businessmen who had connections with an eastern Gentile firm and were thus importing eastern goods at the time the church was pushing for the use of domestically produced "home manufacture," was the object of a church-sponsored boycott in 1869. Sleater's family says that resulting hurt may have been the cause of some of Sleater's religious neglect which they saw toward the end of his life. However, it did not seem to have unduly affected him at that time, for three years later he was seeking counsel from Brigham Young and was to be a "defender of the faith" in publishing circles in Provo.

By 1871 Sleater had become president of Local 115 of the typographers and in November called a strike against the fledgling Salt Lake *Tribune* for dismissing two union members (Salt Lake *Tribune*, November 7, 1871). In view of Sleater's later antagonism toward the *Tribune* because of its bitterly anti-Mormon editorial policy, one may well wonder if the strike action had more than the dismissals themselves behind it.

In 1872 Sleater became a permanent member of the International Typographical Union (McVicar, 1891) which had given a charter to Deseret Typographical Union Local 115 (Sleater was the only such member from Utah until 1890). That same year, 1872, he represented his local and was elected one of two vice presidents of the International Typographical Union at its convention in Richmond, Virginia (Executive Council, 1964, p. 403), possibly the first Utahn and Mormon in a union leadership capacity at the international level and possibly the first to attend a convention of an international union.

Sleater had been foreman of the printshop at the Salt Lake *Daily Telegraph* and, according to family members, was probably foreman of the shop of its successor, the Salt Lake *Herald* (secretly owned by the church).

Sleater's Provo Years

In the fall of 1872, Sleater became associated with a church friend and fellow Englishman, John C. Graham, an actor and manager of the Salt Lake Theatre, who had worked as a journalist before moving to Salt Lake City. The two men proposed to go to Provo to start a newspaper, first seeking the counsel of Brigham Young. President Young approved, but Graham was counseled to remain in Salt Lake City, later being called on a mission to England to work with the church's *Millennial Star*. Sleater decided to go to Provo, taking with him three experienced printers as partners: Oscar Lyons, Robert T. McEwan, and Joseph T. McEwan (Beckham, 1972, pp. 46, 47). All three men were members of the church. Joseph McEwan, like Sleater, was a charter member of Deseret Typographical Union Local 115, and Robert McEwan was to be a long-term member of the local. Lyons and the McEwans were related by marriage.

On August 1, 1873, the first issue of Utah County's first newspaper, the Provo *Daily Times*, was published as "the official paper of Utah County . . . a paper for the people." Over the next four years, the paper was to change its name to the *Utah County Times*, the *Utah County Advertiser*, and the *Utah County Enquirer*. During that time, Sleater lost his partners and became sole proprietor. He was evidently the principal editor through most of this period (Alter, 1938, pp. 201–03).

The Provo *Daily Times* and its successors were avid supporters of the church and its leaders, participating vigorously in the Utah newspaper war of the 1870s, attacking the Salt Lake *Tribune* and other anti-Mormon newspapers. This was no "gentlemen's war" but a knockdown conflict of editors. According to Beckham (1972, p. 66), Sleater was the more vigorous of the partners. He points out that "a change came over the *Times* after its reorganization. Sleater must have left, because the harsh attacks on the *Tribune* ceased immediately and did not return until Sleater came back nearly three months later."

At one time, Sleater referred to the *Tribune* editors as "Godless, prayerless, profane" (Beckham, 1972, pp. 71, 72). A crude editorial, typical of his slashing attacks, took place in June 1877, a few weeks before his return to Salt Lake City (Beckham, p. 74, quoted from the *Utah County Enquirer*, June 6, 1877):

The cowardly [*Tribune*] editor dare not tell us to our face that we justified treason, for if he did so, we would wring the dirty claret from his snipe nose, and make the corrupt blood of his dirty snout atone for his impudence and lies. (Brackets are Beckham's).

On the other hand, the *Tribune* editors had no more love for Sleater. In January 1876 they referred to the *Times* as

. . . an obscure little Mormon sheet. . . . During its brief and inglorious existence, it has been the born thrall of the Church . . . edited without ability, and its virulent abuse of the *Tribune* and Methodism in Utah has . . . rendered it obnoxious to its own supporters (Salt Lake *Tribune*, January 14, 1876, quoted in Beckham, p. 74).

The *Tribune* editors later referred to Sleater as a "2-ply polygamist and slave of Brigham Young" (Salt Lake *Tribune*, April 20, 1877).

This newspaper fight was especially interesting in view of the fact that the anti-Mormon leaders were the men tried for their church membership at the same time that Sleater's one-time partner — Watt — was tried for his membership.

Sleater evidently honored the calling of printer, feeling a partnership with the entire profession. Perhaps prophetic of his future role as a union organizer, he also recognized other trades. In January 1877, a few months before ending his publishing career, he said (Beckham, 1972, quoted from *Utah County Enquirer*, January 13, 1877):

Our avocation in life is. . . printing. We have learned the art after steady apprenticeship of years, and we say confidently that we can do our duty at the case, and press, that commends us to our brethren of the art everywhere. . . . That is our choice of the calling, and we are acknowledged by the craft everywhere. We have had experience in the printing, publishing of newspapers from our youth up. . . . We feel we have as good and great a right to print and publish a newspaper as the tailor, carpenter, or smith has to begin business in any place for which he is qualified.

Sleater was not afraid of taking on government officials — local, state, and federal — periodically lashing out at Provo city officials for their administrative lapses. In 1877 he also attacked his former commanding general, then President Ulysses S. Grant, for his support of programs of persecution of the Saints. He wrote: "He is a good commander of men who must obey, but bad with intelligent, reasoning men" (Beckham, 1972, p. 76). In addition to his impassioned crusades in defense of Brigham Young and the church, and his attacks on government officials, Sleater — following the policy of the church at the time — was a staunch advocate of women's rights (Beckham, 1972, p.81).

These often intemperate attacks were evidently the emotionalism and rashness of youth. They were indeed a far cry from the deliberativeness and objectivity that must have characterized the later period when he was able to arbitrate and mediate in disputes between labor unions and managements.

On September 5, 1877, Sleater left his newspaper business in the hands of his old friend John C. Graham, printer and also editor of the Salt Lake *Daily Times* (Beckham, 1972, pp. 90, 91), returning to Salt Lake City. He had not been able to make the newspaper a profitable enterprise, for he was in constant need of money to pay his bills. He also must have felt that he didn't have the support of the city officials whom he had felt free to criticize. In addition, the mid-1870s were hard depression years, a difficult period in which to be in any business.

Return to Salt Lake City and Business Activities

After Sleater's return to Salt Lake City in the fall of 1877, his two wives gave birth to ten additional children (each had delivered two while in Provo). The last child was born and died in 1893. It would seem that Sleater was not too punctilious in seeing to the church ordinances for his children — while church doctrine provides for baptism at eight years of age, his first child was not baptized until eleven years of age, his second son (of Mary) had no record of baptism (according to a family group sheet), another daughter was not baptized until she was twelve, and the remaining children of Mary were baptized, if at all, from eight to ten years of age. A granddaughter reports that the delay was probably caused by Mary who felt that because her parents had been "religious fanatics and had forced religion down her," she would not do the same with her children, letting them decide for themselves. However, only one child by his second wife has a record of a live baptism, the others have been baptized for after they were deceased.[3] This is evidence that Sleater's religious

---

[3]Baptism for the dead is an ordinance of the church in which a church member, as proxy for an unbaptized deceased person, is baptized in his or her behalf.

neglect was due to more than Mary's wishes. He himself may not have been too active in the church.

It was a new world into which Sleater entered in 1877. In 1879–80, 1883–84, and 1885–86, Sleater was listed as a compositor with J. C. Graham and Co., a printing and bookbinding firm, the owner of which was his old friend who had taken over Sleater's newspaper interests. In 1888 Sleater was foreman for the *Journal of Commerce*,[4] according to the Utah directory for those years. The journal was a semimonthly newspaper published by a non-Mormon fellow countryman H. L. A. Culmer, who was to gain renown as a Utah leader, explorer, and artist.

In 1889 Sleater was associated in the Grocer Printing Company with Graham and Culmer, and a year later we find him as its manager. In 1894, W. C. F. Grimsdell, a member of the church, became his partner in the Grocer Printing Company. They remained partners until 1900. The following year he had A. B. Richardson and W. S. Willis as partners in the Century Printing Company. Richardson was not a member of the church, although he was married to an LDS woman, the daughter of Utah's pioneer photographer C. R. Savage. Willis probably was not a member. In 1902 Richardson moved to California, dissolving his share of the partnership, but Willis remained until 1907. In that year, Sleater became associated with William George Romney, an inactive church member and son of pioneer Mormon leader Miles Park Romney, and J. C. Ryan, who was evidently not a church member.

Sleater remained with Century until 1912 when he retired, possibly because of poor health. But there may have been other problems, for according to the 1911 Salt Lake City directory, while he was still at Century he managed the Tuxedo Apartments. While with Century, Sleater was called upon by the *Deseret News* (which was publishing a new edition of the *Book of Mormon*) to straighten out some type which had become pied (mixed up). To a printer, this was akin to "family tradition," and he complied. This bit of information is interesting in view of the 1903 declaration of the typographers that the *Deseret News* was unfair to organized labor, and they had placed a ban on any relationship of union printers doing any work for the *News* (data taken from the minutes of the Salt Lake Typographical Union Local 115, November 8, 1903), but dating from 1890 (see chapter 9).

---

[4]In 1885–86, the Salt Lake City directory lists the *Grocer & Trade Journal* owned by the Culmer brothers. H. L. A. Culmer in 1888 was the publisher of the *Journal of Commerce*. Sleater was associated in 1890 with the Grocer Printing Company, possibly an offshoot of the earlier enterprise.

Union Activity

Within two years of returning to Salt Lake City, Sleater was an active member in Local 115. Indeed he probably retained his membership while he was publisher of the Provo newspaper (at least, one would expect this consistency from such a man). He later maintained that a typographer was always a typographer and should pay his dues so long as he was working at his trade (I.T.U. convention report, 1896, p. 43).

In 1879, 1880, and 1881 Sleater was on the executive committee of Deseret Typographical Union Local 115, a position he held again in 1884. In 1882 and 1883, he was president of the local. In 1885 he was listed only as a member, but was elected vice president of the local in 1886; and in 1888 he was once more president. During the last two years, most of the offices as well as the executive committee were controlled by non-Mormons. In 1888 Sleater was a delegate once again to the International Typographical Union convention in Kansas City, Missouri. One must speculate that Sleater faced some embarrassment since Local 115 was in arrears in its payments to the international union's general fund, and he was therefore not allowed to vote as the convention began. However, approximately half way into the convention, he started to exercise his right to vote, evidence that the local must have cleared up its delinquency (I.T.U. convention reports, 1879–88).

In the fall of 1888, he organized and led Utah's first Labor Day parade. Within a few months, Salt Lake City's labor central, the Utah Federated Trades and Labor Council, was formed; Sleater was the prime mover and its first president. At the inaugural ball on February 28, 1889, he must have caused a great deal of consternation as he entered with a wife on each arm. In fact, a number of people reportedly left in protest (a family tradition). Of course at that time the antipolygamy and antichurch campaign in Utah was at its height, with General Authorities and local church members in the state penitentiary for unlawful cohabitation. Most of the remaining General Authorities, including President John Taylor, were either in hiding or "on the run" to avoid arrest. So far as we know, Sleater was never arrested for his defiance of this law — which is an interesting commentary: Why was he able to live a public life and not be arrested for polygamy? His union leadership at that time must indicate either that there were numerous Latter-day Saints in the labor movement or that Sleater had become known as an apostate and was supported by the anti-Mormons. However, his later actions would seem to belie the latter conclusion.

According to the Salt Lake *Tribune* (March 1, 1889), Sleater had told the people at the inaugural ball that:

> ... for the first time in the history of Utah, the various trades and labor unions throughout the Territory had federated and formed a central organization for the purpose of uniting their strength and framing such laws for their government as would be of benefit to the working class. ... Many people supposed that labor unions were formed to order strikes, create boycotts. This organization had no such purpose. Its purpose was to preserve order and prevent strikes by maintaining just and proper relations between labor and capital. [See chapter 10 for the speech in its entirety.]

Sleater's speech reveals his conservative philosophy for which he was to become known, as did his speech to a labor assembly a week later in which he stated the purposes of the federation (Salt Lake *Tribune*, March 9, 1889):

(1) To urge and assist the spread of intelligence and education among members

(2) To foster social and friendly relations among members

(3) To elevate the cause of labor

(4) To encourage amicable relations between employer and employee

(5) To reconcile interests of both when they conflict

(6) To help make working men enjoy home and keep out of saloons

Even the Salt Lake *Herald* (March 9, 1889), the church-controlled newspaper, reported him as advocating "conservative" unionism. While there may have been some lapses, essentially this philosophy seems to have dominated the union activity of Sleater, for he became known as a peacemaker in labor negotiations in Salt Lake City, and even on occasion in Ogden.

The formation of the Utah Federated Trades and Labor Council in 1889 was followed by a major union organizing effort. The federation under Sleater's direction became the single most effective source of unionizing support, while the Knights of Labor organization was on the decline (see chapter 7 for more details). By July 1889, Sleater had succeeded in organizing several new unions in the city, there being in that year at least thirteen different union locals in the Federated Trades (Pawar, 1968, pp. 198-09). His effort was part of a nationwide resurgence of craftconscious unionization taking place under the auspices of the newly formed (1886) American Federation of Labor.

Sleater attended the annual convention of the AFL in Boston, December 14, 1889, representing the Utah Federated Trades and Labor Council. He was appointed to the labels and boycotts committee and addressed the opening session. This committee submitted a resolution to the convention urging some discipline against any union member persisting in the use of products of "scab" labor, Sleater's signature leading the others. He voted in favor of the resolution, urging states to outlaw ironclad contracts[5] forced on workers out of work because of strikes or boycotts. According to the AFL annual convention report (1889), Sleater attended all sessions of the convention. By 1890, two more union locals had been organized in Salt Lake City, and Sleater was considered an official local organizer for the AFL (Pawar, 1968, p. 125).

In April 1890, Sleater acted as arbitrator in a dispute involving the printers of Ogden, the dispute being concluded in favor of the union (Salt Lake *Tribune*, April 30, 1890). He also acted as arbitrator in an Ogden typographers and a Salt Lake City plumbers dispute in July of that same year (Pawar, 1968, pp. 145–46). Also in the summer of 1890, the carpenters decided to enforce their demands for an eight-hour day, threatening a strike. When management failed to grant it, the carpenters also included a demand for a closed shop. A great public furor was created by the strike threat, and Sleater attempted to quiet the fears of the citizenry, then riding toward the crest of prosperity and economic expansion, by calling a mass meeting at which he assured them that the "laboring men will work for the interest of our city, they will work with the chamber of commerce, with the city government, and . . . build up in this valley a beautiful city" (Pawar, 1968, p. 128, quoted from the Salt Lake *Tribune*, April 30, 1890). According to the Salt Lake Typographical Union Local 115's 1968 centennial publication, Sleater in that same year urged the formation of a building trades council to help protect building trades craftsmen.

---

[5]Ironclad or "yellow dog" contracts were often required of employees in which they "contracted," as a condition of employment, that they would not join a union or be involved in union action against the employer. If they did so, they could be fired for breaking the contract.

Political Activity

In August 1890, Sleater became involved in politics. The Liberal Party (anti-Mormon) was reportedly attempting to take over the Salt Lake County government, with the People's Party (Mormon) fighting to maintain its power. It is uncertain who instigated the relationship, but Sleater formed the Workingmen's Party with essentially the same slate of candidates as the People's Party. This political alliance between a union, or at least a Sleater-sponsored political party, and the church — which had earlier that year, through the *Deseret News*, denounced the carpenters for their strike — aroused considerable antagonism among unionists. This antagonism was especially strong after the *Tribune* printed an article claiming that all of the candidates on the slate either were at that time or had been members of the church (Pawar, 1968, pp. 134–40).

In an interview with a reporter from the Salt Lake *Herald*, Sleater disavowed union involvement, saying that the political movement was outside the union. However, his disavowal carried little weight in union circles, especially among the carpenters. Even his own typographers rose up against his political efforts, a group of members in a letter to the newspaper referring to him as "that foxy individual [who] has clothed his ideas in such language that as will permit no direct charge against himself. . . . At the same time he has implied the meaning that all the labor unions support the ticket" (Pawar, 1968, p. 137, quoted from the Salt Lake *Tribune*, August 2, 1890).

They also accused him of violating his oath as president of the Federated Trades and Labor Council by revealing the proceedings of a meeting. They went on to claim that Sleater

> . . . . as president of the Federated Trades . . . did not submit the ticket made up at a private pow wow and printed by himself at the Grocer Office to the delegates of the various trades unions . . . instead referring it to the People's Party managers to be cut and slashed to suit themselves and their ends. And if it was an "Independent Workingman's" ticket, why did he not put some workingmen on it? (Pawar, 1968, pp. 137, 138, quoted from the Salt Lake *Tribune*, August 4, 1890).

This turn of events resulted in the creation of the Liberal Labor League, which then became allied with the Liberal Party to bring defeat to the People's–Workingmen's alliance (Pawar, p. 139). This rupture, largely caused by Sleater, was the first within the fledgling Utah labor movement, a rupture evidently predicted shortly before by AFL President Sam Gompers, who had warned of the consequences should the union movement become involved in politics (Pawar, pp. 138, 139). This occurrence would indicate that Sleater was at least on friendly terms with the church at that time.

Continued Utah Labor Activity

Sleater's alienation of some unionists did not end with the political foray. In the fall of that year the streetcarmen, associated with the Federated Trades, conducted an unsuccessful strike. After it was over, Sleater, following the lead of the AFL leadership who emphasized craft unionism, said that he regretted the fact that the "unskilled" streetcarmen were in the Federated Trades — that their being there was "detrimental in place of beneficial" (Pawar, 1968, pp. 143, 144). It was evident that Sleater was not interested in organizing the unskilled or industrial-type workers, at least not within the Federated Trades.

While Sleater may have been at least temporarily on the way out of his position of union leadership, it did not prevent his hosting Gompers' visit to Salt Lake City on March 2, 1891 — Gompers' first visit to the city in a nationwide swing to enlist the participation of coal miners in the growing union movement. This was a "red letter day" both for Sleater and for the Utah labor movement. At the evening meeting, attended by some twelve hundred people, Sleater, still president of the Federated Trades, escorted Gompers onto the stand amid cheers. After calling the meeting to order, Sleater introduced Governor Arthur L. Thomas, former head of Salt Lake Union No. 1, who officially presided over the affairs. After Gompers' speech, Sleater, on behalf of the reception committee, presented the guest of honor with a gold-headed cane. At the banquet which followed, sponsored by the Plumbers Union, Sleater served as the toastmaster and offered a toast to "the organized trades of Utah," speaking on the advantages to unions of federation (Salt Lake Tribune, March 3, 1891).

That same year Sleater was also a general organizer for the AFL in Utah, probably being named in connection with Gomper's visit. In a letter from the secretary of the AFL (dated April 9, 1891, a copy of which is in the possession of this author), Sleater, addressed as "President," was informed about the mailing of some letterhead paper and was asked to enforce the brewers' boycott. He evidently had action taken to suspend a boycott of Anheuser-Busch beer products, action

taken without the approval of the brewers union or the AFL. The Salt
Lake *Tribune* for at least March 30 and 31 and April 1, 1891, had the
following notice from Sleater:

> ... I am in receipt of satisfactory information that the
> Anheuser-Busch Brewing Association of St. Louis is strictly an
> American institution and in perfect harmony with good
> organized labor, and the boycott theretofore existing against
> said brewery is hereby suspended.
>
> > (Signed) R. G. Sleater, Organizer,
> > American Federation of
> > Labor for Utah

Sleater received a sharp letter of reprimand from Samuel Gompers
(dated April 22, 1891), in which Gompers said:

> Now I desire to call your attention to the fact that the
> boycott upon that company was placed upon it by a unan-
> imous vote of the delegates to the convention of the
> American Federation of Labor ... that nothing has
> transpired between that time and now to change the con-
> dition. . . that on the contrary the Anheuser-Busch Com-
> pany have been . . . not only antagonistic . . . but have
> [resorted to] all sorts of tricks and maneuvering [an-
> tagonistic to] the eight hour movement of the carpenters
> and joiners. . . . I therefore, in view of the above, request
> you to make known to the organized wage-workers of Utah
> that the boycott . . . is still in full force . . . until the firm
> concedes fair conditions to its wage-workers. . . . Earnestly
> hoping that you will comply with the request . . . and in-
> form me thereof and what actions you have taken . . . .

In May 1891, Sleater was displaced as president of the Federated
Trades (according to the Salt Lake City directory of that year). The
following year, he was in trouble with President Gompers again. In
another sharp letter to Sleater as general organizer (dated August 9,
1892), Gompers said:

> I am in receipt of a number of letters from Salt Lake in
> which it is alleged that you have induced the Trades and Labor
> Council to withdraw from the American Federation of Labor
> and also make statements calculated to bring the A.F. of L. into

contempt. It is also asserted that the local unions that are organized in Salt Lake City are urged by you not to affiliate with the National Unions of their trade, and also local unions of which there are no National Unions in existence you have induced not to apply to the American Federation of Labor for charters. . . . Having known you for a number of years and believe you are [a consistent trade union member] I am desirous of believing that these statements are at variance with your conduct, but I desire your answer in reference to them, explicit and authenticated by the Trades and Labor Council.

While we have no record of Sleater's or the council's reply, and no further correspondence from Gompers on the subject, the following year Sleater's name was among those on an application of the Utah Federated Trades Council for a charter. He was also listed as the secretary of the council at that time (copy of application for affiliation is in my files). Evidently the Utah Federated Trades Council had either lost its charter between August 9, 1892, and January 12, 1893, the date of the charter application, or the Federated Trades had never been an official member of the AFL. The charter application is the earliest known documentation of such membership. It is possible that the attacks on Sleater were the residual effect of his abortive political effort in the 1890 county elections.

Sleater's return to the good graces of the union movement is evident — not only from his activities with the Utah Federated Trades and Labor Council but also with his own local, 115, of the typographers union. In 1893 he was elected president of the local once again (*Typographical Journal*, April 15, 1893). His election may well have been made possible by the depression of 1893–94, during which there was a mass exodus of typographers (probably mostly Gentile) from Salt Lake City, due not only to the depression itself but also to the introduction of the linotype machine that put many typographers out of work, inducing the more transient non-Mormons to leave the state or seek alternative employment.

In the depression year of 1894, Sleater was chairman of a committee to raise money for and to assist "Coxey's Army" to get to Washington, D.C., to protest the depression and heavy unemployment then wracking the nation and Utah (Salt Lake *Tribune*, April 18, 1894). During that same depression, Sleater's beloved Federated Trades Council became inactive (Pawar, 1968, pp. 156–71), the victim of the depression of 1893–94 and of schism. However, it was not alone, for the same thing was happening throughout the nation. Unionism was typically faltering throughout the country in those depression years. In 1895–96 he served as president of Local 115 of the typographers, as documented in the Salt Lake City directory (1896).

From 1896 to 1898, Sleater was the International Typographical Union's organizer for District 13, which encompassed Utah, Wyoming, Montana, and Idaho (I.T.U. convention reports, 1896–98). As such, he had the responsibility of holding the locals together during a most difficult period. Business was reviving from the depression of 1893–94, but the typographers faced a new threat: Typesetting machines were becoming popular in the larger cities, putting scores of typographers out of work and reducing the membership of I.T.U. locals. In a letter to the national convention in 1896, Sleater said (I.T.U. convention report, 1896, p. 43):

> Reports received from the various unions in this district show that a large majority have suffered a material decrease in membership during the past year or two. This is principally due to the introduction of typesetting machines in many of the daily newspaper offices, the men thrown out of employment being forced to seek other fields. Already sixteen machines have been put in operation in Salt Lake City, seven in Helena [Montana], and five in Butte [Montana] . . . four in Cheyenne [Wyoming], two in Laramie [Wyoming], not counting Anaconda [Montana] (as I do not at present know the number in that town), and many offices now employing hand compositors are preparing to put in machines.

Sleater's common-sense conservative approach to the problem is seen further (I.T.U. convention report, 1896, p. 43):

> The time scale, varying from $3.50 to $5 per day, has been adopted for machine work in all of the towns except Salt Lake City, which has been working under a piece scale for two years past. Careful observation of the two plans in practical operation leads me to the conclusion that the piece system is not only just as feasible for machine as hand composition, but vastly more satisfactory in its results to all concerned. Under the time scale the tendency is naturally to discriminate in favor of swift workmen, which causes those

desirous of retaining situations to wear themselves out in the effort to become record-breakers, and makes it impossible for those classed as slow operators to obtain employment either as regulars or substitutes. The employers always expect the product of the machines to reach the highest possible figures, and are not slow to complain when the average shows a decrease, no matter from what cause. The time system was thoroughly tried in Salt Lake City, and found so unsatisfactory, both to employers and employees, that a piece scale of thirteen (13) cents a thousand was adopted, since which time there has not been a single complaint from any source. The employers know they are not required to pay for a single line of work not performed, while the operators have the satisfaction of receiving pay exactly in proportion to their speed. Under this arrangement men who make no claims to phenomenal skill are able to hold their own in company with swifter workmen, and the serene conditions which prevailed in the old-style composing rooms are again noticeable.

The effect of the technological change on the Salt Lake City Typographical Union is shown by Sleater (I.T.U. convention report, 1896, p. 43):

> The loss in membership through the introduction of machines has been considerable. Many, being unable to procure employment, have retired from the business and sought other fields of labor; others have gone into country towns and engaged in the newspaper business, while many have gone into small job offices, either as proprietors or stockholders. In Salt Lake alone the loss in membership has been upwards of 100 in the past two years, and this has been the experience of most of the unions throughout the district.

Sleater reports that the only real trouble, aside from a loss of membership, was with Local 236 in Ogden, which evidently was barely kept afloat. However, his faculty as a mediator is shown (I.T.U. convention report, 1896, p. 44):

> After many conferences an agreement was effected between the union and the principal daily paper in the town

[where the original trouble occurred], and a contract made whereby the office would become strictly union. This necessitated, on my part, many visits to Ogden, but in the end everything was arranged satisfactorily, both to the union and the proprietors; and I am glad to say, with the exception of a few matters, I have heard of no trouble since. . . . I hold that all union men actually working at the business should be required to pay dues, as they receive the same benefits as others, and at the same time it tends to keep up prices.

Two years later, Sleater saw the slump in silver as a contributory cause of the decline in membership in his district (I.T.U. convention report, 1898, p. 62):

I must confess that the condition of the craft throughout the district is not encouraging, partly owing to the introduction of the machine, but mainly to the great slump in silver as mining is the principal industry in the western country.

He was quite discouraged over conditions, for his words are recorded in the same report (pp. 62–63):

I have been very much discouraged during the past year over the state of the trade in many portions of the district, so many men being out of employment, and the membership of the unions reduced accordingly. I have endeavored by correspondence to work up an interest in some of the cities and towns, but have met with poor success, many of my letters remaining unanswered.

His ability as mediator was tested by a conflict in Helena, Montana. He was able to work the conflict out by a compromise (I.T.U. convention report, 1898, p. 63):

After many conferences with the pressmen's union and those directly interested, I recommend that the non-union pressman make application for membership in the pressmen's union. [The man's record seemed straight, and nothing was brought against him.] The proposition was agreed to by all parties concerned.

He placed at least some of the blame on the local, as can be seen from the same page of the convention report:

> The matter had been passed upon, but the sting still remains. From my observation while in Helena, I thought No. 95 a little too arbitrary, as matters could have been adjusted to the satisfaction of all parties, if the union had been a little more conservative.

And on that same page of the report, he recognized that the *Deseret News* was a nonunion shop, but he was moderate in tone:

> The *Deseret News*, the church organ (non-union) has recently put in five machines. The union has made several attempts to unionize this office and also the job offices, but . . . to date [it has been] unsuccessful.

In the March 2, 1896, issue of the *Typographical Journal*, Sleater was honored as the president of Local 115 as well as the I.T.U. organizer for district 13 of the union. The article includes a picture and the caption "R. G. Sleater" and refers to his "conservative" brand of unionism:

> This gentleman is president of Salt Lake Typographic Union No. 115. Although fifty-six years of age, Mr. Sleater is as active as in all his former years. He first went to Utah in 1865, after coming out of the late war with a wound as a reminder of his connection therewith. He was one of the charter members of No. 115, of which he has held the office of president at frequent intervals for many years. He has three times represented his union in sessions of the International body, and at Richmond in 1872, was elected its vice president. He is now organizer for the thirteenth district; one of the organizers of the Utah Federated Trades and Labor Council, its first president and its representative to the American Federation of Labor at the Boston session. Though rather conservative, he is firm in union matters and a great friend of arbitration. He has been frequently complimented with tokens of esteem for his measures of assistance in the settlement of troubles in other trades, notably the steam and gas fitters, as also the clerk's union, and is held in generally high esteem by trades-unionists of all classes.

But to return to 1896 — Sleater also made a comeback as the first president of Salt Lake City's newly chartered central, the Utah Federation of Labor (UFL), his reinstatement perhaps due to the decline of membership (this, according to the Salt Lake City directory for that year). At the Labor Day celebration he introduced Edward Boyce, president of the Western Federation of Miners, as the guest of the day (Pawar, 1968, p. 174). In 1897 he welcomed the delegates to the fifth annual convention of the Western Federation of Miners (Pawar, p. 175), and was displaced that year as president of UFL (according to the Salt Lake City directory).

In 1902 Sleater was appointed a member of the committee of the UFL to establish a Labor Temple. In March 1903, as a delegate from the Pressmen's Union, he attended the first organizing meeting of the Allied Printing Trades Council and was appointed, along with a Mr. Holdsworth, to draw up a constitution and bylaws. On March 12, the two men reported to the union, having completed their assignment. The constitution and bylaws were presented and adopted by the delegates. Sleater was later defeated as president of this council. On July 13, Sleater, along with a Mr. McCanna, was nominated for the office of secretary-treasurer of the council, but was again defeated. He attended the meetings of the council until November 18, 1902, but no mention is made of attendance or activity from that point on.

In 1904 he played an as yet undefined role in the formation of the Utah State Federation of Labor that year (Minutes, Salt Lake Typographical Union, May 3, 1904). In the account books of the Typographical Union, Sleater is shown to have kept his dues current until November 5, 1905, when he officially retired (Salt Lake Typographical Union ledgers).

The Grand Army of the Republic

By 1899 Sleater had begun to devote himself to work with the Grand Army of the Republic (G.A.R.), serving in that year as assistant quartermaster general for the Salt Lake post, later as assistant adjutant general and as aide-de-camp to the staff commander-in-chief in 1909 and 1910, being instrumental in bringing to and hosting the national encampment of the G.A.R. in Salt Lake City in 1909. By 1913, the year before his death, Sleater dropped out of the G.A.R. activities (Salt Lake City directories for those years).

Memorialized

After his death on March 26, 1914, Sleater's Typographical Union Local 115 memorialized him as a "western organizer" for the AFL. They declared that he was responsible for organizing Salt Lake City's unions before 1900, that he had organized the first Labor Day parade in Utah, and that he had served as Grand Marshal of that parade for three years. They also referred to him as the local's "representative in the councils of the International Typographical Union and as vice president of the body . . " (taken from the minutes of the local, May 3, 1914) — a fitting tribute to a man who had five decades of union activity at the state and national levels of both his trade union and the union movement.

Postscript

According to his family, Sleater's polygamous marriages were very happy. One granddaughter reports that she remarked to her Grandmother Mary toward the end of her life, "Grandma, polygamy must have been awfully hard to live."

Her grandmother replied, "Dear, don't ever say that. Next to your grandpa, I loved Lizzie [Eliza, who died in the late 1890s] more than anyone else in the world." The two had lived as neighbors all of their lives.

While Sleater was not too active in the church, according to a granddaughter, he always believed in Mormonism. We are not aware of any action or word of disloyalty to the church or its leaders, unless church inactivity could be interpreted as such. While his family know of no church position ever held, his political involvement with the church, which temporarily cost him his position of leadership in the union movement, would indicate a positive relationship with the church. We do know that he had a "Word of Wisdom"[6] problem.

Evidently his lack of religious attention predisposed his surviving wife Mary not to be active in the church, and she may have been even antagonistic toward it, for she arranged for him to be buried in his Civil War uniform rather than his temple clothing.[7] Shortly after his burial, she reported to the family that she had been visited by her deceased husband who said: "Mary, why did you not have me buried in my temple clothes? You'll never know how hard you have made it for me here." Apparently Mary repented, for she became (and remained) active in the church until her death at the age of 102 in 1951.

---

[6]The church had an injunction against the use of tobacco and alcohol.
[7]Latter-day Saints who have been "endowed" are entitled to be dressed in their unique temple clothing for burial.

Pawar (1968, pp. 392–93) concludes about Sleater:

> The Utah labor movement had earlier suffered a great loss of leadership when Mr. R. G. Sleater, the founding member of the first central labor organization in Utah, died on March 26, 1914, at the age of seventy-three. Mr. Sleater had been the leading spirit of the Utah labor movement in its early struggles. He was one of the strongest proponents of conservative unionism in Utah, and the influence of his policy of moderation was felt in the Utah labor movement long after he was gone. Mr. Sleater had led the Utah labor movement successfully through many a trying situation, and his insistence on following arbitration and mediation as the initial steps in the settlement of labor disputes made him popular among both the employers and organized labor in Utah.

Indeed it must be concluded that Sleater had led Utah's labor movement through a difficult era. He had a foot in each of two camps: the church and the labor movement. The latter was frequently assumed by church leaders to be antagonistic to the goals of the church, and thus its leaders and members, if they were also church members, were often looked upon as disloyal. His attempts to align the labor movement with the church politically ended disastrously for him, mainly because a large body of unionists resented the negative attitude of the church leaders and the *Deseret News* toward union activities. The nearer one drew to the church, which expected almost absolute loyalty, the less likely he would be able to exercise union leadership. And the more closely one was tied to the union movement, the more critically he was looked upon by the church leaders. At this time, we have no data on how church leaders felt about Sleater as a person. Nor are we certain as to how Sleater felt, personally, about the church. For all we know, he may have been loyal to both, although there would be those who would look upon a particular act of his as one of disloyalty. At least Sleater evidently never forsook either the church or his union.

References

Allied Printing Trades Minute Book, 1903–1914. Salt Lake City: University of Utah Archives. Various years.

Alter E. Cecil. *Early Utah Journalism*. Salt Lake City: Utah Historical Society. 1938.

Application for Admission to AFL, January 12, 1893.

Beckham, Raymond. "One Hundred Years of Journalism in Provo, Utah." Carbondale: University of Southern Illinois. 1972. Doctoral dissertation.

Executive Council, International Typographical Union. *Study of the History of the I.T.U.* Volume I. Colorado Springs: International Typographical Union. 1964.

International Typographical Union (I.T.U.) convention reports. Salt Lake City. 1896, 1897, 1898.

Journal History. Salt Lake City. July 3, August 2, September 6, October 4, November 1, 1855; May 22, June 28, October 4, 1868; February 14, March 4 and 26, June 25, 1870; May 3, 1874; October 2, 1899.

McVicar, John. *Origin and Progress of the Typographical Union, 1891.* Lansing, Michigan; Darius D. Thorp, Printer & Binder. 1891.

Pawar, Sheelwant Bapurao. "An Environmental Study of the Development of the Utah Labor Movement, 1860–1935." Salt Lake City: University of Utah. 1968. Doctoral dissertation.

Salt Lake City Directories, various years.

Salt Lake *Herald*, March 9, 1889.

Salt Lake *Tribune*, November 7, 1871; January 14, 1876; April 20, 1877; March 1 and 9, 1889; April 30, August 2 and 4, 1890; March 3, 30, 31, and April 1, 1891; April 18, 1894.

Salt Lake Typographical Union Ledgers. Salt Lake City: University of Utah Archives. Various years.

Samuel Gompers' Letters, April 22, 1891; August 9, 1892.

Typographical Journal. Salt Lake City. April 15, 1893; March 2, 1896.

Utah County Enquirer, Provo, January 13, 1877; June 6, 1877.

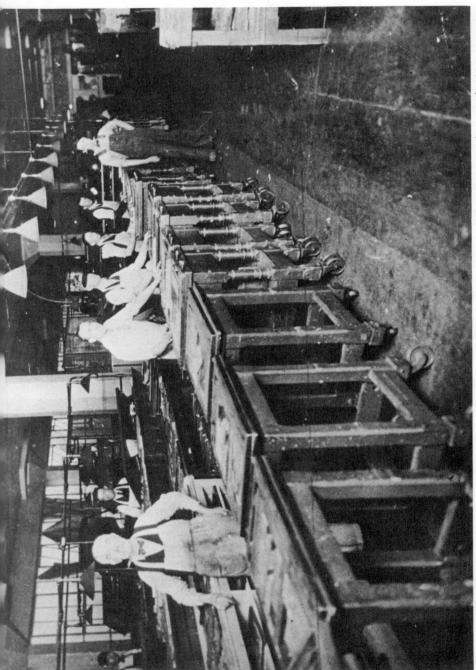

By the time this photo was taken of the *Deseret News* composing room (*circa* 1918), the typographers at the *News* were no longer members of the Typographical Union.

9

Utah's Secularized Printers 1886 to 1896

While the decade of the 1880s was kind to Utah printers, in terms of numbers, it also produced radical changes and their share of problems. As previously shown, the membership of Local 115 was 35 persons in 1885, with the admission that year of twelve typographers by card from other locals in the country, and nine initiates. The indigenous local had evidently been unable to meet the sudden increase in demand for typographers as Salt Lake City became the printing capital of the Intermountain West. Nor had Mormondom itself been able to supply the needs. The antipolygamy raids and the national anti-Mormon campaign, the effects of which were being felt throughout the world, were taking their toll on the number of persons the Mormon missionaries were able to convert. In addition, the assets of the church's Perpetual Emigration Fund were escheated by the federal government and could no longer be used as a recruiting device to bring workmen "out of Babylon," not even typographers.

Despite the sudden influx of new typographers in 1885, as shown earlier, the local leadership was still dominated, although barely, by church members, with two devout LDS old-time typographers Henry McEwan and John Priestley respectively serving as president and vice president. Of the four remaining officers and executive committee members, two — Henry Sconberg and Robert C. McEwan — are known to have been members of the LDS Church.

Table 6

Membership Activities of the Salt Lake Typographers Local 115
(1885–90)[a]

Status of Member	1885	1886	1888	1890
Initiated	9	8	16	
Admitted by card	12	22	17	
Rejected			5	
Withdrew by card	4	20	37	
Deceased				
Expelled		1	1	
Suspended		5	5	
Reinstated	4		1	
Members	35	50	44	80
Members in good standing		38		
Number of non-union "rats"				
Apprentices				
Females, union				
Non-union females		9		

[a] The years 1887 and 1889 were omitted because there were no reports for those years.

Source: International Typographical Union convention reports, 1885-90.

A Change in the Guard

Table 6 presents the membership figures for Local 115 for the years 1885 to 1890. It can be seen that 1886 saw another substantial increase in membership, swollen that year once again by the admission of 22 members by card from other locals of the country. In addition, eight persons were initiated into the union, making a total of fifty members, compared with 35 the year before.

Membership tallies were not the only changes that occurred: For the first time in its history, the local reported that a number of women were employed as typographers — nine of them, and none was unionized. The use of women in the printing business represented a new problem for the typographers, for it came simultaneously with an increase in the demand for typographers, and there were evidently insufficient unionized men typographers available. It may have also represented an attempt by the employers to reduce the power of the union, substituting non-unionized women for unionized men.

We have some detail on one woman typographer, Sadie Asper (U), who was to become treasurer of Local 115 in 1892. She had been working at the typographical trade with the Salt Lake *Herald* before 1888, but resigned before that year to enter the university (Salt Lake *Herald*, September 5, 1888). In its announcement of her resignation, the *Herald* proclaimed that she could "lay claim to being the quickest and most expert lady compositor ever known in this section of the country," which would seem to indicate that there were other female typographers. She was evidently not a member of the union at that time.

That same year, 1888, Minnie McDonald (U) "deposited" her card with the local, probably transferring from another. From an I.T.U. convention report (1890), it would appear that the non-union women were principally employed by the Salt Lake *Tribune*, which in the 1870s had been strongly pro-union, although whether that was an ideological or a tactical attachment is not certain.

As might be expected within a democratic organization, the large relative increase in membership, mostly non-Mormon, resulted in a "change of the guard" in which church members were "turned out" of office. This change is clearly shown from data of the International Typographical Union convention reports for (1885–88):

1885:

Title	Name	
President	Henry McEwan	(M)
Vice president	John Priestley	(M)
Financial and corresponding secretary and treasurer	R. C. McEwan	(M)
Recording secretary and treasurer	J. F. Webly	(U)

Title	Name	
Executive committee	R. C. McEwan	(M)
	William Zeidler	(U)
	Henry Sconberg	(M)

1886:

President	H. L. White	(U)
Vice president	R. G. Sleater	(M)
Financial and corresponding secretary and treasurer	P. J. McIntyre	(U)
Recording secretary and treasurer	J. F. Webly	(U)
Sergeant at arms	William Zeidler	(U)
Executive committee	Henry McEwan	(M)
	A. F. Taysum	(N)
	John Priestley	(M)
	P. J. McIntyre	(U)
	J. Buckmaster	(U)

1888:

President	R. G. Sleater	(M)
Vice president	J. T. Snyder	(U)
Financial and corresponding secretary and treasurer	E. D. Burlingame	(N)
Recording secretary and treasurer	S. M. Stenhouse	(U)
Sergeant at arms	J. E. Cowley	(M)
Executive committee	Theodore Lovendale	(U)
	J. E. Cowley	(M)
	J. E. Bosch	(N)
	William Zeidler	(U)
	John Priestley	(M)

In 1886 H. L. White (U), a member of the local since at least 1879, but never having previously held a union office, was elected president, with R. G. Sleater as the only known member of the church holding local union office. The executive committee was increased from three to five members, only two of the five — Henry McEwan and John Priestley — being known members of the church. The others were relatively new members of the local, joining between 1883 and 1886, and so far as is known, were not church members. For the first time since the local's founding, the role of president was not filled by a known Mormon, nor by either Henry McEwan or R. G. Sleater, although the latter was made vice president and the former was on the executive committee. It should be noted that if the executive committee had not been increased from three to five persons, it would have been dominated by church members.

One of the results of the "change of the guard" was the change of the name of Local 115. Called "Deseret Local 115" since 1868, a carryover from the days it was an "association," in 1886 the name of the local was changed to "Salt Lake City Local No. 115," the uniquely Mormon appellation "Deseret" being lost. The change of title was portentous of things to come: Serge M. Stenhouse (U) was recording secretary and treasurer in 1888, having joined the local only that year; S. Stenhouse (U) had become a member of Local 115 in 1884; B. Stenhouse (U) joined in 1886, and Lorenzo Stenhouse (U) in 1888. Their membership represented another step in the secularization process. T. B. H. Stenhouse, possibly their father, had been a prominent member of the LDS church, serving as a mission president in Switzerland. However, he became disaffected with the church around 1870, becoming involved in the Godbeite movement and, with his wife, had become one of the bitterest foes of the church. The involvement of the four Stenhouses in Local 115 (one of them was an officer of the local in 1888) couldn't help but widen the breach between the church and Local 115.

The Printers in the Late 1880s

The officers and membership of Local 115 are not known for 1887, for the local didn't publish a membership list in the I.T.U. convention report of that year, perhaps a sign that it was experiencing internal friction. However, in 1888 R. G. Sleater (M) was elected once again (see chapter 8) to the office of president and then served as delegate to the

I.T.U. convention. When Sleater appeared in Kansas City for the convention, he found that he was not entitled to a vote because the local was in arrears in its per capita tax (I.T.U. convention report, 1888). This may be further evidence of internal conflict. But toward the end of the convention, Sleater was registering his vote, evidence that the local had probably paid its debt; evidence also that Sleater had pluck, for he had remained at the convention despite the affront.

Sleater must have been a most persuasive and forceful man to have been elected head of a local union, dominated by non-Mormons, at a time when the anti-Mormon campaign was near its zenith — and this in spite of the fact that he was a polygamist and, as publisher of a series of newspapers in Provo, had been a leader in support of the church in the newspaper war with the *Tribune* in the mid-1870s.

The only other known church members among the officers and executive committee in 1888 were John Priestley (M), and John E Cowley (M) who were evidently loyal church members as well as faithful typographers.

The typographers played a key role in the organization of Utah's first Labor Day parade in 1888, and the Federated Trades and Labor Council in the following year, with R. G. Sleater playing the most prominent role in both celebrations. Local 115 was one of the dominant and most faithful of those associated with the Federated Trades Council. In 1889 F. M. Pinneo (U), a newcomer to the local that year, was elected corresponding secretary of Local 115 (*Typographical Journal*, 1889), but the other officers are unknown.

In 1887 Ogden Local 236 of the typographers was organized (Scorup, 1935, p. 76), and by the following year was reporting to the International Typographical Union (I.T.U. convention report, 1888). Table 7 shows the membership figures of that local for the years 1888 and 1889, increasing from fourteen to thirty in those years. The first known leader of the Ogden local was George Grove Taylor, an endowed member of the church, who was the local contact man (possibly the secretary) of the International Typographical Union in August 1889.

Also in 1889, the Salt Lake pressmen organized Local 41, an affiliate of the Pressmen's Union, with W. J. Lewis (M) representing the local and with only six members. Wages were $12 to $18 per week, the lowest reported in the country for any local of the Pressmen's Union.

Table 7
Membership Activities of the Ogden Typographers Local 236
(1888–89)

Status of Member	1888	1889
Initiated	14	8
Admitted by card	10	35
Rejected		1
Withdrew by card	9	15
Suspended		1
Expelled		
Reinstated		
Members in good standing		
Members	14	30
Females, union	1	
Non-union females	12	

Source: International Typographical Union convention reports, 1888–89.

Local 115 and the 1890s

The secularization of Local 115, so strongly evidenced in 1886, was to continue into the 1890s, and that decade was to prove to be especially troublesome for the typographers. They had to deal with several problems:

(1) The increasing antagonism between Mormons and non-Mormons

(2) The battle between the Salt Lake *Tribune* and the *Deseret News*

(3) The increased use of women operators in printing establishments

(4) The serious general depression of 1893–94

(5) The introduction of the linotype machine, which reduced employment possibilities in the years following the depression

(6) The increasing antagonism between unions and church leaders

In terms of numbers, Local 115 was to grow in 1890–92, as Utah itself grew and the Salt Lake City publishing business continued to expand. The known growth can be seen in Table 8. The year 1891 saw the biggest increase yet, more than doubling membership from 55 to 115. In the course of the year, some 268 typographers were admitted by card, with 247 withdrawing by card.

Unfortunately, detailed membership information was discontinued in the I.T.U. convention reports after 1892, but with the introduction of the linotype machines and with the general depression of the 1893–94 period, the membership of the local must have shown a considerable decline. Evidence of the effect of these machines is seen in a convention report on January 15, 1894, showing that in two offices (using sixteen machines), which had previously employed 33 regulars and 28 substitutes, after the installation only 25 regulars and nine substitutes were employed, displacing eight regulars and nineteen substitutes.

In 1891, for the first time we see evidence of a characteristic unique to the typographers — the existence of a two-party system within the union, for there were two candidates for each of the three major offices. Of this group of candidates, at least three were members of the church, with seven whose church affiliations are not known. In 1892, 1893, and 1896, two different sets of officers served in the course of a year.

In 1892 Mrs. E. E. Sylvester (U) served as recording secretary and Miss Sadie Asper (U) (now a union member) as treasurer of Local 115. They were the first known women in Utah to serve in a union office. Of the officers of Local 115 in the 1880–85 period, during which Mormons controlled the local, only four remained active as local officials: R. G. Sleater (M), John Priestley (M), William F. Grimsdell (M), and J. E. Bosch (N). Of the four McEwans, Henry was dead and only R. C. (M) remained professionally active (in Ogden), being expelled from the Ogden local in 1892 for "ratting" (*Typographical Journal*, September 1892). (See pages 182, 183.)

C. S. Williamson (U) represented Local 115 at the I.T.U. convention in 1890, according to its report for that year. The convention must have been somewhat embarrassing to Williamson, unless he agreed with and condoned it, for the report of the international's district organizer attacked Utah and especially Salt Lake City. The convention report, which was not always clear as to its meaning, is indicative of the internal friction that characterized the local at the time, as well as the problem of women printers:

Table 8

Membership Activities of the Salt Lake Typographers Local 115
(1890–92)

Status of Member	1890	1891	1892
Initiated		14	6
Admitted by card		268	213
Rejected		3	
Withdrew by card		247	195
Suspended		3	10
Expelled			
Reinstated		1	2
Deceased			3
Members in good standing	80	112	130
Members	55	115	138
Nonmembers		63	
Apprentices		45	
Female, union		12	13
Non-union females		14	

Source: International Typographical Union convention reports, 1890–92; *Typographical Journal* (January 15, 1892).

For a long time the printers of Salt Lake City patiently worked under the double affliction of cheap female labor and the order system of payments. So offensive was this to the stalwart printers of the coast and those traveling thither that even an International card issued by Salt Lake Union received barely the tribute which its possessor could demand. Yet with this sentiment arrayed against them and impotent for any good their Union seemed to be, Mormon and Gentile printers contrive to hold their little organization together, biding the day of their deliverance.

Payment of wages in part cash and part orders is one of the Mormon methods of business obtaining yet throughout the

Territory. Yielding up one-tenth of what labor produces as
"tithing" is one of the tenets in the creed of the Church of the
Latter-day Saints. But the onus of cheap female labor may
properly rest upon the head of the Gentile, not confined to
Utah, but, unhappily, throughout the length and breadth of the
land.

The day which hastened the deliverance of the Utah
printer will yet dawn upon the wage-workers everywhere . . . .

A municipal election was pending, the like of which was
never before felt in this country. It was an election without
politics — an election wherein the perpetuation of church rule
on the one hand and its annihilation on the other struggled for
mastery. From the inception of the canvas the Union printers
of Salt Lake, Mormon and Gentile, were awakened to the opportunity which the situation presented and realized that now
or never was the time for action. Good men in Salt Lake,
however, prevented undue haste, and prevailed upon the majority to await the arrival of an International officer . . . .

At a special meeting of the Union, held on the second Sunday of January, the gratifying report was made that the *Herald*
management [Mormon] in the future would pay wages in
cash alone, and the female employees of the
Tribune . . . made application for admission to the Union.

Having gained this much, the Union felt strong enough
to win over the chief publishing house of the Mormon
Church . . . *Deseret News*. This house also enjoyed the
monopoly of publishing all territorial reports and
everything of a public character not directly connected with
Federal patronage. . . . The business methods and discipline
of the Mormon Church had a baneful effect on outside competition. Calling to his aid the President of the Utah
Federated Trades Council [R. G. Sleater], and such candidates as were nominated on the People's [Mormon] ticket,
[the organizer] got so far as to have their leading bishop and
managing editor of the *News* place himself on
record . . . as . . . addressing those under his employ in aid
of the Organizer's plans. From the commencement,
however, the business manager threw obstacles in the way,
and . . . his influence arrayed the Board of Directors against
any change . . . .

Right at this moment, when success seemed to crown our efforts, a sudden change of heart took place among the employees. Every printer among them had one reason or another for non-affiliation. They all found argument for remaining with the *Deseret News*, claiming that no benefit outside the Mormon Church would be commensurate with Union membership. All of this was doubtless inspired by the business manager.

Thereupon the Organizer, in his report to Salt Lake Union, recommended that the office be closed to Union men and such Union men as were at present employed be called out. This was done, but one remaining in the office so called out [probably Watkin Lewis Rowe].

Dating from the meeting in January, Salt Lake Union had made metropolitan progress . . . no better evidence of its spirit can be attested than the presence of a delegate [C.S. Williamson] sitting in Atlanta.

Additional evidence of this break was the expulsion of Watkin Lewis Rowe (U) from the local's rolls in April 1890 for "having refused to cease work on the *Deseret News*, after the union had declared the same closed to union men" (*Typographical Journal*, April 15, 1890).

The internal friction in Local 115 can also be seen in the response of a substantial number of the members of the local to the political activities of R. G. Sleater (M). In 1890 Sleater, who at the time was president of the Utah Federated Trades Council, organized the Workingmen's Party which collaborated with the People's Party, the political arm of the church, in the nomination of a common slate for the county offices. Sleater vowed there was no formal connection between the slate of candidates and the council, but his action brought the condemnation of fellow unionists, both in the Federated Trades Council and in Local 115. In a letter attacking Sleater, 34 of his typographer brothers said (Salt Lake *Tribune*, August 4, 1890):

In the publication of the *Herald* interview, with R. G. Sleater in regard to the position taken by labor unions of this city toward so called workingmen's ticket that foxy individual has clothed his ideas in such language that as will permit no direct charge against himself, knowing that if he did so he would have unceremoniously [been] sat down upon as on former occasions under similar circumstances. At the same time, he has implied the meaning . . . that all the labor unions support that ticket.

If he himself says, the subject was not allowed to be discussed by the unions, how does he know what their position will be?

In the second place his statements are not to be relied upon, for when he states that the matter sprang from the Carpenters' Union, he violated his oath as a member of the Federated Trades for disclosing the proceedings of a meeting, even if it was true; and to throw all the disgrace of such a shameful piece of business upon the Carpenter's Union is certainly ungenerous, to say the least. And we ask Mr. Sleater why, as a president of the Federated Trades, he did not submit the ticket made up at a private pow-wow and printed by himself at the Grocer office [Sleater's print shop] to the delegates of the various trades unions, the Salt Lake Typographical Union for instance, instead of referring it to the People's party managers to be cut and slashed to suit themselves and their ends? And, if it was an "Independent Workingman's" ticket, why did they not put some workingmen on it?

We do not believe the workingmen are in sympathy with the ticket, and we, as individuals, members of the Salt Lake Typographical Union No. 115, hereby express our contempt for such a move, and our disapproval of any such transparent fraud and deception.

Signed:

G. J. Playter, Clint P. Rice, Charles McCarthy, W. H. Bell, T. J. Oeirich, R. R. Graham, Ed. M. Killough, F. L. Wilson, H. Schaekelford, J. F. McClure, H. L. Evans, E. A. Hinecheliffe, A. F. Schaff, C. M. Kimball, John Marren, W. S. Willis, Chas. Mulack, E. D. Burlinghame, P. E. Tierney, J. S. Daveler, A. J. Johnson, H. E. Glenn, A. G. Wright, F. Banfield, H. J. Syms, Jas H. Tillett, F. M. Pinneo, S. K. Spann, Larry Lyon, K. K. King, C. P. Walker, Frank H. Root, H. C. McDonough, F. Daniel.

The Mormon attempt to retain political control of the county failed, the People's and Workingmen's parties going down to defeat. And Sleater was displaced as head of the Federated Trades and Labor Council.

A letter to the I.T.U. *Journal* (written by George J. Playter (U), the first to sign the letter attacking Sleater) later that year indicates even more the friction among the members of the Salt Lake local. Also the

The Salt Lake *Tribune* Building was located at 133 South West Temple.

fight between the *News* and the *Tribune* is evident (*Typographical Journal*, December 1890):

> For the first time in years, if not in its history, No. 115 will have a spirited fight for president next month, a caucus and a number of secret and deep laid combinations have brought forth the nominations of J. A. Kavanaugh [Cavanaugh], late of New York, and C. C. Cline. . . . Both morning papers are getting up holiday numbers. Last year the *Herald* [Mormon] printed a very creditable Christmas number, the entire work of which was done here. Much to the surprise and regret of all, this year it is having the entire work for its holiday number done in some obscure town in the east. This is all the more singular as "Salt Lake workingmen" was the slogan in a recent political campaign by the Mormon People's Party of which the *Herald* is the champion. The *Tribune*, on the other hand, true to its history in this respect, will be a home production. . . . The *Deseret News* [Mormon organ], an institution in which our organization has failed to effect a lodgement, where the employees are compelled to pay ten percent tithing for the redemption of souls in Europe and the propagation of the principles of the so-called Mormon religion, and withall the "granniest" of old granny newspapers, is threatening to come out as an eight page paper soon.

One of the interesting applicants for admission to the local early in 1890 was Andrew Jensen (M). According to his application, he had worked as a compositor in Provo for two and a half years and for two years in Denmark (*Typographical Journal*, July 1890). (Jensen was later to become the assistant church historian.) The disposition of his application is unknown. Perhaps the friction within the local over political and religious questions was too much for him. He may even have been rejected in his application, for he was well known as an active, prominent Latter-day Saint. However, he applied again in October 1892, reporting that he had worked on the *Enquirer* and *Gazette* in Provo (*Typographical Journal*, October 15, 1892). But once again the disposition of this application is not known. In his autobiography (1938), Jensen does not mention anything of this application or of securing union membership.

The friction within the local, especially over Sleater, is seen again in a letter to the *Typographical Journal* in November 1891. The letter is also indicative of the battle between Local 115 on one hand and the *Deseret*

News and the Mormon church on the other. In addition, it shows progress in the unionization of women:

> Zion was one of the cities of the great West represented in the Atlantic seaboard "Hub" International convention last June. . . . In a little over a year, after a neck-and-neck struggle, fighting tooth and nail, we have unionized the *Tribune* day force of girls, numbering sixteen to twenty . . . driven plates out of the city, with the exception, of course, of the non-union *Deseret News*, which has had the same force of Swedes, English, Welsh, etc., as it had in the '60's, with the addition, now and then, from the nomadic hordes gathered by the Latter-day missionaries from the slums of Europe and the leper-ridden regions of Molokai, Hawaiian Islands; and finally got a scale of prices and constitution that will compare favorably with any in the country. . . . There will not be any exaggeration in saying that the man who did more to bring about this happy state of affairs . . . was S. K. Spann, lately deceased. . . . We buried him three weeks ago in our lot in the cemetery. . . . Before his demise, he held cases and was chairman of the *Tribune* chapel. . . . S. P. Rounds . . . took hold of the *Tribune* job room . . . [and] . . . pulled it out of the slough . . . and has made a metropolitan office of it. . . . C. C. Cline, for over a year foreman of the *Evening Times*, made his debut in the city editor's department of the *Tribune*. . . . It is whispered that charges are to be preferred against a hitherto prominent member of this union next regular meeting [evidently R. G. Sleater]. He has lately been active in endeavoring to form a new political party, and let his spleen get the better of his good sense by publishing an article in the *Labor Sentinel* calling into question the procedure of this union.

While the friction with the *Deseret News* and the church was to continue, there is no record of a trial for Sleater, and he was to bounce back into union leadership later on. It can be seen from the following list of officers (taken from Salt Lake City directories, I.T.U. convention reports, and the *Typographical Journal* for the subject years) that the campaign of 1890–91 to rid Local 115 of Sleater failed, and in 1893 and 1896, he was again elected president of the local. These elections may have resulted from the removal, from the city and from the local, of many of the more transient non-Mormon typographers, leaving behind the longer term workers, many of whom were Mormons.

1892:

Title	Name	
Group One		
President	George W. Armstrong	(U)
Vice president	E. J. Parks	(U)
Secretary	F. M. Pinneo	(U)
	George Playter	(U)
Group Two		
President	H. C. Fenstermaker	(U)
Vice president	H. R. Freeman	(U)
Recording secretary	Mrs. E. E. Sylvester	(U)
Financial secretary	S. M. Stenhouse	(U)
Treasurer	Sadie Asper	(U)
Sergeant at arms	Irving Coutant	(U)
Executive committee	J. H. Lincoln	(U)
	C. W. Barnes	(U)
	J. L. Barter	(U)
	A. B. Bennett	(U)
	S. A. Mann	(U)

1893:

Group one		
President	H. C. Fenstermaker	(U)
Vice president	J. B. Van Gorden	(U)
Financial secretary	S. M. Stenhouse	(U)
Secretary	Philip Corcoran	(U)
Group Two		
President	R. G. Sleater	(M)
Vice president	H. L. Evans	(U)
Recording secretary	J. E. Bosch	(N)
Financial secretary	C. I. Coutant	(U)
Reading secretary	L. A. Lauber	(U)
Treasurer	G. J. Playter	(U)
Sergeant at arms	H. W. Cherry	(U)
Executive committee	J. E. Cowley	(M)

	E. T. Hyde	(U)
	E. T. Morris	(U)
	A. G. Wright	(U)
	A. L. Rivers	(U)
Board of Trustees	Oliver Gallup	(U)
	F. L. Gray	(U)
	C. A. Jones	(U)

1894–95:

President	George G. Wells	(U)
Vice president	T. C. Crawford	(U)
Secretary	S. M. Stenhouse	(U)
Treasurer	George J. Playter	(U)

1896:

Group One

President	R. G. Sleater	(M)
Financial secretary	H. C. McDonough[1]	(N)

Group Two

President	W. S. Willis	(U)
Vice president	Joseph Jepperson	(U)
Financial secretary	S. M. Stenhouse	(U)
Recording secretary	H. C. McDonough	(N)
Treasurer	George J. Playter	(U)
Sergeant at arms	John Priestley	(M)
Executive committee	John Kavanaugh (Cavanaugh)	(U)
	A. E. Graham	(U)
	M. H. Daniels	(U)
	Frank L. Harte	(U)
	R. G. Sleater	(M)

The depression of 1893–94, as well as the introduction of labor-saving linotype machines, must have driven many of those with less firm roots from the city and state. Not only did Sleater reassume local leadership, he also became a district organizer for the International Typographical Union in 1896, serving in that capacity for three years (I.T.U. convention reports, 1896–98).

[1]Later joined the church.

In 1892 the rumors began to spread that linotype machines were coming to Salt Lake City. The Salt Lake reporter to the *Typographical Journal* (October 1892) said: "Talk of putting in type-setting machines on the *Herald* and *Tribune* within the next six months is why the boys are working for a stake to go elsewhere." By the following year, the picture was clear: In January 1893, George Armstrong (U), the local president, informed the *Journal*: "According to the executive committee's report, we have more than two members for each regular station . . . and things are getting worse. . . . [There is] considerable talk of machines . . . which will not help."

Machines were installed during the depression, resulting in a semipermanent decline in the need for typographers. By 1896 the machines had become a way of life to which typographers had learned to adjust. Sleater (at the time I.T.U. district organizer), in his report to the international union convention that year said:

> Reports received from the various unions in this district show that a large majority have suffered a material decrease . . . principally due to the introduction of type-setting machines . . . the men thrown out of employment being forced to seek other fields . . . and many offices now employing compositors are preparing to put in machines.

The *Deseret News* apparently took that step in 1897, for in his report in 1898, Sleater said, "The *Deseret News*, the church organ [non-union], has recently put in five [linotype] machines. The union has made several attempts to unionize this office . . . but up to date they have been unsuccessful" (I.T.U. convention report, 1898). Evidently even the conciliatory Sleater was unsuccessful in unionizing the *Deseret News*.

Despite internal dissension, Utahns almost monopolized the district leadership of the International Typographical Union during the decade of the 1890s. In 1891 Charles Abernethy (U) of Ogden Local 236 was district organizer, being succeeded by F. M. Pinneo (U) of Salt Lake Local 115 in 1892. Pinneo served through most of the following year when he resigned, perhaps the victim of the depression, moving to Coalville (Utah) as a publisher of the Coalville *Times*. In addition, the Salt Lake local was represented at the International Typographical Union conventions by C. S. Williamson (U) in 1890, C. P. Rice (U) in 1891, F. M. Pinneo (U) in 1892, Phillip Corcoran (U) in 1893 (I.T.U. convention reports for subject years), and John Kavanaugh (U) in 1896 (*Typographical Journal*, September 15, 1896).

The Pressmen and Stereographers

The Pressmen, Local 41, affiliated with the international union, was active in 1890 with at least six members and William Jack (M) as president; he and the local's members marched in the Fourth of July parade of that year (*Typographical Journal*, July 1890). The known officers of the local for the decade of the 1890s are as follows, showing considerable turnover (data from I.T.U. convention reports, Salt Lake City directories, and the *Typographical Journal* for pertinent years):

1890:

Title	Name	
President	William Jack	(M)
Vice president	J. C. Poulton	(M)
Recording secretary and Treasurer	A. M. Merwin	(U)
Corresponding and financial secretary	Theo. T. Gross	(U)
	O. H. Patchel	(U)
Sergeant at arms	O. S. Thompson	(M)
Executive committee	B. S. Hoag	(U)
	O. H. Patchel	(U)
	J. C. Poulton	(M)

1891:

President	Burdette S. Hoag	(U)
Corresponding and financial secretary	Charles W. Young	(U)
Executive committee	Thomas Tisdale	(U)
	Frank Merwin	(U)

1892:

President	A. M. Merwin	(U)
Vice president	J. C. Poulton	(M)
Financial and corresponding secretary	T. T. Gross	(U)
Secretary and Treasurer	Peter N. Hann	(U)

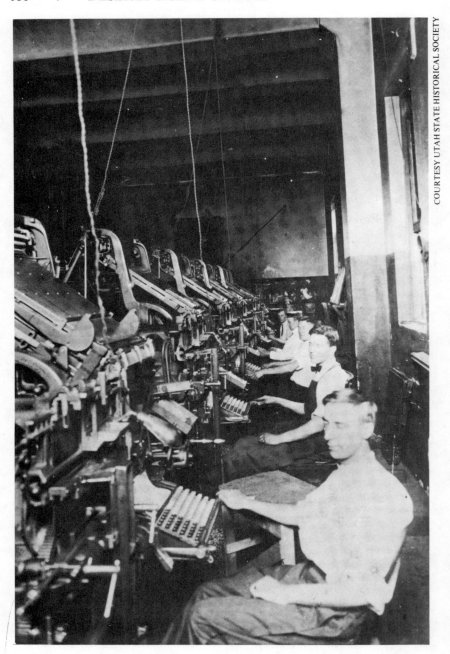

Linotype machine operators at the Salt Lake *Tribune* (*circa* 1903 or 1906) were members of Typographical Union Local 115.

1893:

Title	Name	
President	B. S. Hoag	(U)
Vice president	Thomas Tisdale	(U)
Financial and corre- sponding secretary	C. G. Watson	(U)
Secretary-treasurer	A. J. Charon	(U)

1894–95:

Secretary-treasurer	John Jack	(U)

In 1896, the local officially added the stereographers, with the addition of that trade to the local's name. Mormons evidently played a limited role in the local, as seen in the above list of officers (data taken from I.T.U. convention reports, Salt Lake City directories, and the *Typographical Journal* for subject years):

1896:

Title	Name	
President	Thomas Tisdale	(U)
Secretary	J. Carl Poulton	(M)

Ogden Typographers Local 236

The Ogden typographers Local 236 remained active in the 1880s, although it was not without problems, many of them concerning the question of the closed shop. On Tuesday April 8, 1890, a lockout occurred in the office of the Ogden *Commercial* (a local newspaper of that era), and was reported in the I.T.U. convention report for that year.

It arose over the refusal of [the] Ogden Union to grant the demand of the business manager to hire an "ad" man at a lower rate of wages. . . . The organizer decided, after a fruitless conference with the business manager . . . to appeal to the united trades of Utah and Idaho. That the *Commercial* office to-day is a Union office is just as much a victory for the trade unions as for the Printers interested.

Local 236's known member figures for 1891–92 are shown in Table 9. It may be seen that no report was issued in 1890, and only a very sketchy one in 1891. The report for 1892 shows a decline in membership.

Table 9

Membership Activities of the Ogden Typographers Local 238
(1891–92)[a]

Status of Member	1891	1892
Initiated		4
Admitted by card		38
Rejected		2
Withdrew by card	48	32
Suspended		7
Expelled		7
Reinstated		
Members in good standing		18
Members		25

[a] The year 1890 was omitted because there was no report for that year.

Source: International Typographical Union convention reports, 1890-92.

In 1891 and 1892, at least eight persons were expelled from the local for nonpayment of dues. In September 1892, the following persons were listed as working on the *Daily Post*, apparently a non-union shop (*Typographical Journal*, September 1892):

Rats		*Unfair*	
W. W. Browning	(M)	Miss May Graham	(U)
R. C. McEwan	(M)	John Cooney	(U)
G. B. Dankers	(U)	W. D. Hamilton	(U)
------ Becker	(U)	Will Kenner	(U)
		John Van Boskirk	(U)
		Guy Partridge	(U)
		Fred Baldwin	(U)
		Alex Wasmer	(U)
		Christina Michaelson	(U)
		J. D. Ferguson	(U)

These must have constituted the reported seven expelled and the seven suspended from the local that year.

The known officers of Local 236 in the 1890s are listed below. Of these officers, Theo A. Smith (U) had been associated with the typographers since 1868, when he was charter member of Deseret Local 115 (data from *Typographical Journal* for subject years):

1890:

Title	Name	
President	M. W. Sills	(U)
Secretary	Charles Abernethy	(U)

1891:

Group One

President	Thomas E. Browning	(M)
Financial secretary	J. O. Woody	(U)
Secretary- treasurer	Charles Abernethy	(U)
Sergeant at arms	Fred Zitzman	(U)
Executive committee	Theo A. Smith	(U)
	William Wallin	(U)
	Fred Zitzman	(U)

Group Two

President	Charles Abernethy	(U)
Vice president	W. M. Wallin	(U)
Secretary	J. H. Randall	(U)
Secretary-treasurer	Joseph Odell	(U)
Corresponding secretary	Fred Zitzman	(U)
Executive committee	O. H. Barber	(U)
	Thomas Chatland	(U)
	Jesse Carter	(U)
	G. S. Capps	(U)
	Robert Probst	(U)
Auditing or financial committee	J. O. Woody	(U)
	T. A. Smith	(U)
	C. J. Pettee	(U)

Title	Name	
Group Three		
President	T. A. Smith	(U)
Vice president	G. G. Taylor	(M)
Secretary-treasurer	R. A. Canine	(U)
Corresponding secretary	Joseph H. Randall	(U)
Executive committee	George G. Taylor	(M)
	William L. King	(U)
	Joseph S. Adams	(U)
Auditing or financial committee	T. A. Smith	(U)
	T. E. Browning	(M)
1892–93:		
President	E. H. Picker	(U)
Vice president	T. A. Smith	(U)
Secretary-treasurer	D. W. Probst	(U)
Financial secretary	F. A. Zitzman	(U)
Sergeant at arms	A. H. Rollo	(U)
Executive committee	T. A. Smith	(U)
	R. A. Canine	(U)
	G. G. Taylor	(M)
Auditing or financial committee	E. H. Picker	(U)
	Miss F. Hall	(U)
	C. C. Wolf	(U)
1894:		
President	T. A. Smith	(U)
Vice president	A. T. Hestmark	(U)
Secretary-treasurer	D. W. Probst	(U)
Financial secretary	R. A. Canine	(U)
Sergeant at arms	W. H. Adams	(U)
Executive committee	A. T. Hestmark	(U)
	William L. King	(U)
	E. D. Stack	(U)

Title	Name	
1895:		
President	O. H. Barber	(U)
Vice president	Charles Pascoe	(U)
Financial secretary	R. A. Canine	(U)
Secretary-treasurer	J. H. Miracle	(U)
Executive committee	J. A. Anderson	(U)

The existence of three sets of officers in one year (1891) is indicative of considerable internal strife. As already discussed, Charles Abernethy (U) attained national recognition when he was named district organizer for the international union in 1890 (*Typographical Journal*, September 1890).

Once again, Local 236 took action against "unfair people and rats," this time singling out the Ogden *Standard Examiner* (*Typographical Journal*, November 15, 1894):

Rats		Unfair	
E. H. Lund (Salt Lake City)	(U)	Francis Brussand	(U)
		John Q. Critchlow	(U)
Hiram M. Coombs (Salt Lake City)	(U)	Miss May Graham	(U)
		Mrs. --- Martin	(U)
W. G. Shields (Salt Lake City)	(U)	F. W. Chamber	(U)
		W. B. Martin (Salt Lake City)	(U)

Summary

Utah's printers went through an interesting and wrenching metamorphosis between 1846 and 1896. They went from informal group meetings in the intimate home surroundings of one of the senior apostles (John Taylor) to the formal encouragement by the president of the church and the involvement of several prominent General Authorities, as well as the leadership of a brother of the church president (Phineas Young). This religiously dominated organization was followed by the gradual secularization of the printers' organization as the church-controlled Deseret Typographical Association gave way to a Mormon-dominated local union associating with the International Typographical Union in 1868. Then the Mormon-dominated local gave way in 1886 to domination by non-Mormons, often antagonistic toward the church and its institutions. The antagonism finally came into full blossom in 1890 in the apparent attempt to force the church-owned *Deseret News* to become a union shop. Evidently *Deseret News* workers were free before 1890 to choose to join or not to join with the typographical union and, in Utah at least, unionized typographers could, without serious problems, work for a non-union shop, particularly the *Deseret News.*

Church resistence to compulsory unionism became most apparent when *Deseret News* employees, in the face of the union shop demands by the union, were required to make a choice between working for the *News* or belonging to the union. Had this been in the time of depression, the choice would have been more difficult, but the early 1890s were prosperous years and the *Deseret News* employees had a viable option: They could have left the *News.* As there were almost no fringe benefits, they were also economically free to leave and seek employment elsewhere, and there were jobs available in 1890. The evidence would seem to indicate that on the whole the *Deseret News* employees remained non-union by choice — although no doubt influenced by church leaders — only to face a new problem as the introduction of linotype machines severely reduced the need for typographers.

References

International Typographical Union convention reports, 1885 - 98,

Jensen, Andrew. *Autobiography of Andrew Jensen.* Salt Lake City: Deseret News Press. 1938.

Salt Lake *Herald, September 5, 1888.*

Salt Lake *Tribune*, August 4, 1890.

Scorup, Dee. "A History of Organized Labor in Utah." Salt Lake City: University of Utah. 1935. Master's thesis.

Typographical Journal. Salt Lake City. August, October 1889; April, July, September, December 1890; November 1891; September, October 1892; January 1893; January 15, September 15, November 15, 1894; September 15, 1896.

10

The Utah Federated Trades and Labor Council 1888 to 1896

Nationally the Knights of Labor peaked in 1886, declining thereafter in the face of the rise of the American Federation of Labor. The AFL's immediate predecessor, the International Federation of Trades and Labor Unions, was created in 1881 in Terre Haute, Indiana, with the International Typographical Union playing a prominent role (Federation of Trades and Labor Unions, 1881). Differing from the Knights, this federation maintained the integrity of the separate trade unions, considering them as autonomous entities which formed a federation for their mutual benefit. The International Federation of Trades and Labor Unions met yearly until 1886, when it became the American Federation of Labor at a convention in Columbus, Ohio. By 1888, the Knights were probably defunct in Utah.

Utah's First Labor Day

As discussed in previous chapters, Utah workers had marched as trade and craft groups in a number of Fourth of July parades as early as 1861 and at least as late as 1880. On the first Monday of September 1888, the Utah trade unions held their first Labor Day parade, with R. G. Sleater (M) of the typographers as grand marshal (*Deseret Evening News*, September 4, 1888), with Governor Caleb West (N) and Major E. M.

Bynon (U) as speakers. Eight trades were represented: Salt Lake Typographical Union No. 115, cigarmakers; plumbers and gasfitters; stonecutters; tailors; the Brotherhood of Painters, barbers; and bricklayers.

Inauguration of the first Monday of September as Labor Day by Utah unionists is evidence of the intensive involvement of the fledgling Utah union movement in national union affairs, for it was one of the earlier states or territories to hold a Labor Day parade. Nationally the Knights had begun celebrating Labor Day on the first Monday of September — as distinguished from May Day, which was celebrated by most of the labor world — in 1882 to 1884, with parades in New York City. In 1884 the Knights passed a resolution that called for setting aside such a day throughout the country. In 1887 Oregon was the first state to legislate the establishment of Labor Day, but it was not until 1894 that the U.S. Congress set the day apart as a national legal holiday.

Of this group of participants in 1888, the bricklayers, the painters, the plumbers and gasfitters, and the stonecutters were represented in the 1874 protest meeting. The typographers, while not at the meeting, were in existence. The cigarmakers, the tailors, and the barbers had not been represented in the 1874 meeting, but had been in the parades of the 1860s. For an unknown reason, the plasterers, the carpenters and joiners, the tinners, the telegraphers, and the brewery workers were not represented in the parade, although they had recently been organized. Nor were the miners or the railroaders present.

Organization of the Utah Federated Trades and Labor Council

By January 1889 unionization had developed to the extent that there were about twenty local unions in Salt Lake City, many of them associated with national unions. Later that year, fourteen of these locals, representing more than 2,500 men, organized into a central body, the Utah Federated Trades and Labor Council, under the leadership of R. G. Sleater (M). It was anticipated that at the next meeting of this council (to be held February 24), "delegates from a number of miner's unions will be in attendance" (Salt Lake *Tribune*, January 29, 1889). There is no evidence, however, that such an affiliation took place. Table 10 gives the slate of officers of the council. At least seven of the sixteen men (or 43.7 percent) were Mormons.

What the exact relationship of the locals was to the Knights of Labor vis-à-vis the American Federation of Labor is still uncertain.

Table 10

Officers of the Utah Federated Trades and Labor Council

(1889)

Title	Name		Trade
President	Robert Gibson Sleater	(M)	Typographer
Vice president	G. [George W.] Cushing	(M)	Rail clerk
Corresponding and recording secretary	H. H. Stephens	(U)	Unknown
Finance secretary	A. Haig [Arthur Haigh]	(U)	Brick mason
Treasurer	H. Hamlin [Henry C. Hamblin]	(N)	Carpenter
Sergeant at arms	T. [Thomas] Morris	(M)	Stonecutter
Board of Directors:			
Chairman	S. Hansen	(U)	Tailor
Member	E. [Edward] Ashton	(M)	Railroad worker
Member	W. J. Lewis	(M)	Pressman
Member	C. M. Olsen	(N)	Cigarmaker
Member	G. [George] Parimore	(M)	Stone mason
Executive committee:			
Chairman	G. [George] Fullman	(U)	Unknown
Member	F. [Frank] Sage	(U)	Architect
Member	T. [Thomas S. or F.]Rowland	(U)	Train dispatcher or mason
Member	R. M. Porcher	(U)	Painter
Member	G. G. Taylor	(M)	Typographer

Source: Salt Lake *Tribune*, March 1, 1889; and Salt Lake City directories.

From 1881 to 1886, on the national level the Knights of Labor and the Federation of Organized Trades and Labor Unions had attempted to live side by side. By 1886 it was realized by the leaders of both organizations that they could not peacefully coexist. The result was that they made dual association impossible. Nationals and union members were forced to make a choice. The year 1886 is usually dated as the zenith of the Knights, with the AFL (organized that year from the International Federation of Trades and Labor Unions) gaining ascendency and becoming the dominant, overarching federation as the Knights sank into oblivion.

While the use of the appellation "Federated Trades and Labor Council" in Utah indicates at least a philosophical alliance with the International Federation of Organized Trades and Labor Unions, Utah was not represented at its conventions in the 1881–86 period, nor had any known direct contact been established. Why this name was retained in the face of the new name of the American Federation of Labor, with which Utah's Federated Trades and Labor Council became associated — although infomally — in 1889, is uncertain. The desertion of the Utah unionists from the Knights may have been influenced somewhat by the conflict between the Knights and the church leadership as well as the unpopular strike of Knights in 1886. At that point of time, active LDS unionists would have had a tendency to eschew the Knights in the face of church criticism.

On February 28, 1889, the Federated Trades and Labor Council held an inaugural concert and ball at the Emporium Hall, "probably the largest ever seen at Emporium" (Salt Lake *Tribune*, March 1, 1889). President Sleater addressed the assembled workers and companions. This address established Sleater's philosophy of unionism, holding out an olive branch to the unaffiliated unions as well as the Chamber of Commerce, while at the same time insisting on justice for the working man. Because of its importance, the address is reproduced in full (Salt Lake *Tribune*, March 3, 1889), its Declaration of Principles being an amalgam of the principles of both the Knights of Labor and the A.F.L.:

> Members of the Federated Trades, Ladies, and Gentlemen: My name having been placed on the program for the opening address, I think I cannot do better, in occupying a few minutes of your time, than by explaining, to the best of my ability, in a brief manner, some of the principles of our organization.

For the first time in the history of Utah, the various trades and labor unions throughout the Territory have federated and formed a central organization for the purpose of uniting our forces to attain strength and achieve success, by framing, to this desideratum, laws for the benefit of the working classes.

I deem it wise at this time to present to you the principles as adopted by the Utah Federated Trades and Labor Council, although they have already been published in the leading journals and newspapers of the Territory.

Preamble

Whereas, The necessity of unity of action among the working classes has been fully demonstrated and we believe such unity of action can be best accomplished by an organization composed of delegates elected or appointed by the various trade and labor unions, therefore,

Resolved, That we, representatives of the various trades and labor unions, in order to form a central organization for the benefit of all laboring men, do adopt the following

Declaration of Principles

First — While we are opposed to entering any political party as a body, we declare it our duty to use our influence with the law-making power to secure the following objects: the regulation of the employment of children; securing the adoption of proper laws regulating the hours constituting a day's work; reforms in prison labor, so as to prevent the product of the convict coming into competition with honest industry.

Second — We declare it the duty of every laboring man to use his utmost endeavors to secure the amelioration of the conditions of the laboring classes generally, and, to accomplish this, we believe that a central organization should exist, whereby all branches of labor may prove allies to any particular one that may be oppressed by capital.

Third — We hereby pledge ourselves to assist each other in securing fair wages to the laboring man, by all honourable means; and we shall withdraw, and use our influence to have others withdraw, all patronage from any unfair employer, let his calling be what it may.

Fourth — We declare that all beneficial labor laws should be rigidly enforced, especially those requiring compulsory education and the abolition of the truck system [payment in kind], and we pledge ourselves to take such measures as will secure enforcement.

Fifth — We are in favor of arbitration whenever differences exist between employer and employed.

Sixth— We favor the self-employment of labor, as only complete independence can be obtained when the laborer is no longer dependent on other individuals for the right to work; and especially do we recommend that, whatever trades intend striking for the accomplishment of any just purpose, if the funds of the organization will allow it, the resistance, instead of being passive, should become active and aggressive, by using the funds productively instead of unproductively.

A great many persons have the impression that labor unions are formed for the purpose of ordering strikes and creating boycotts. This is an error in many cases, but more especially in our organization. Our purpose is to create harmony and good feelings between the employers and employees, and only in cases of oppression to use the power of our organization to obtain our just rights.

It has been remarked by some persons, on learning of our organization, that the next thing they expect to hear of is strikes in Utah, even to the tie-up of the streetcar line. I do not anticipate anything of the kind, especially such a disaster as the latter.

Knowing so well the gentlemen who compose the Federated Trades and Labor Council, I do not think there need be any apprehension of strikes or lockouts: yet, at the same time, we intend to maintain our rights as citizens and honorable artisans in a firm and gentlemanly manner.

I will be excused for stating that having belonged to and taken a prominent part in trades organizations during the past twenty-five years, I have not been engaged in any strikes whatever. On the contrary, I have always exerted my influence against strikes and tried to settle all differences by arbitration.

Within the past few years only two strikes have taken place in Utah, to my knowledge, that have been successful, and two unsuccessful, but the parties engaged in the latter were not members of any organization. This goes to prove that strikes only succeed where the cause is just and there is organization and unity of action. But I am only in favor of strikes as a last resort, where real oppression is imposed upon the working classes, and where there is no other way to get a redress of grievances. The many errors committed by the societies of organized labor in the East will be of great benefit to us in our legislative capacity and work. It will be our duty to study well our surroundings, and to so legislate and act, that it will not only place us on a firm foundation but will receive the sanction of the public. In my estimation, the power of our organization will increase in the proportion as we use it in wisdom and with consideration to the ends sought. We have not organized to fight, but to maintain our rights, and obtain security in the exercise of them; and I think the occasion will be rare indeed when we shall be called upon to exert all the strength there is in us; but we must be prepared, at proper moments, to exhibit all the forces we have, and at times of emergency, to use our strength for all it is worth. But as I have said, it will only be necessary, at most times, to prove the measure of our capacity, and our points will be gained, for few will have the hardihood to array themselves against it. If we were weak, I might say, let us be up and battle for the victory; but being strong, I am anxious that we do not abuse our power. Our strength lies not so much in our numbers as in the human justice of our aims. . . . Thrice is he armed that hath his quarrel just.

We are for right, and right is might. We are for the mental, moral, physical and monetary improvement of the working classes, and under that standard we should feel mighty to achieve success and substantial progress as we stand shoulder to shoulder, supported by and supporting each other. And to men who are bound together by ties of this importance, we must keep our hands in good check, putting forth our strength, yet only when the noble and honourable principles of our platform are to be supported and accomplished.

It pleases me to note the harmonious relations which bid peace to exist between our Labor Council and other organizations which have been created for other purposes of self-defense and public good. For instance, I know with what singleness of purpose and what sacrifice of time and energy the Chamber of Commerce of this city has been brought to its present powerful condition, and if its membership represents a different element to ours, that is a good reason why we should work pleasantly together. We are mutually necessary to each other; if they originate work, we perform it; and by maintaining pleasant relations we may secure the first of all our [objectives] — an equitable relation between capital and labor.

It is within our power to a great extent to give popularity or unpopularity to any public measure, and I think it behooves us to give at least our moral support to those enterprises which the Chamber of Commerce inaugurates from time to time.

In conclusion, I hope this, our Inaugural Ball, will begin a new era for the trades classes of Utah, and that we may often meet together in a social manner and become better acquainted with one another.

On March 8, the Federated Trades and Labor Council met, with George Fullman (U) as chairman and President Sleater and Major E. M. Bynon (U) addressing those present (Salt Lake *Tribune*, March 9, 1889). Sleater presented the "principles" of the body, stating that "no union can strike without the consent of the main body." This tenet was more in keeping with the principles of the Knights than with the AFL, as is also true of the tenet that "the union does not encourage strikes. On the contrary, its aim will be to prevent them." Both Sleater and Bynon advocated temperance and staying away from saloons. The Federated Trades member unions led in the celebration of the Fourth of July 1889 with a "great barbecue and celebration at Liberty Park" (Salt Lake *Tribune*, July 4, 1889).

The Second Labor Day Parade

On the first Monday of September 1889, Utah's second Labor Day celebration was held under the auspices of the same central body, with J. C. Dowlin (U) as grand marshal. Over fifty business houses closed for the occasion. Thirteen unions marched behind the grand marshal and President Sleater, an increase of five unions over the previous year (Salt Lake *Tribune*, September 1, 1889). The carpenters and the plasterers had joined in the festivities, along with the iron moulders, the hod carreirs, and the blacksmiths. For a reason unknown, the tinners, the telegraphers, and the brewery workers, along with the independent railroad brotherhoods and the miners, were not involved. The participating unions were:

Typographers	Iron moulders
Cigarmakers	Barbers

Tailors	Carpenters
Plumbers	Hod carriers
Painters and decorators	Blacksmiths
Stonecutters	Plasterers
Brick and stone masons	

The Ogden unions also paraded in that city under Thomas E. Browning, an endowed Mormon, as grand marshal. The Ogden contingent then entrained for Salt Lake City to enjoy the remainder of the day with the Salt Lake unions at Lake Park. The marshals and aides for the day were (Salt Lake *Tribune*, September 1, 1889):

Trade	Name	
Ogden:		
Typographer	T. E. Browning	(M)
Plasterer	W. G. Chesshire	
	(Cheshore)	(M)
(Unknown)	M. Fluellen	(U)
Salt Lake City:		
Painter	Lorenzo Cracroft	
	(Craycroft)	(M)
Rate clerk, Union		
Pacific Railroad	G. W. Cushing	(M)
Painter	Thomas Dangerfield	(M)
Builder	J. C. Dowlin	(U)
Painter	W. S. Harlow	(U)
Blacksmith	Ezra Huntsman	(M)
Bookbinder	A. H. Kelly	(M)
Stonemason	S. Newton	(M)
(Unknown)	T. M. Olsen	(U)
Stonecutter	A. M. Ross	(U)
Barber	J. Sheets	(M)
Typographer	R. G. Sleater	(M)
Typographer	George G. Taylor	(M)

Approximately one thousand "sons of toil" marched in the parade, and nearly five thousand people joined in the activities at Lake Park. In addition to the traditional banners of the Salt Lake unions, the Ogden tin, sheet iron, and cornice workers had a unique metallic banner. Speeches were delivered by the new Utah governor, Arthur L. Thomas (N), who saw America's "intelligent labor" as helping to pass the nation "safely to posterity." Major Bynon, whose theme was the eight-hour day, saw it as enhancing the enjoyment of the home and giving to working men the "opportunity for [the] self to improve the skills and education of themselves and their children through their own educational facilities." President Sleater, who closed the festivities by pointing to the aims and purposes of the Federated Trades, outlined the following objectives (Salt Lake *Tribune*, September 3, 1889):

(1) Mental advancement

(2) Enjoyment of the home

(3) Mutual dependence and support

(4) Doing justly by all men

(5) Raising the standard of workmanship

(6) Maintaining free institutions

The 1889 Salt Lake Labor Supply and Wages

In November 1889, the Salt Lake *Tribune* attempted to analyze the labor supply of Salt Lake City and Ogden. Its findings were (November 5):

Category	Number
Salt Lake City:	
Federated trade union members	810
Nonfederated union members	515
Workers not in trade unions	900
Ogden:	
Federated trade union members	350
Nonfederated union members	135

The *Tribune* estimated that the "number of skilled laborers is about equal to the demand, excepting carpenters [and] brick and stone masons" which were "15 per cent short of the actual demand." While the carpenters and blacksmiths worked ten hours a day, the remainder worked nine hours. The wages of the various trades were:

Trade	Per Diem Wage
Bricklayer	$4.50 to $5.50
Blacksmith	3.00 to 4.00
Carpenter	2.75 to 3.50
Hod carrier	2.50
Laborer	1.50 to 2.00
Plasterer	4.00 to 4.50
Plumber	3.60 to 5.00
Printer	3.60 to 5.00
Stonecutter	4.00 to 4.50
Stone mason	4.50 to 5.50
Tinner	3.50 to 4.00

A Tentative Association with the American Federation of Labor

In December 1889, Utah and Salt Lake City were represented by R. G. Sleater (who was also representing the Utah Federated Trades and Labor Council members) at the "ninth" convention of the fledgling American Federation of Labor in Boston (AFL convention report, 1889). The Utah Federated Trades was one of the earliest city or state-territory central federations to be represented and was actually the only known Territory represented in the AFL. Apparently no other Utahns attended an AFL convention unitl 1896, when George A. Whitaker (U), a cigar-maker from Salt Lake City, officially represented the Cigar Makers International Union (AFL convention reports, 1889–96 and, unofficially, the new state of Utah. While Sleater spoke and participated otherwise in the 1889 AFL convention as a representative of the Utah Federated Trades and Labor Council and was an organizer for the AFL in 1891–92, the first evidence we have of official association with that body as a constituent member was in 1893 when a charter was applied for and granted.

Utah Unions in 1890

In 1890, the year for which there is the most complete information on the individual Salt Lake City unions and their leaders until that time, the Salt Lake City labor movement consisted of the officers and executive committee shown in Table 11 (data taken from the city directory for 1890). The unions that were listed for that year are shown in Table 12. In addition, Pawar (1968, p. 115) lists the unions existing in 1889 and on

Table 11

Officers of the Utah Federated Trades and Labor Council

(1890)

Title	Name		Trade
President	R. G. Sleater	(M)	Typographer
Vice president	James Devine	(N)	Carpenter
Recording secretary	Lorenzo Cracroft	(M)	Painter
Financial secretary	Hugh Wallace	(U)	Painter
Treasurer	John G. Robinson	(M)	Carpenter
Sergeant at arms	G. W. Cracroft	(M)	Painter
Executive committee:			
President	A. D. Cowles	(U)	Carpenter
Member	Mark Cohen	(N)	Cigarmaker
Member	G. W. Cracroft	(M)	Painter
Member	J. J. Dodds	(U)	Lather
Member	John S. Dangerfield	(M)	Tinner
Member	J. H. Lovendale	(N)	Printer
Member	Theo T. Grove	(U)	Pressman
Member	George Parker	(U)	Tailor
Member	H. Fisher	(U)	Brewery worker
Member	John Ryan	(U)	Hod carrier

Source: Salt Lake City directory, 1890, p. 115.

January 1, 1891; while they are not listed in the Salt Lake City directory in 1890, they were probably in existence:

Blacksmiths	Machinists
Brick and stone masons	Amalgamated Carpenters and Joiners
Plasterers	
	Teamsters and laborers

It would appear that, in addition to the Federated Trades and Labor Council, there were at least 27 local unions in Salt Lake City in 1890. Of the thirty different Salt Lake labor leaders listed, at least twelve (or 40 percent) were members of the church, with at least four of the six federation officers being church members; three crafts were represented among

Table 12

Officers and Unions of Salt Lake City[a]

(1890)

Title	Name		Trade Union
President	I. J. Dofflemyre	(U)	Barbers Protective Union
President	Nicholas Veeser	(U)	Brewers Union
President	H. B. Button	(U)	United Brotherhood of Carpenters and Joiners No. 489
President	George A. Whitaker	(N)	Cigar Makers Union No. 224
President	J. J. Dodds	(U)	Lathers Union No. 1
Chief engineer	Gilbert A. McLean	(M)	Brotherhood of Locomotive Engineers, Wasatch Division No. 222
Master	T. J. Buckley	(U)	Brotherhood of Locomotive Firemen
President	Edward King	(M)	Moulders Union
President	H. Waldo	(U)	Brotherood of Painters and Decorators No. 98
President	Robert B. Harper	(U)	Plumbers Union
President	William Jack	(M)	Pressmen's Union
Master	G. M. Jones	(M)	Brotherhood of Railroad Trainmen
President	George Mason	(M)	Stationary Engineer Association
President	R. W. Lloyd	(U)	Stone Cutters Union
President	Hyrum Harris	(M)	Street Car Men's Union, 1st Division
President	George Parker	(U)	Tailors Union
President	John S. Dangerfield	(M)	Tin, Sheet Iron, and Cornice Union

[a]Also listed was Typographical Union 115, but no officer was listed, perhaps because of turmoil within that local (see chapter 9).

Source: Salt Lake City directory, 1890, p. 115.

Table 13

Officers and Unions of Ogden (1890)

Title	Name		Trade Union
President	I. Williamson	(U)	Central Labor Union
Vice president	Charles Abernethy	(U)	Central Labor Union
Secretary	A. J. Welty	(U)	Central Labor Union
President	D. Catchpole	(U)	Bricklayers Union
Chief conductor	J. W. Metcold	(M)	Order of Railway Conductors, Wahsatch Division No. 124
President	W. A. Heath	(U)	Brotherhood of Painters and Decorators, Ogden Local No. 100
President	John O'Fallon	(U)	Plasterers Union No. 1
President	John McCune	(U)	Inter-Stone Masons Union No. 3
President	Solomon A. Lindle	(N)	Tailors Union No. 111
President	Thomas E. Browning	(M)	Typographical Union No. 236
President	James J. Leahey	(U)	Hod Carriers Union

Source: Ogden City directory, 1890.

the officers: typographers, carpenters, and painters (Salt Lake *Tribune*, 1869–96; *Deseret News*, 1869–96; Salt Lake City directories, 1869–96; Pawar, 1968).

In 1890, the Ogden labor movement consisted of at least those shown in Table 13. Pawar lists two additional Ogden local unions in 1889, and these were probably still in existence in 1890: the Brotherhood of Locomotive Firemen, Perseverance Lodge No. 98, and the Brotherhood of Railway Trainmen, Ogden Lodge No. 68.

In addition to the Central Labor Union and the affiliates, it appears that Ogden had at least ten local unions in 1890. As in Salt Lake City, the typographers played a key role in the formation of the Ogden Central Labor Union, with Charles Abernethy (U) as secretary-treasurer of Local 236 of that union, who served as vice president of the city central. Of the eleven listed Ogden labor leaders, only one, Thomas E. Browning of the typographers, is known to have been a member of the church.

In addition to the Salt Lake and Ogden local unions, there were locals of miners and smelterers scattered throughout the state, but at this writing, little is known of them. Provo, Utah's third largest town, had no known local unions at that time. While some Provo typographers may have been organized in 1888, they were probably either associated with Salt Lake Local 115 or not formally associated with any local. As complete a list as we have of the organized workers in Ogden is taken from the city directories for the years shown (there are no directories available for 1894–96):

Year	Organized Workers
1885	Knights of Labor
	Tinners
	Typographers
1890–91	Bricklayers
	Central Labor Union
	Hod carriers and laborers
	Painters, decorators, and paper hangers
	Plasterers and cement finishers
	Railway conductors
	Railway firemen
	Railway trainmen
	Stone masons
	Tailors
	Typographers
1892–93	Brick layers
	Central Labor Union
	Painters, decorators, and paper hangers
	Plasterers and cement finishers
	Railway car men
	Railway conductors
	Stone masons
	Tailors
	Trainmen
	Typographers

The Eight-Hour Day

One of the great thrusts of the American union movement in the 1880s was that of securing an eight-hour day. Nationally, the labor movement had made great strides in obtaining such through negotiation in the early 1870s. However, the depression of that decade wiped out those gains. In 1884, the Federation of Organized Trades and Labor Unions, the predecessor of the American Federation of Labor, started again to fight for it. In 1886 the AFL resolved to move toward the legal protection of such a day, having seen how easily employers could get around contracts that supposedly limited the hours of work. A nationwide general strike was called to press for such legislation. Leaders of the Knights of Labor, opposed as they were to strikes, denounced the efforts. Utah was a leader in the movement, having won by a number of negotiated agreements with employers the limitation of the required working day to eight hours. But Utah workers had also soon found that these contracts were easily subverted. By 1892 sufficient undercutting had taken place that the Utah unions changed their tactics to that of securing government enforcement of such limitation.

In 1892 the *Deseret News* editorially supported the concept of an eight-hour day but opposed a law requiring limitation, looking on such a law as an abrogation of the freedom to contract (*Deseret News*, August 17, 1892). The Salt Lake City Commission passed an ordinance outlawing work in excess of eight hours, but the mayor vetoed the ordinance, and the workers were denied the effective means of enforcement. However, in 1894 the Momon-dominated territorial legislature passed a law limiting the hours of work on public work to eight hours (Beal, 1923, p. 35).

The Independent Workingmen's Party

The forces existing to prevent a complete rupture between the Mormon church and the unions in Utah can been seen in the Salt Lake County elections of August 1890. In the election were three political parties: (1) the People's Party (Mormon), (2) the Liberal Party (non-Mormon), and (3) the Independent Workingmen's Party,[1] under R. G. Sleater (M), founder and president of the Utah Federated Trades and Labor Council.

---

[1]The union movement generally looked on Sleater as the founder of the Workingmen's Party. Whitney (p. 718) refers to James Devine (N), the vice president of the Federated Trades, as one of the foremost leaders of that group.

In his *History of Utah*, Whitney (1898, vol. 3, pp. 716–19) reports that before the February elections of that year the Liberals, to obtain the support of the working men, had promised Salt Lake work to Salt Lake City. Whitney maintains that the Liberals had not followed through on their promise but had given jobs to imported "hobos" instead. The working men were reported to have decided to put up an independent ticket for the Salt Lake County offices, to be voted on in August. They waited for the Liberal Party convention, but were dissatisfied with its nominees. On July 25, 1890, they formed an organization, the Independent Workingmen, adopted a platform, passed resolutions, and nominated a ticket. On the following day, according to Whitney, the People's Party met in convention and, with only one exception, accepted the ticket of the Workingmen's Party.

The Salt Lake *Tribune*, opposed to the "fraudulent" People's and Workingmen's parties, listed the combined ticket (Table 14). This list was submitted by S. H. Carlisle (M), a stonecutter and disaffected member of the church who had spoken out so strongly against Brigham Young in the 1874 protest meeting. Carlisle demanded of the Workingmen's Party: "Why did you select all Mormons with two or three exceptions?" (Salt Lake *Tribune*, August 4, 1890, quoted in Pawar, 1968, p. 136). This was actually an unfair charge. Of this group, five — Clive, Cushing, Kenner, Toronto, and Cracroft — have been verified as church members, and of these only two, Kenner and Toronto, appear to have been active members. Kenner was not even on the Workingmen's Party slate, that party having Joseph H. Hurd (U) instead.

The slate appears to have been a legitimate one. It was certainly not pro-church. Ferguson was deputy clerk for the Third District Court; Rumel was a recorder teller at the Deseret National Bank and his father had been the representative of the masons, painters, brick and adobe makers in the Fourth of July parade in 1861; Clive was a real estate man, the son of Claude Clive, a veteran leader of the Dramatics Association and the tailors; Burt was sheriff; Cushing was a builder; Kenner was an attorney and later a judge; Toronto was a professor of mathematics and history; Cracroft was a union leader, serving as preceptor of the painters and decorators in 1890, recording secretary of the Utah Federated Trades that same year, and treasurer of that body in 1893 (most of the data are from the city directory for 1890).

The alliance was unable to prevent the Liberals from taking most of the county offices (Whitney, vol. 3, 1898). In name, at least, there was a

Table 14

List of Nominees for the People's and Workingmen's Parties (1890)[a]

Office	Candidate	Church Affiliation
County clerk	Fergus Ferguson	Ex-Mormon
Recorder	J. H. Rumel, Jr. (John)	Mormon born
Assessor	J. H. Clive	Mormon born
Sheriff	A. J. Burt	Mormon born
Selectman	G. Cushing (George R.)	Mormon born
Attorney	S. A. Kenner	Mormon
Treasurer	J. B. Toronto	Mormon born
Coroner	Lorenzo Cracroft	Very little mormon

[a] The Workingmen's Party slate had the name of Joseph H. Hurd (U).

Source: Salt Lake *Tribune*, August 4, 1890; Sheelwant Bapurao Pawar, "An Environmental Study of the Development of the Utah Labor Movement, 1860–1935" (Salt Lake City: University of Utah, 1968), p. 135, doctoral dissertation; Orson F. Whitney *History of Utah*, Volume 3 (Salt Lake City: George Q. Cannon and Sons Co., 1898), p. 718.

kinship of Utah's Workingmen's Party to the Workingmen's parties of the early 1800s, America's first labor-sponsored political parties.

New Non-Mormon Union Leadership and an AFL Charter

The leadership of Sleater in allying the Independent Workingmen's party with the church's People's Party caused a rupture in the newly amalgamated Utah union movement, with the newly created Liberal Labor League forming an alliance with the anti-Mormon Liberal Party. The non-Mormon labor leaders organized effectively, and in 1891 Sleater was defeated as president of the Utah Federated Trades by Norman D. Corser (N), a Baptist carpenter and newcomer to the state (1890).

The internal rupture occasioned by this attempt at politicalization of the labor movement, a move strongly condemned in general by AFL President Samuel Gompers, was widened by the failure of the streetcar men strike of 1890. While the strike was at first supported by the

Federated Trades, its failure induced Sleater to speak out against including unskilled or semiskilled workers in an organization consisting primarily of skilled craftsmen, such as the Federated Trades. This action could have been at least partially responsible for the creation of a radical industrial block in the Utah labor movement, composed largely of unskilled and semiskilled workers, in the form of the Western Federation of Miners. Corser was succeeded in 1892 by another non-Mormon newcomer (1889), John V. Woodburn (N), a plumber. On January 12, 1893, the Federated Trades and Labor Council applied for a charter from the AFL. The charter, granted on January 24, was signed by Samuel Gompers, making it the only territorial federation belonging to the AFL as well as one of the earliest local or regional federations. The application was signed by H. M. Willard (U) as president, with R. G. Sleater (M) as secretary. In addition, it was signed by John Woodburn (N), L. Cracraft (M), Edward King (M), L. Brodie (U), and J. W. Lapsley (U). Of this group Sleater, Cracroft, and King were church members. Only Sleater was endowed at the time although King later was.

The Collapse of Utah Unions

The nationwide depression of 1893–94 hit Utah in full force in the winter of that year. The result was, as was characteristic nationwide, the suspension of much labor union activity. Workers lose interest in an organization which cannot help them, and unions had proved powerless in coping with the extensive depression. The Utah Federated Trades, with cigarmaker John Hanhauser (N) as president, ceased operation, a reduced Board of Labor taking its place. This caretaker board was lead consecutively by Stephen Tyne, stone mason (possibly LDS), and Arthur E. Graham (N), a typographer, in 1894–96. Even the newly created Building Trades Congress became defunct (data from city directories).

Once again the Utah labor movement was funneled into broader social action. Arrington (1961, p. 3) reports that unemployment of workmen in Salt Lake City reached over 48 percent in the spring of 1894. As a result, Utah workers formed a "Workingmen's Association" which evolved into the "Industrial Army of Utah" after the arrival from the West Coast of Industrial Army units in Salt Lake City. While it was apparently intended that Utah's representatives would join in the march, meeting up with "Coxey's Army" in Ohio for a march on the national capital, enthusiasm soon waned, ending with the raising of money by Utah's unionists to help the marchers on their way (Pawar, 1968, pp. 166-68). Coxey's Army was one of many industrial armies formed to march on Washington, demanding relief from unemployment. It was actually the only one to reach the nation's capital, but its leader was arrested for trespassing on the White House lawn.

What remained of the leaders of the Utah Federated Trades attempted to organize the Workingmen's Cooperative Manufacturing and Mercantile Association (Salt Lake *Tribune*, June 20, 1894; quoted in Pawar, 1968, p. 169) in 1894, but with no long-term results. The church was more successful in forming an "Industrial Employment Bureau" which provided employment for a recorded 1,637 persons. (Arrington, 1961, p. 10). By January 1895, both the Federated Trades and the Building Trades Congress had relinquished their charters in trust to the Board of Labor, the functions of which were mainly social. But even it soon became inactive. The most lively unionism was found among the rambunctious miners who miners who established a home, if a radical one, in the rapidly growing Western Federation of Miners.

In 1894, at the depth of the depression the railroad brotherhoods became involved in a strike in sympathy with socialist Eugene V. Debs's American Railway Union, which was engaged in an abortive nationwide strike against the Pullman Palace Car Company (Scorup, 1935, pp. 10–11). This was to prove to be a landmark labor dispute. Debs had become converted to socialism and had moved away from his conciliatory position of the 1880s, forming the American Railway Union in 1893. By 1894, its membership exceeded that of the brotherhoods, many of the latters' locals having been weaned away. In 1894, the union had begun to focus its attention on the Pullman Palace Car Company to protest wage cuts. A strike resulted with violence on both sides. The company appealed for federal intervention on the grounds that the mails were being interfered with. Federal troops became involved in protecting company property, and court injunctions were issued against the strikers. Upon the refusal of Gompers of the AFL to support the strikers with a call for a general strike, the unpopular strike failed, leaving railroad unions throughout the nation in a weakened condition, fractured by dual unionism and defeat.

The effect of the national railroad problem on Utah locals is uncertain. In Ogden, when *Polk's Directory* began publishing again in 1897, of the earlier railroad unions, only the conductors remained organized, but with a new railroad union, the Order of Railroad Telegraphers, Division 1449. In Salt Lake, in 1895, the locomotive engineers, locomotive firemen, and railroad trainmen remained organized. While they may have been affected by the strike, they had apparently continued their existence.

11

Processes of
Secularization and
Accommodation

As the Utah labor movement developed in the last half of the nineteenth century, two separate but interrelated processes were at work — a process of secularization and one of accommodation. They were not unique to the labor movement of the Territory of Utah but were part of the socio-politico-economic developments of that period. While other communities were also undergoing similar developments, Utah's were unique.

The clarity with which the working of these processes may be seen results from the unique separatist beginnings of the Mormons. When the Mormon pioneers entered the Great Basin, they had separated themselves from their Anglo neighbors by hundreds of miles and hoped to establish a separate commonwealth in the form of the State of Deseret. They dominated most of what is now Utah, Nevada, southeastern Idaho, and western Wyoming, with strong influence in additional contiguous areas. In fact there was almost no challenge to the authority — both religious and secular — of Brigham Young, the Mormon prophet. His word was law, at least among the faithful.

His singular dominance was not to last. With the Utah war of the late 1850s, Deseret's borders were collapsed — first by church edict when the Saints were called in from many of the colonial outposts — and then by congressional decree. In addition, the U.S. Army entered the core of the Rocky Mountain empire in support of new federally appointed territorial officers. The secular power of Brigham Young and the church, while great, was no match for the overwhelming power of the federal government, which was to increase with the successful conclusion of the Civil War.

Federal troops and officials were followed by an unending stream of railroaders, miners, craftsmen, and merchants. Deseret became a battleground for a thirty-year socio-politico-economic war. There were two camps. On one hand were Gentiles and apostates and on the other hand were the Saints. The Saints were determined to exercise their freedom of conscience and religion for the building of a politico-economic-religious system or kingdom, uniquely Mormon. Their antagonists were out to destroy the ubiquitous power of that system. From the non-Mormon point of view the system was characterized by undemocratic theocracy, uncapitalistic cooperation, and un-Christian polygamy — all of them abhorrent to the American public and therefore "un-American." Mormons were considered rebels and traitors to the American ideals of that day. Democracy, capitalism, and monogamy became the war-cry of the enemies of the Saints. And there was little room for neutrals — not in Utah.

While the church's missionary system brought in new recruits for the "army of the Saints," not all stayed faithful, substantial numbers falling by the wayside, frequently the unbloodied victims of the war. Some of these joined the camp of the enemy, finding greater comfort there than in the beleaguered camps of the Saints. The church fought its enemies valiantly through the 1880s, but its secular power was no match for that of the Gentiles, aided by the overwhelming combined power of the executive, legislative, and judicial branches of the federal government with its extensions into the territorial affairs. With the imprisonment, exile, and death of much of the Mormon hierarchy, the escheatment of church properties, and the disfranchisement of the Mormon people, the Mormon secular power was broken by 1890.

So long as the Mormon power was dominant and so long as the battle progressed, there was little secularization and little accommodation. The Mormon society could remain religiously motivated and directed. With defeat, accommodation became essential for survival, but for it to take place, some secularization was necessary. The victorious Gentile community was not about to allow unique Mormon church-dominated politics and economics. It was not even about to allow the unique Mormon marriage system of multiple wives, at least not in practice.

The secularziation of the business community, making possible the accommodation of Mormon and Gentile economic interests, was relatively painless. By the 1880s the economic superiority of capitalism had become self-evident. Mormon economic cooperation had gone through three stages — cooperatives, United Orders, and Boards of Trade — each short lived. Economic self-interest, the key to the success of capitalsim, was too strong, and while church leaders may have been able to induce the Saints to enter into some form of cooperation, especially in hard times, their interest and sustainability did not last long. By the time of the most intense of federal persecution in the late 1880s, the Mormon economic system was essentially dead, Mormon men of property being freed to pursue their own self-interest — the pursuit of profits. It was probably with a sigh of relief that they greeted the end of cooperation, although nostalgia and time might soften the memories.

The secularization of politics and the accommodation of Mormon and Gentile political designs and activities were not quite so easy, and yet there were long-run trends which would eventually accomplish these ends. Evidently as a condition of statehood, the church had to give up its People's Party, accepting involvement in the national two-party system. With the end of a Mormon political party, it would be difficult for church leaders to give political "marching orders" to the Saints. The Republican Party had become so strongly anti-Mormon that it must have been difficult for the Saints to become "bedfellows" with these, their former enemies. However, the transition would be made easier with the turn of the century as Republicanism became more and more conservative, representing more and more the capitalistic-oriented citizenry. As Mormon business and professional men were free to pursue their own self-interest, with almost no interference from church leadership, the switch to Republicanism became natural for many.

While the accommodation of Mormons to capitalism and a two-party political system were relatively easy and well on the way by the time of statehood in 1896, the same is not true of a concomitant of capitalism in a democratic (or republican) environment — namely unionism. While the free enterprise capitalism of the nineteenth century bred vast differences in the accumulation of political and economic power, the democratic system produced its own correction to abuse. Once the franchise was extended to common men, they could protect themselves from the ravages of capitalistic exploitation through the ballot box. Thus the Granger Movement of the late 1800s produced protective legislation to control monopoly power. That same democracy also meant the eventual democratization of the workshop through the establishment of unions and collective bargaining, though that development was to await fulfillment until the 1930s.

Just as the American society of 1896 had not accommodated itself to unionism, so the Mormon society had not accommodated itself. In fact, the conflict between the two value systems had seemed to worsen. Contrary to the results of secularization of business and politics which had resulted in accommodation, the secularization of unionism, which had preceded that of the former, did not produce accommodation. Whereas Mormonism had come to accept Republicanism and capitalism, the same was not true for unionism. Perhaps the difference can best be understood by looking at the nature of the secularization of Utah's worker movement between 1852 and 1896.

(1) There was a heavy, almost overwhelming influx of non-Mormon workmen in the mining, railroading, and construction industries, eventually touching even the typographical union — the last known stronghold of Mormon dominance in worker organizations.

(2) The church's cooperative movements drew off many Latter-day Saints — especially the more devout — from the budding union movement, depriving local unions of Mormon leadership, membership and, consequently, influence.

(3) Radical and violent activities frequently were associated with the organizing activities of the Knights of Labor and the miners.

(4) The vestiges of secrecy remaining with the Knights helped to make it feared by church leaders as were all secret fraternal bodies.

(5) The Knights of Labor in Utah, the dominant labor organization at the height of the anti-polygamy campaign, had become associated with the principal home-grown persecutors of the church, the Liberal Party, and had taken positions against statehood and polygamy.

(6) The conservative unions, once established, insisted on closed union shops frequently resulting in discrimination against those Mormon workmen who, obedient to the counsel of church leaders, refused to join unions.

(7) The church firmly resisted closed union shops even though workshops closed to non-Mormons had existed when Mormons controlled Deseret's worker organizations.

(8) The unions, in "feeling their oats" in the late 1880s, refused to take into account the Mormon position against compulsory unionism. In a day when church secular power was waning, there was felt little need to accommodate union practice to the church position.

(9) The strong anti-union pronouncements of the church organ, the *Deseret News*, and individual church leaders unquestionably influenced many of the more devout church members to leave union activity as well as to be critical of it.

(10) By the time the church cooperative movement died out, the attitude of church leaders toward unions had been firmed up. The unions were in the camp of the enemy and Mormons who became involved with them were considered apostate, or at least weak in the faith. That conclusion was not to change even when Mormons in practice were no longer required to sacrifice everything for the building up of Zion, as had been true under cooperation.

(11) Just as Mormon workmen had been expected to be obedient to church leaders in secular affairs during the cooperation era, they were still expected to be obedient to the same leaders during the new capitalistic era. While the role of leaders had changed, they could not accept a change in the role of workmen. Unionism meant "rebellion against duly constituted authorities."

(12) The few surviving Mormon union leaders found themselves in a most difficult position. Unions being highly democratic, union leaders had to respond to worker-member demands if they were to stay in office. If the Mormon union leader responded to worker demands to the point of confrontation with business leaders, who were frequently church leaders, or even with Mormon or non-Mormon business leaders who were supported by church leaders, they were considered rebels — unfaithful Saints. On the other hand, if they "obeyed counsel" of church leaders, against the perceived interests of the workers, they

would lose all influence within the union movement. Such a position at the time of an almost complete lack of accommodation was untenable. Mormon union leaders either quit the union or quit the church (or at least decreased church activity). The less faithful members of the church, who found little need to follow "counsel" but who had leadership abilities and aspirations, would naturally filter into union leadership positions. Their way was often eased by their criticism of the church leaders or by divergence from church standards of personal conduct. By the same token, non-Mormon union leaders who were critical of the dominant "enemy of the union movement in Utah" would find that their way into union leadership positions was eased.

(13) Once local unions became associated in national union activites, their sovereignty became limited as their goals and practices became merged and harmonized with those of their union brothers throughout the country. The loss of sovereignty, while sometimes compelled, generally took place naturally as new influences of unionists outside of the community became felt.

The net effect of these peculiarities was an estrangement which was to last for decades. While the endowed (though probably inactive) Mormon, Robert Gibson Sleater, had led in the development of Utah's trade union movement and was the Utah Federation of Labor's first president, the Utah movement became secularized, essentially coming under the control of non-Mormons and inactive church members. There was almost no accommodation between the church and the unions, as institutions, although some individuals made personal accommodations.

Appendix A

Known Pioneer Mormon Organized Crafts or Guilds 1846 to 1877

Year	Place	Craft or Guild
1846	Nauvoo	Boot- and shoemakers Coopers Saddle and harness makers Smiths Spinners Tailors Theater workers Typographers or printers Wagon or carriage makers
1852	Salt Lake City	Theater workers Typographers or printers Wagon or carriage makers
1852	Salt Lake City	Theater workers Typographers or printers
1861	Salt Lake City	Agriculturists Artists Bakers and confectioners Basket makers Blacksmiths

Year	*Place*	*Craft or Guild*
1861 (cont.)	Salt Lake City (cont.)	Bookbinders and paper rulers
		Boot- and shoemakers
		Brick and adobe makers
		Bridge builders
		Broom makers
		Butchers
		Cabinet makers, carvers, wood turners, and upholsterers
		Carpenters and joiners
		Chemists
		Civil engineers
		Comb makers
		Coopers
		Dyers
		Edge tool makers
		Engravers
		Foundrymen
		Gun and locksmiths
		Hair dressers
		Hatters
		Horticulturists
		Jewelers
		Locomotive engineers
		Lumbermen and sawyers
		Masons
		Match makers
		Millers
		Millwrights
		Painters and glaziers
		Paper makers
		Plasterers
		Potters
		Quarrymen
		Rope makers
		Saddle and harness makers
		Schoolteachers
		Silver smiths
		Stock raisers
		Stonecutters
		Tailors
		Tanners and curriers
		Theater workers
		Tin and coppersmiths
		Tobacco manufacturers
		Typographers or printers
		Watch and clock makers

Year	Place	Craft or Guild
1861 (cont.)	Salt Lake City (cont.)	Weavers Wheelwrights Whitesmiths Wool carders
1863	Provo	Blacksmiths Boot- and shoemakers Carpenters and joiners Machinists Millwrights Tanners and curriers Theater workers
1865	Salt Lake City	Agriculturists Blacksmiths Butchers Gun and locksmiths Horticulturists Musicians Shipwrights Stable men Telegraphers Theater workers
1877	St. George	Brick and adobe makers Cabinet makers, carvers, wood turners, and upholsterers Carpenters Coopers Laborers Lime burners Masons Painters and glaziers Plasterers Quarrymen Stonecutters Wagon or carriage makers

Appendix B

Biographical Notes

Each biographical note begins with the name of members or associates or guilds or unions in Utah from 1852 to 1896. Part I gives the names of those who participated or were active in pioneer Mormon worker groups or guilds from 1852 to 1874, while part II lists the names of leaders of Utah labor unions from 1868 to 1896; however, a few go beyond 1896 in their union activity. The name is followed by possible variations in parentheses, then by letters designating any known relationship to the Mormon church (see key for symbols and abbreviations), which in turn is followed by the place of participation and the dates of birth and death, if they are known. Next is the reference to the group, guild, or union activity, followed by the year or years of participation. We have excluded those whose only known activity was in a United Order.

Key

M	=	Mormon
ME	=	Endowed Mormon
N	=	Non-Mormon
U	=	Religious affiliation unknown
Un	=	Union
SLC	=	Salt Lake City
Og	=	Ogden
Pr	=	Provo
GC	=	Grass Creek
ZCMI	=	Zion's Cooperative Mercantile Institution

Part I — Leaders of Pioneer Mormon Guilds (1852–74)

Allen, Benjamin, M; SLC; ——1841; Typographical Association of Deseret, 1855; Deseret Typographical and Press Association, 1856.

Allman, Thomas, ME; Pr; 1819–89; carpenters, joiners, and millwrights, 1863.

Amy, Dustin, ME; SLC; tin- and coppersmiths, 1861.

Benson, Ezra Taft, ME; SLC; 1811–69; participated in the Typographical Association of Deseret, 1855; Deseret Typographical and Press Association, 1856.

Binder, William L., ME; SLC; 1832–1902; bakers and confectioners, 1861; 15th Ward United Order, 1874.

Bollwinkel, John Murray, ME; SLC; 1837–73; Deseret Typographical and Press Association, 1856.

Bond, James, ME; SLC; 1830–77; Printers of Deseret, 1852; Typographical Society of Deseret, 1854.

Bringhurst, Samuel, ME; SLC; 1812–88; wheelwrights, 1861.

Brower, Ariah Coats, ME; SLC; 1817–84; Printers of Deseret, 1852; Typographical Society of Deseret, 1854; Typographical Association of Deseret, 1855.

Brown, George, ME; Pr; 1814–75; machinists and blacksmiths, 1863.

Bull, Joseph, ME; SLC; 1832–1904; Typographical Association of Deseret, 1855; Mechanics Dramatic Association, 1860.

Burton, Robert T., ME; SLC; 1809–73; Deseret Dramatic Association, 1852.

Calkin, Asa, ME; SLC; 1821–1907; Deseret Dramatic Association, 1855.

Cammomile, Daniel (Camomile), M; SLC; basket makers, 1861.

Campbell, Robert Lang, ME; SLC; 1825–72; Deseret Dramatic Association, 1849; Territorial Association of Teachers, 1870; Deseret Teachers Association, 1874.

Candland, David, ME; SLC; 1819——; Deseret Dramatic Association, 1856.

Cannon, George Quayle, ME; SLC; 1827–1901; Typographical Association of Deseret, 1855; General Order of the United Order, 1874.

Carrington, Albert, ME; SLC; 1813–89; attended Typographical Association of Deseret, 1856; General Order of United Order, 1874.

Chambers, John Garratt, ME; SLC; 1818–92; Typographical Association of Deseret, 1855; Deseret Typographical and Press Association, 1856; Mechanics Dramatic Association, 1850s.

Clark, Samuel, ME; Pr; 1798–1885; tanners, curriers, and shoemakers, 1863.

Clawson, Hiram Bradley, ME; SLC; 1826–1912; Deseret Dramatic Association, 1852, 1855, 1856; ZCMI, 1870s.

Clayton, William, ME; SLC; 1814–79; Deseret Dramatic Association, 1852; ZCMI.

Clive, Claude, ME; SLC; 1821–79; tailors, 1861.

Cowley, Matthias, ME; SLC; 1829–65; Typographical Society of Deseret, 1854.

Cowley, William Michael, ME; SLC; 1836–1915; Typographical Association of Deseret, 1855; Deseret Typographical Union Local 115, 1880s.

Cummings, James Willard, ME; SLC; 1819–83; Deseret Dramatic Association, 1856.

Curtis, Theodore, M; SLC; ——1903; wool carders, 1861.

Dart, Robert, U; SLC; edge tool makers, 1861.

Davis, John S., M: SLC; —— 1907; Typographical Association of Deseret, 1855; Deseret Typographical and Press Association, 1856.

Derr, William, M; SLC; 1813–97; comb makers, 1861.

Derrick, Zachariah Wise, ME; SLC; 1814–98; foundry workers, 1861.

Doremus, John Henry (or Henry John), ME; SLC; 1801–89; Deseret Teachers Association, 1860.

Dusenberry, Warren N., ME; SLC; Deseret Teachers Association, 1872, 1874.

Dusenberry, Wilson Howard, ME; SLC; 1841–1925; Deseret Teachers Association, 1872, 1874.

Eardley, John, ME; SLC; 1826–1900 (or 1910); potters, 1861.

Ellerbeck, Thomas W., ME; SLC; 1829–95; Deseret Dramatic Association, 1856; General Order of United Order, 1874.

Ellsworth, Edmund Lovell, ME; SLC; 1819–93; Deseret Dramatic Association, 1850; lumbermen and sawyers, 1861.

Evans, John, ME; SLC; 1807–96; dyers, 1861.

Ferguson, Henry Anson, M; SLC; 1840–1913; Typographical Association of Deseret, 1855.

Ferguson, James, ME; SLC; 1828–63; Deseret Dramatic Association, 1852.

Fletcher, Francis, M; SLC; 1818——Deseret Dramatic Association, 1855.

Fox, Jesse William, ME; SLC; 1819–94; civil engineers, 1861.

Glover, William, Jr., ME; SLC; 1813–92; Deseret Dramatic Association, 1852.

Grant, Jedediah Morgan, ME; SLC; 1816–56; attended the Deseret Typographical Association, 1856.

Groo, Henry, (Grow) ME; SLC; 1817-91; bridge builders; 1861; 19th Ward, United Order, 1874.

Hague, James, ME; SLC; 1823–71; gun- and locksmiths, 1861.

Hales, George, ME; SLC; 1822–1907; Typographical Association of Deseret, 1855; Deseret Typographical and Press Association, 1856.

Hampton, Benjamin, ME; SLC; 1837–1917; tobacco manufacturers, 1861.

Hawkins, Leo, M; SLC; 1834–52; Deseret Dramatic Association, 1855.

Hennefer, William Henry, ME; SLC; 1824—; Deseret Dramatic Association, 1855.

Howard, Thomas, ME; SLC; 1843--1915; paper makers, 1861.

Hutchinson, Jacob Flynn, ME; SLC; 1816--67; Deseret Dramatic Association, 1852; Typographical Association of Deseret, 1855.

Judd, Joseph, ME; St. George; 1849-1929; St. George Builders Union, 1877.

Kelly, John Bookbinder, ME;
SLC; 1824–83; Typographical
Association of Deseret, 1855;
Deseret Typographical and
Press Association, 1856;
bookbinders and paper rulers,
1861; Deseret Dramatic
Association, 1860s; 7th Ward,
United Order, 1874.

Kesler, Frederick, ME; SLC;
1816-99 (or 1900); millwrights,
1861; 6th Ward, United Order,
1874.

Kidgell, Charles, M; SLC; 1833–
72; jewlers, 1861.

Kimball, Heber Chase, ME; SLC;
1801–68; participated in
printers' festivals, 1852, 1856.

Kiskadden, Annie Adams, ME;
SLC; 1848–1916; Deseret
Dramatic Association, 1864.

Lamb, Abel, ME; SLC; 1801–74
coopers, 1861.

Lambert, Charles, ME; SLC;
1816-92; stonecutters, 1861; 7th
Ward, United Order, 1874.

Long, Joseph Varah, ME; SLC;
1826–69; Deseret Typographical
Association, 1855.

Lyman, Amasa Mason, ME; SLC;
1813–77; Deseret Typo-
graphical and Press Association, 1856.

Lyman, Leonard, ME; SLC; 1793–
1877; hatters, 1861.

Lyon, John, ME; SLC; 1803–89;
Deseret Dramatic Association,
1855.

Lyon, Thomas, ME; SLC; 1826-63;
weavers, 1861.

Maiben, Henry, ME; SLC; 1819–
83; Deseret Dramatic Society,
1852; associated with Deseret
Typographical and Press
Association, 1856.

Maeser, Karl Gottfried, ME; SLC;
1828-1901; Deseret Teachers
Association, 1872, 74.

Martin, Edward, ME; SLC; 1818–
82; Deseret Dramatic Association, 1852; painters and glaziers,
1861.

McEwan, Henry, ME; SLC and
Pr; 1830–94; Deseret Dramatic
Association, 1860s; Provo
Dramatic Association, and
Typographical Association of
Deseret, 1855; typographers,
1861; Deseret Typographical
Union Local 115, 1868–88.

McKenzie, David, Jr., ME; SLC;
1833–1914; Deseret Dramatic
Association, 1856; engravers,
1861; General Order of United
Order, 1874.

McKnight, James, ME; SLC;
1830–1900; Printers of Deseret,
1852; Typographical Society of
Deseret, 1854; Typographical
Association of Deseret, 1855.

McMaster, William Athol, ME;
SLC; 1816–87; rope makers,
1861, 11th Ward United Order,
1874.

Miller, Jacob, ME; SLC; 1835–
1911; agriculturists, 1861;
ZCMI, Farmington (Utah)
cooperative.

Miller, Reuben, ME; SLC; 1811–
82; agriculturists, 1861;
Millcreek United Order, 1874.

Mills, William Gill, ME; SLC;
1822-95; Deseret Typographical
Association, 1855; Deseret
Typographical and Press
Association, 1856.

Morriss, William Vaughn, ME;
SLC; 1821—; artists, 1861.

Musser, Amos Milton, ME; SLC;
1830–1909; Deseret Dramatic
Association, and Leather
Goods Cooperative, 1852.

Neff, John, ME; SLC; 1794-1869; miller, 1861.

Neibaur, Alexander, ME; SLC; 1808–76 (or 1883); match makers, 1861.

Park, John Rocky, M; SLC; 1833–1900; Deseret Teachers Association, 1872, 1874.

Phelps, William Wines, ME; SLC; 1792–1872; Typographical Association of Deseret, 1855; Typographical and Press Association, 1856.

Pickett, Horatio, ME; St. George, 1848–1918; St. George Builders Union, 1877.

Pitt, William, ME; SLC; 1813–73; Deseret Dramatic Association, 1852.

Platt, Francis, ME; SLC; 1825–85; saddlers and harness makers, 1861; 13th Ward United Order, 1874.

Pratt, Orson, ME; SLC; 1811-81; Deseret Typographical Association, 1850s.

Pratt Orson, Jr., M; SLC; 1837–1903; Territorial Teachers Association, 1860.

Pugmire, Jonathan, ME; SLC; 1823–80; blacksmiths, 1861.

Pyper, Alexander Chruikshanks, ME; SLC; 1828–82; chemists, 1861; 12th Ward United Order, 1874.

Rawlins, Joseph L., ME; SLC; Deseret School Teachers Association, 1872; South Cottonwood United Order, 1874.

Richards, Henry Phineas, ME; SLC; 1831–1912; Deseret Dramatic Association, 1855; ZCMI.

Richards, Samuel Whitney, ME; SLC; 1824-1909; talked at a meeting of the Typographical Association of Deseret in 1855.

Richards, Willard, ME; SLC; 1804–54; participated at printers' festival, 1852.

Riding, Henry, ME; St. George; 1845-1900; St. George Builders Union, 1877.

Riggs, Obadiah Higbee, ME; SLC; 1843-1907; Deseret Teachers Association, 1872, 1874.

Robson, James, ME; SLC; 1841–1926; tanners and curriers, 1861.

Rodgers, John, ME; SLC; 1837–1920; silversmiths, 1861.

Romney, Miles, ME; SLC; 1806–77; carpenters and joiners, 1861.

Romney, Miles Park, ME; St. George; 1843-1904; St. George Builders Union, 1877; carpenters, United Order of St. George, 1874.

Rumell, John H., Sr., ME; SLC; 1819–94; masons, painters, brick and adobe makers, 1861.

Sayers, E., M; SLC; horticulturists, 1861.

Scott, John, ME; SLC; 1811–76; agriculturists, 1861.

Sharp, Adam, ME; SLC; 1827–90; quarrymen, 1861.

Smith, Elias, ME; SLC; 1804–88; attended Typographical Association of Deseret's festival, 1856.

Smith, George Albert, ME; SLC; 1817–75; participated in printers' festival, 1852; General Order of the United Order, 1874.

Smithies, James, ME; SLC; 1807–79; Deseret Dramatic Association, 1852.

Snelgrove, Edward, ME; SLC; 1820–1900; boot- and shoemakers, 1861; 12th Ward United Order, 1874.

Snow, Erastus, ME; SLC; 1818–88; Typographical Association of Deseret, 1855; Deseret typographical festival, 1856; General Order of United Order, 1874.

Spencer, Claudius Victor, ME; SLC; 1824–1910; Deseret Typographical and Press Association, 1856.

Squires, John Fell, ME; SLC; 1846–1933; hairdressers, 1861.

Staines, William Carter, M; SLC; 1818–81; Deseret Dramatic Association, 1855; 12th Ward United Order, 1874.

Stewart, James Zebulon, ME; SLC; 1844–1931; Deseret Teachers Association, 1874.

Stringham, Briant (Bryant), ME; SLC; 1825–71; stock raisers, 1861.

Taylor, Charles B., ME; SLC; 1819–95; butchers, 1861.

Tripp, Robert Billings, U; SLC; 1852–1937; Deseret Teachers Association, 1872.

Ursenbach, Octave, ME; SLC; 1832–71; watch and clock makers, 1861.

Wade, Moses, ME; SLC; 1792–1869; broom makers, 1869.

Watt, George Darling, ME; SLC; 1815–81; Typographical Association of Deseret, 1855; Deseret Typographical and Press Association, 1856.

Wells, Daniel Hanmer, ME; SLC; 1814–91; attended Deseret typographical festival, 1856; General Order of United Order, 1874.

Whitney, Horace K., ME; SLC; 1823--84; Typographical Association of Deseret, 1855; Deseret Dramatic Association, 1852.

Whitney, O. K., ME; SLC; 1830–84; Deseret Dramatic Association, 1852.

Wilkie, Matthew Forbes, ME; SLC; ——1861; Typographical Association Deseret, 1855.

Willis, William, ME; SLC; 1810–77; Deseret Teachers Association, 1860.

Woodbury, Orin N., ME; St. George; 1828–90; St. George Builders Union, 1877.

Woodruff, Wilford, ME; SLC; 1807--98; Deseret Typographical and Press Association, 1856; General Order of United Order, 1874.

Young, Brigham, ME; SLC; 1801–77; helped found Deseret Dramatic Association, 1852, and Printers of Deseret, 1852; ZCMI; General Order of the United Order, 1874.

Young, Brigham Hamilton, ME; SLC; 1824–98; Typographical Association of Deseret, 1855; Deseret Typographical and Press Association, 1856.

Young, John, Jr., ME; SLC; 1791–1870; attended the printers' festival, 1853.

Young, Phineas H., ME; SLC; 1799--1879; attended the printers' festival, 1853; Typographical Association of Deseret, 1855; Deseret Typographical and Press Association, 1856.

Part II — Leaders of Utah Unions (1868–96)

Abernethy, Charles (Abernathy), U; Og; Typographical Union No. 236, 1890–91; Ogden Central Labor Union, 1890–91; International Typographical Union, 1891.

Ackerman, J. H. (John Henry), N; SLC; 1851–1907; Deseret Typographical Union Local 115, 1879–86.

Adams, Joseph S., ME; Og; 1861–1936; Typographical Union No. 236, 1893.

Allece, Charles W., U; Og; Hod Carriesr Union, 1890–91.

Allen, George, U; Og; Order of Railway Conductors No. 124, 1890–91, 1906–07, 1910–11.

Anderson, J. A., U; Og; 1860–1943; Typographical Union No. 236, 1895.

Anderson, W. N. (William Nephi), ME; SLC; 1818–1904; Moulders Union, 1890.

Andrew, R. S. (Richard Septimus), ME; SLC; 1858–83; Deseret Typographical Union Local 115, 1881–82.

Armstrong, George, W., U; SLC; Typographical Union Local 115, 1891-93; Jordan Assembly No. 3543 and District Assemby No. 205, Knights of Labor.

Armstrong, T. C., (Thomas Columbus), U; Jordan; 1843-1900; Knights of Labor No. 3543, 1887.

Ashton, E. (Edward), ME; SLC; 1821–1904; Utah Federated Trades and La bor Council, 1889.

Asper, Sadie, U; SLC; Typographical Union Local 115, 1891–92.

Attley, Henry W. (William), ME; SLC; 1822–1911 Deseret Typographical Union Local 115, 1869.

Aubrey, F. D. (Franklin D.), U; SLC; ——1915; Barbers Protective Union, 1890.

Auterson, David, U; SLC; Stone Cutters Union, 1890–92.

Aveson, Robert (Avison), ME; SLC; 1847–1939; Deseret Typographical Union Local 115, 1868.

Baker, John, U; SLC; National Association of Stationary Engineers No. 1, 1896.

Ball, Charles, U; Og; Plasterers Union No. 1, 1890–91.

Barber, Orrin Hallett, U; Og; 1866--1936; Typographical Union No. 236, 1895.

Barnes, C. W., (Charles) U; SLC; Typographical Union Local 115, 1892.

Barnum, E. W., U; SLC; Telegraphers Union, 1881.

Barter, J. L. U; SLC; Typographical Union Local 115.

Beless, James, U; SLC; 1855–1940; Brotherhood of Locomotive Engineers Local 713, and Wasatch Division No. 222, 1890–96.

Bennett, A. B. (Athel), U; SLC; Typographical Union Local 115, 1890–93; Utah Federated Trades and Labor Council, 1890.

Berry, C. L. (Charles), U; SLC; Salt Lake Musicians Protective Association, 1896.

Berry, J. F., U; Og; Order of Railway Conductors, Wasatch Division No. 124, 1890–91; Brotherhood of Railway Conductors, 1892–93.

Berry, James, U; Og; Inter-Stone Masons Union No. 3, 1890–91.

Berry, Joseph, U; SLC; Hod Carriers and Laborers Union No. 1, l891-92.

Besten, W. V. (William), U: SLC; Barbers Protective Union, 1896.

Bond, John W., U; SLC; ——1905; Moulders Union, 1890.

Boog, B. S., U; SLC; Pressmen's Union, 1893.

Bosch, J. E. (Jacob Emanuel), N; SLC; 1852–1918; Deseret and Salt Lake Typographical Union Local 115, 1879–80, 1886, 1888, 1893. Bostwick, G. W., U; SLC; tinners, 1874.

Breeze, Alfred (Alfred Hardy), ME; SLC; 1870–1946; Hod Carriers and Laborers Union No. 1, 1890.

Brewster, Edwin H., ME; SLC; 1843–1926; Tin, Sheet-Iron, and Cornice Union, 1890–92.

Brodie, L. (Louis M.), U; SLC; Utah Federated Trades and Labor Council, 1893.

Brown, Alfred, U; SLC; Stone Cutters Union 1894–96.

Brown, Emil C., U; Ogden Tailors Union No. 111, 1892–93.

Brown, R. C. (Robert), U; SLC; Brotherhood of Locomotive Firemen, Salt Lake Lodge No. 178, 1894–1896.

Browning, Thomas E. ME; Ogden, 1861–1921; Labor Day parade, 1889; Typographical Union No. 236, 1890–91, 1893.

Bryan, W. J. (James W.), U; SLC; Utah Federated Trades and Labor Council, 1891–92.

Bucher, L. J., U; Og; Builders and Contractors Exchange, 1892–93.

Buckley, T. J. (Timothy), U; SLC; Brotherhood of Locomotive Firemen, 1890–92.

Buckmaster, J. (John), U; SLC; Typographical Union Local 115, 1886.

Burlingame, E. D. (Everett Douglas), N; SLC; 1858–1930; Typographical Union 115, 1888.

Burns, Andrew, N; SLC; 1866–1928; Brewers Union, Salt Lake No. 1, 1890.

Burns, James, N; SLC; 1862–1934; Tin, Sheet-Iron, and Cornice Union, 1890-92.

Burns, William J., U; SLC; Utah Federated Trades and Labor Council, Carpenters and Joiners Union, 1891.

Burrows, J. H. (John), U; SLC; Brewers Union, Salt Lake No. 1, 1890–92.

Burt, A. J., ME; SLC; 1852–1922; candidate for sheriff in Salt Lake County, Workingmen's Party, 1890.

Bush, Monroe, U; SLC; United Brotherhood of Carpenters and Joiners No. 489, 1890.

Bussman, T. A. (Theodore L.), U; SLC; United Brotherhood of Carpenters and Joiners No. 263, 1893.

Button, H. B. (Herbert G.), U; SLC; United Brotherhood of Carpenters and Joiners No. 489, 1890.

Button, J. S. (John E.), U; SLC; United Brotherhood of Carpenters and Joiners No. 489, 1890.

Bynon, E.M., U; SLC ——1891; first and second Labor Day parades, 1888, 1889; Utah Federated Trades and Labor Council, 1888-89.

Bywater, George H. (George G.)
ME; SLC; 1828-98; Stationary
Engineers Association, 1890.

Caggie, James, U; Og;
Brotherhood of Painters and
Decorators No. 100, 1890–91.

Cain, J. (John Wesley), N; GC;
1850 or 1851–1938; Knights of
Labor outing, Fidelity
Assembly No. 3286, 1885.

Calhoun, A. B., U; SLC; delegate
to convention of the International Typographical Union,
1893.

Cambron, W. B. (Cambrow), U;
SLC; United Brotherhood of
Carpenters and Joiners No. 263,
1893.

Campe, John H., U; Jordon;
Knights of Labor No. 3543 and
District Assembly No. 205,
1887.

Canine, R. A., U; Og; No.
Typographical Union No. 236,
1893, 1895.

Capps, G. S., U; Og;
Typographical Union No. 236,
1891.

Carlisle, S. H. (Samuel H.), M;
SLC; stonecutters, 1874.

Carney, T. F. (Thomas), U; SLC;
Building Trades Congress,
1894–95.

Carter, Jesse, U; Og;
Typographical Union No. 236,
1891.

Catchpole, D., U; Og; Bricklayers
Union, 1890.

Cavanaugh, John T. (John A.
Kavanaugh), U; SLC;
Typographical Union Local
115, 1890; International
Typographical Union conven-
tion, 1896.

Charon, A. J. (Arthur), U; SLC;
Pressmen's Union, 1893.

Chatland, Thomas C., ME; Og;
1864–1914; Typographical
Union No. 236, 1891, 1906.

Cherry, H. W. (Howard), U; SLC;
Typographical Union Local
115, 1893.

Chesshire, W. G. (William George
Cheshore), M; Og and SLC;
1885-1921; Labor Day parade,
1889; Plasterers Union No. 1.

Clark, E. E., U; Og; Order of
Railway Conductors, Wasatch
Division No. 124, 1890–91.

Clark, Hiram (Hyrum), U; SLC;
Stone Cutters Union, 1894–95.

Clark, S.L., U; Murray; Knights of
Labor No. 6854 and District
Assembly No. 205, 1887.

Clements, J. C. (John or John T.);
U; SLC; ——1930; Brotherhood
of Painters and Decorators No.
98, 1890.

Clements, Sirus (Cyrus Henry),
ME; SLC; 1864--1949;
Brotherhood of Painters and
Decorators No. 98, 1890.

Cline, C. C., U; SLC;
Typographical Union Local
115, 1890.

Clive, J. H. (Jedediah Hume), ME;
SLC; 1858-1918; candidate for
assessor, Salt Lake County,
People's and Workingmen's
parties, 1890.

Coats, A., U; SLC; Hod Carriers
and Laborers No. 1, 1891–92.

Cody, T. A. (Thomas A.), U; SLC;
Hod Carriers and Laborers No.
1, 1890.

Cohen, Mark (Cohn), U; SLC;
Utah Federated Trades and
Labor Council, 1890; cigar
makers, 1893.

Collier, George P., U; SLC; Utah
Federated Trades and Labor
Council, 1891–92.

Corcoran, Philip (James P.), U; SLC; 1876-1951; Utah Federated Trades and Labor Council, 1890-92; Typographical Union Local 115, 1893; International Typographical Union national and district conventions, 1893.

Coutant, Irving (C. I.), U; SLC; Typographical Union Local 115, 1892-93.

Cowley, J. E. (John E.), ME; SLC; 1861-1919; Typographical Union Local 115, 1880, 1888, 1893.

Cowls, A. D. (Cowles), U; SLC; Utah Federated Trades and Labor Council, 1890; United Brotherhood of Carpenters and Joiners No. 489, 1890-92.

Cox, T. J. (Thomas J.), U; SLC; ——1912; Stone Cutters Union, 1890-92.

Cracroft, G. W. (George William), ME; SLC; 1866-67; Utah Federated Trades and Labor Council, 1890.

Cracroft, James, U; Jordan; Knights of Labor No. 3543, and District Assembly No. 205, 1887.

Cracroft, Lorenzo William, M; SLC; 1860-1917; represented Jordan Assembly No. 3543, District Assembly No. 205, Knights of Labor, 1887; Utah Federated Trades and Labor Council, 1890, 1893.

Crawford, Thomas C. (Cartwright), U; SLC; about 1860--1925; Deseret Typographical Union Local 115, 1884-88.

Crocker, E. S., U; Og; Order of Railway Conductors, Wasatch Division No. 124, 1890--92, 1897-99, 1900-02.

Cushen, M. C., U; SLC; International Association Machinists, 1894-95.

Cushing, George R., U; SLC; — 1946; candidate, Workingmen's Party, 1890.

Cushing, George W. (Woods), M; SLC; 1865-1940; Utah Federated Trades and Labor Council and Labor Day parade, 1889.

Cushing, James, ME; Sandy; 1830-1912. Knights of Labor No. 6940 and District Assembly No. 205, 1887.

Cushion, Henry A. (Cushing, Henry), U; SLC; shoemakers, 1874.

Dallis, John (J. W. Dallas), U; SLC; Cigar Makers Union, 1893-95; Cigar Makers International Union No. 224, 1896.

Dangerfield, C. J. (Charles Jabez), ME; SLC; 1860-1913; Tin, Sheet-Iron, and Cornice Union, 1890-92.

Dangerfield, John (John S.), ME; SLC; 1865-1946; Utah Federated Trades and Labor Council, 1890; Tin, Sheet-Iron, and Cornice Union, 1890-92.

Dangerfield, T. (Thomas), ME; SLC; 1848--1925; Utah Federated Trades and Labor Council, 1890; Brotherhood of Painters and Decorators of America No. 98, 1890.

Daniels, J. S. (John), U; SLC; 1874-1956; Federated Trades and Labor Council and Typographical Union Local 115, 1890.

Daniels, M. H., (Mensdorffe), U; SLC; Federated Trades and Labor Council and Typographical Union Local 115, 1893.

Daveler, J. S., U; SLC; Federated Trades and Labor Council and Typographical Union Local 115, 1893.

Davis, A. L. (A. M.), U; SLC; Brotherhood of Locomotive Firemen, 1893–96.

Davis, Edward, U; SLC; Tin, Sheet-Iron, and Cornice Union, 1893–95.

Davis, Walter, U; SLC; Deseret Typographical Union Local 115, 1868.

Devine, James, N; SLC; 1854–1941; Utah Federated Trades and Labor Council and International Association of Fire Engineers, 1890.

Dexter, R. (Richard), M; GC; 1836--88; Knights of Labor outing, Fidelity Assembly No. 3286, 1885.

Dickson, James (Dixon), N; SLC; ——1920; tinners, 1874.

Dixon, George H., U; SLC; Tin, Sheet-Iron, and Cornice Union, 1893.

Dodds, J. J. (John J.), U; SLC; Utah Federated Trades and Labor Council, and Lathers Union No. 1, 1890–92.

Dofflemyre, I. J. (Isaac Jay Dofflemyre), U; SLC; Barbers Protective Union, 1890–92.

Dolan, John, U; SLC; Brotherhood of Railway Track Foremen, 1896.

Donkin, T. J. (Thomas John), ME; SLC; 1844–1916; Typographical Union Local 115, 1879–86.

Donnelly, Joseph R., U; SLC; Stone Masons International Union No. 1, 1896.

Dower, James, U; SLC; Hod Carriers and Laborers Union No. 1, 1891–92.

Dowlin, J. C. (John C.), U; SLC; Knights of Labor convention, 1886; Labor Day parade, 1889.

Drennan, James, U; SLC; Journeymen Stone Cutters Union, 1896.

Drinkwater, J. R. (James Robert), N; Sandy; 1850–1921; Knights of Labor No. 6940, 1887.

Driscoll, James P., U; Eureka; 1860–1910; Knights of Labor No. 7705, 1887.

Duckworth, J. J. (Joseph J.), U; SLC; 1851–1909; Salt Lake Knights of Labor, 1886.

Duffy, James F., U; Eureka; ——1914; Knights of Labor No. 7705 and District Assembly No. 205, 1887.

Duggan, John, U; Eureka; Knights of Labor No. 7705 and District Assembly No. 205, 1887.

Dunn, William (William K. Dunne), N; SLC; 1891–1946; Secretary of the Moulders Union, 1890; Ironmoulders Union of North America Local 231, 1896.

Dunne, Daniel, U; SLC; addressed Knights of Labor, 1887.

Edmond, Alfred (Edmonds, Alfred), U; SLC; Brewers Union, Salt Lake No. 1, 1890.

Edwards, Joseph, U; SLC; Tin, Sheet-Iron, and Cornice Union, 1893.

England, J. (James or John), ME; GC; 1851–1943 (or 1945); Knights of Labor outing, Fidelity Assembly No. 3286, 1885.

Erickson, John (John E.), U; SLC; 1841–1925; Street Car Men's Union, 1st Division, 1890.

Estes, B. F., U; SLC; ——1953; Brotherhood of Locomotive Engineers, Wasatch Division, 1890–92.

Evans, David, U; Og; Tailors Union No. 111, 1890–91.

Evans, H. F. (Henry F.), U; Jordan; Knights of Labor No. 3543 and District Assembly No. 205, 1887.

Evans, H. L. (Homer), U; SLC; Typographical Union Local 115, 1893.

Evans, John Evan, ME; SLC 1844–1897; Deseret Typographical Union Local 115, 1868, 1879–83, 1888; inaugural ball, Utah Federated Trades and Labor Council, 1889.

Evans, Richard (Richard A.), N; SLC; 1869–1932; Street Car Men's Union, 1st Division, 1890.

Eynon, T., Sr. (Thomas F.), M; GC; 1831–1902; Knights of Labor outing, Fidelity Assembly No. 3286, 1885.

Eynon, T., Jr. (Thomas Francis), ME; GC; 1862–1933; Knights of Labor outing, Fidelity Assembly No. 3286, 1885.

Faddis, D. (David Faddies), ME; GC; 1854–90; Knights of Labor outing, Fidelity Assembly No. 3286, 1885.

Faddis, J. (John McCallister [1859--1918] or James Pullock Faddies [1857–1905], U; GC; Knights of Labor outing, Fidelity Assembly No. 3286, 1885.

Faddies, R. (Robert), N; GC; 1838–86; Knights of Labor outing, Fidelity Assembly No. 3286, 1885.

Fagan, J. W., U; SLC; shoemakers, 1874.

Fenstermaker, H. C. (Hollis), U; SLC; Typographical Union Local 115, 1892–93.

Ferguson, Fergus, U; SLC; 1860–1927; candidate for county clerk for Salt Lake County, People's and Workingmen's parties, 1890.

Fisher, H. (Herman), ME; SLC; 1858–1933; represented the brewers on the executive committee of the Utah Federated Trades and Labor Council, 1890.

Fitzsimmons, Jim, U; Silver Reef; Miners Union, 1881.

Fletcher, J. (Jasper), M; SLC; 1857-1920; Telegraphers Union, 1881.

Fluellen, M., U; Og; Labor Day parade, 1889.

Flynn, Z. M., U; SLC; Utah Federated Trades and Labor Council, and Typographical Union Local 115, 1890.

Foreman, M. W., U; Og; Knights of Labor, Ogden Local Assembly No. 3537, 1886.

Foster, E. (Ephraim), M; SLC; 1869–1928; Stone Cutters Union, 1890–92.

Fowler, F., U; GC; Knights of Labor outing, Fidelity Assembly No. 3286, 1885.

Fowler, W. (William), M; GC; 1852–1911; Knights of Labor outing, Fidelity Assembly No. 3286, 1885.

Freeman, H. R. (Harry), U; SLC; Typographical Union Local 115, 1892.

Frey, Henry (Frei), U; SLC; Utah Federated Trades and Labor Council, 1890; Tin, Sheet-Iron, and Cornice Union, 1893.

Fuller, William, ME; SLC; 1845—; Deseret Typographical Union Local 115, 1868; national executive committee, International Typographical Union, 1870–71.

Fullman, G., U; SLC; Utah Federated Trades and Labor Council, 1889.

Fumerton, J. G. (John G.), U; SLC; United Brotherhood of Carpenters and Joiners No. 489, 1890–92.

Gallup, Oliver, U; SLC; Typographical Union Local 115 and Utah Federated Trades and Labor Council, 1893.

Gavagan, James, U; SLC; Plumbers Union, 1890.

Gilberg, C. D. (Carl M.), U; SLC; ——1911; Tailors Union, 1890–92.

Gilbert, E. S., U; SLC; Brotherhood of Railway Car Men Lodge 74, 1896.

Gillcrist, A., U; GC; Knights of Labor outing, Fidelity Assembly No. 3286, 1885.

Glassman, William, U; Jordan; Knights of Labor No. 3543 and District Assembly No. 205, 1887.

Goodwin, H. C. (Harry C.), U; SLC; Salt Lake District Assembly and national Knights of Labor convention, 1886; Utah Federated Trades and Labor Council and Typographical Union Local 115, 1893.

Graham, A. E. (Arthur), U; SLC; Utah Board of Labor, 1896; Utah Federation of Labor, 1899–1900; Typographical Union Local 115, 1899; organizer for American Federation of Labor, 1902; first meeting of Allied Printing Trades Councils of Salt Lake, 1903.

Graham, John Crosthwaite, ME; SLC; 1839–1906; Typographical Union Local 115, 1890.

Gray, F. L., U; SLC; Typographical Union Local 115, 1893.

Gray, Robert, U; Murray; Knights of Labor No. 6854 and District Assembly No. 205, 1887.

Greenwald, K. G. (K. J.), U; SLC; Tailors Union, 1890–92.

Griffin, R., U; Ogden; Plasterers Union No. 1, 1890–91.

Grimsdell, William Charles Frederick, ME; SLC; 1852–1925; Typographical Union No. 115, 1879–93.

Groo, John, N; SLC; 1869–1949; Typographical Union Local 115, 1890.

Gross, T. T. (Theodore T. Gross or Theodore T. Grove), U; SLC; Pressmen's Union No. 1, and Utah Federated Trades and Labor Council, 1890.

Gullixon, G., U; Og.; Tailors Union No. 111, 1890–91.

Haig, A (Arthur Haigh), U; SLC; 1854-1916; Utah Federated Trades and Labor Council, 1889.

Hall, F. (Miss), U; Og.; Typographical Union No. 236, 1892-93.

Hall, P. A., U; SLC; Barbers Protective Union, 1896.

Hallsteat, William (Halstead), U; Sandy; Knights of Labor No. 6940 and District Assembly No. 205, 1887.

Hamblin, H. (Henry Clay) (Hamblin), N; SLC; 1843–1910; Utah Federated Trades and Labor Council, 1889.

Hampin, A. L., U; SLC; United Brotherhood of Carpenters and Joiners of America No. 263, 1893.

Hands, James, U; SLC; Hod Carriers and Laborers Union No. 1, 1890.

Hanhauser, John, U; SLC; Utah Federated Trades and Labor Council, 1893; Cigar Makers Union No. 224, 1894–96.

Hankins, E. L., U; SLC; Brotherhood of Locomotive Engineers, 1893.

Hann, Peter N., U; SLC; Pressmen's Union No. 41, 1892.

Hansen, S., U; SLC; Utah Federated Trades and Labor Council, 1889.

Harington, A.F., U; SLC; United Brotherhood of Carpenters and Joiners of America No. 263, 1893–95.

Harlow, W. S. (W. L.), U; SLC; ——1923; Labor Day parade, 1889.

Harper, Robert B., U; SLC; Plumbers Union No. 19, 1890.

Harris, George W., U; Og; Builders and Contractors Exchange, 1892–93.

Harris, Hyrum (Hyrum Smith), ME; SLC; 1863–1924; Street Car Men's Union, 1st Division, 1890.

Harry, A., U; Og; Bricklayers Union, 1890–91.

Hart, F., U; Og; Brotherhood of Railway Conductors, 1890–93.

Harte, Frank L., U; SLC; Typographical Union Local 115, 1896.

Harvey, J. (I. Harvey), U; SLC; Clerks Union, 1894–95; Retail Clerks Union No. 27, 1896.

Hatch, A., U; SLC; Brotherhood of Locomotive Engineers, Wasatch Division No. 222, 1893–95.

Hauser, Vincent (Vincent Edward), N; SLC; 1852–1903; Brewers Union, Salt Lake No. 1, 1890–92.

Hawkins, C. (Creighton), ME; SLC; 1840–1932; Brotherhood of Locomotive Firemen, 1890–92.

Hawthorne, A., U; Og; Brotherhood of Painters and Decorators No. 11, 1890–91.

Hawthorne, James, U; SLC; Plumbers Union 1891–92.

Heath, W. A., U; Og; Brotherhood of Painters and Decorators No. 100, 1890.

Henefer, W. H. (William Henry Hennefer), ME; SLC; 1824–1913; Deseret Dramatic Association, 1855; Barbers Protective Union, 1891–92.

Herrick, L., U; SLC; International Stone Masons Union, 1894–95.

Herrington, F. W., U; Og; Brotherhood of Railroad Conductors, 1892–93; Order of Railway Conductors, 1903–05.

Hestmark, A. T., U; Og; Typographical Union No. 236, 1894.

Hestmark, C. W. (Carl William), U; Og; ——1832; Brotherhood of Railroad Car Men of America No. 76, 1892–93.

Hewitt, N. W., U; SLC; Brotherhood of Railroad Trainmen Lodge 325, 1896.

Hilton, Thomas (Thomas H.), ME; SLC; 1870–1915; Street Car Men's Union, 1st Division, 1890.

Hitch, Charles, U; Og; Plasterers Union No. 1, 1890–91.

Hoag, Burdett S. (Burdette), U; SLC; Pressmen and Stereographers Union No. 41, 1891.

Hodges, W. W. (Hodge, William W.), M; SLC; 1826--1909; Moulders Union, 1890.

Hogan, Dennis, U; SLC; plumbers and gasfitters, 1874.

Hoggan, A. (Alexander), M; SLC; 1860-1937; Lathers Union No. 1, 1891-92.

Hoodless, R., U; SLC; United Order of Carpenters and Joiners of America No. 263, 1893.

Hook, Louis (Lewis), ME; SLC; 1845-1915; Harness Makers Union, 1890.

Horn, W. F., U; SLC; Amalgamated Carpenters and Joiners, 1894-95.

Houston, J. (James N.), M; GC; 1848-1922; Knights of Labor outing, Fidelity Assembly No. 3286, 1885.

Howe, C. R. (Charles R. [Ross]), ME; SLC; 1860--1939; Moulders Union, 1890.

Hunter, James, M; SLC; spoke at protest meeting, 1874.

Huntsman, Ezra, ME; SLC; 1845-1927; Labor Day parade, 1889.

Hurd, Joseph, H., U; SLC; Workingmen's Party, 1890.

Hyde, E. T. (Ezra), U; SLC; Typographical Union Local 115, 1893.

Ibenthall, W. J., U; Og; Inter-Stone Masons Union No. 3, 1890-91.

Inch, John, U; SLC; Pressmen's Union No. 41, 1894-95.

Ingelbretson, John, U; Og; Brotherhood of Painters and Decorators No. 100, 1890-91.

Isaacson, Otto, U; SLC; Hod Carriers and Laborers Union No. 1, 1891-92.

Jack, John, U; SLC; Pressmen's Union No. 41, 1894-95.

Jack, William (William M.), ME; SLC; 1857-1934; Pressmen's Union No. 41, 1890-91.

Jackson, A., U; Og; Bricklayers Union, 1890-91.

Jackson, Lon, U; Og; Bricklayers Union, 1890-91.

James, William, U; SLC; Utah Federated Trades and Labor Council, 1893.

Jensen, Andrew (Andreas), ME; SLC; applied for membership in Typographical Union Local 115, 1890 and 1892.

Jepperson, Joseph (Joseph E.), U; SLC; Typographical Union Local No. 115, 1896.

Johnson, Amos. J., U; SLC and Og; Typographical Union Local 115, 1891.

Johnson, A. J., U; Og; Brotherhood of Railroad Trainmen, 1892-93.

Jones, C. A. (Charles), U; SLC; Typographical Union Local 115, 1893.

Jones, G. M. (George Leadley Martin), ME; SLC; 1858-1929; Brotherhood of Railroad Trainmen, 1890-93.

Kar, C. P., U; Og; Brotherhood of Railroad Trainmen, Salt Lake Lodge No. 68, 1892-93.

Kastrup, J. F., U; SLC; Utah Federated Trades and Labor Council, 1893.

Kavanaugh, John A. (John T. Cavanaugh), U; SLC; Typographical Union Local 115, 1890; International Typographical Union convention, 1896.

Keeler, E. C., U; SLC; Overland Circuit, Telegraphers Union, 1883.

Keim, J. T. (John Fullmer), U; SLC; ——1931. Brotherhood of Locomotive Firemen, 1890.

Kelly, A. H. (Albert Hiram Quick), ME; SLC; 1851–1924; Labor Day parade, 1889.

Kelly, John, U; SLC; Plumbers Union 1894–95.

Kelson, Joseph (Joseph H.), ME; SLC; 1862——; Harness Makers Union, 1890.

Kenner, Scipio Africanus, ME; SLC; 1846–1913; candidate for county attorney for Salt Lake County People's and Workingmen's parties, 1890.

Kesler, L. W. (Leonard Wilford), ME; SLC; 1856--1916; Brotherhood of Locomotive Firemen 1890–92.

Kiernan, Thomas, U; SLC; Lathers Union, 1874.

Kimball, Nathan, N; Og; about 1822–1899; addressed second annual meeting of Local Assembly No. 3533 of Kinghts of Labor, 1886.

King, Edward (E. A.), ME; SLC; 1868 (between 1925 and 1930); Moulders Union, 1890; Utah Federated Trades and Labor Council, 1893.

King, Fred, U; SLC; Brotherhood of Locomotive Engineers, Wasatch Division No. 222, 1893–95.

King, George, U; Og; Order of Railway Conductors, Wasatch Division No. 124, 1890–91.

King, S. B. (Sidney Beatty), U; SLC; 1857–1922; Tin, Sheet-Iron, and Cornice Union, 1890–93.

King, Will L. (William), U; Og; Typographical Union No. 236, 1893, 1897–99.

King, William, U; Og; Brotherhood of Railway Car Men of America, Ogden Lodge No. 76, 1892–93.

Kirk, Tom, U; Og; Inter-Stone Masons Union No. 3, 1890–91.

Knowles, James, U; Eureka; Knights of Labor No. 7705 and District Assembly No. 205, 1887.

Koldervyn, W. A. (Kolderwyn or Koldewyn), U; Og; Tailors Union No. 111, 1890–93, 1900–01, 1905–09, 1911–12.

Lambourne, George, U; SLC; Tin, Sheet-Iron, and Cornice Union, 1893, 1895.

Lapsley, J. W. (James William), U; SLC; ——1942; Utah Federated Trades and Labor Council, 1893.

Lauber, L. A., U; SLC; Typographical Union Local 115, 1893.

Laughlin, M. O., U; Silver Reef; Miners Union, 1880.

Lawrence J. (John or Joab), U; GC; Knights of Labor outing, Fidelity Assembly No. 3286, 1885.

Leahey, James J., U; Og; Hod Carriers Union, 1890.

Lenhart, C. C., U; SLC; Stationary Engineers Association, 1890.

Levedahl, L. J., U; Og; Tailors Union No. 111.

Lewis, A. H., U; Silver Reef; Miners Union, 1880–81.

Lewis, W. J. (Walter Joseph), ME; SLC; 1854–1924; Salt Lake Pressmen's Union No. 41, 1889.

Lincoln, J. H. (Jerome), U; SLC; Typographical Union Local 115, 1892.

Lindblad, John (Linsblad, Linsbad), U; Og; Tailors Union No. 111, 1890–1905.

Lindeberg, Charles, U; SLC; Tailors Union, 1893.

Lindh, Soloman A. (Lindle), U; Og; Tailors Union No. 111, 1890-1906, Utah State Federation of Labor, 1904.

Lloyd, R. W., U; SLC; Stonecutters Union, 1890-92.

Longfellow,— —, U; SLC; carpenters, 1874.

Love, James, M; SLC; 1867-1945; Brotherhood of Railroad Trainmen, 1890-92.

Love, Joseph, U; SLC; Brotherhood of Locomotive Firemen, 1894-95.

Lovendale, J. H. (Julius H.), N; SLC; 1856-1948; Typographical Union Local 115, 1888; Utah Federated Trades and Labor Council, 1890.

Lovendale, Theodore, U; SLC; 1860-1936; Typographical Union Local 115, 1888, 1890; Utah Federated Trades and Labor Council, 1890.

Lynch, J. T., U; Jordan; Knights of Labor No. 3543, 1887; addressed Knights of Labor in SLC, 1887.

Lyon, Larry, U; SLC; Federated Trades and Labor Council, 1890; Typographical Union Local 115, 1890.

Mahan, H. J. (Hugh Mohan), U; SLC; Labor Day Parade, 1888.

Mallory, C. W. (Dr.), U; Stockton; Knights of Labor No. 6162 and District Assembly No. 205, 1887.

Mande, William, U; SLC; Tin, Sheet-Iron, and Cornice Union, 1890-92.

Mann, S. A. (Samuel A.), U; SLC; Typographical Union Local 115, 1892.

Marriot, T. E. (Thomas Edward Marriott), M; Sandy; Knights of Labor No. 6940, 1887.

Marshall, J. (John), N; GC and SLC; Knights of Labor outing, Fidelity Assembly No. 3286, 1885.

Marshall, R., N; GC; 1864-1905; Knights of Labor outing, Fidelity Assembly No. 3286, 1885.

Martin, Anthony, ME; SLC; 1833-1905; tinners, 1874.

Mason, George, ME; SLC; —— 1906; Stationary Engineers Association, 1890.

Masterman, H. J., U; SLC; Salt Lake Musicians Protective Association, 1896.

Mastom, A. B., U; SLC; Brotherhood of Railway Track Foremen, Division No. 102, 1896.

Mathers, Andrew, U; Og; Inter-Stone Masons Union No. 3, 1890-91.

Mayerhoffer, John (Meyerhoffer), ME; SLC; 1853-1917; Tailors Union, and Utah Federated Trades and Labor Council, 1890-92.

McAffrey, P. W., U; SLC; Utah Federated Trades and Labor Council, 1890.

McCune, John, M; Og; Inter-Stone Masons Union No. 3, 1890-91.

McDonald, Minnie, U; SLC; Typographical Union Local 115, 1888.

McDonald, W. (William or William, Jr.), ME; 1857 or 1859-1942; Knights of Labor outing, Fidelity Assembly No. 3286, 1885.

McDonough, H. C., (Harry Coffey), N; SLC; 1857–1937; Typographical Union Local 115, 1896. Later joined the church.

McEwan, Henry, ME; SLC; 1830–1893; Provo Dramatic Association, 1853; typographers in Fourth of July parade, 1861; executive committee of International Typographical Union, representing Deseret Local 115, 1872; Deseret Typographical Union Local 115, 1879–88.

McEwan, Joseph T. (Thompson), ME; SLC and Pr; 1840–1913; Fourth of July parade in Provo, 1865; Deseret Typographical Union Local 115, 1879–81.

McEwan, Robert C., M; SLC and Og; 1856——; Deseret Typographical Union Local 115, 1879–86.

McEwan, R. T. (Robert Thompson), ME; SLC; 1877——; Deseret Typographical Union Local 115, 1879–86.

McIntosh, George F., U; Og; Brotherhood of Railway Conductors, 1892–93.

McIntyre, P. J., U; SLC; Typographical Union Local 115, 1886–88.

McLain, J. A., U; SLC; Brotherhood of Locomotive Engineers, Wasatch Division No. 222, 1890–92.

McLean, Gilbert A., M; SLC; 1851–1926; Brotherhood of Locomotive Firemen, 1893.

McPeak, Charles A., U; SLC; Brotherhood of Locomotive Firemen, 1893.

McPhie, A. (Alexander McPhee), M; GC and Og; 1862–1931; Knights of Labor outing, Fidelity Assembly No. 3286, 1885.

McPhie, Charles A., U; SLC; Brotherhood of Locomotive Firemen, 1893.

McPhie, J. (John McPhee), ME; GC; 1850–1907; Knights of Labor outing, Fidelity Assembly No. 3286, 1885.

McRane W., U; GC; Knights of Labor outing, Fidelity Assembly No. 3286, 1885.

McWenie, J., U; SLC; Cigar Makers Union, 1893.

Meakin, J. T., U; SLC; sang at a Knights of Labor meeting, 1887.

Medina, Frank M., U; SLC; telegraphers, 1881.

Meier, Chris, U; SLC; Brewers and Malters Union No. 1, 1896.

Mercer, H. A., U; SLC; Salt Lake Musicians Protective Association, 1896. (Later joined the church.)

Merwin, A. M. (Andrew N.), U; SLC; Pressmen's Union No. 41, 1890–92.

Merwin, F. (Frank), U; SLC; Pressmen's Union No. 41, 1890.

Metcalf, J. W. (James W.), ME; Og; 1857–1935; Order of Railway Conductors, Wasatch Division No. 124, 1890–91.

Middleton, Robert, U; Og; Brotherhood of Railroad Car Men of America, Ogden Lodge No. 76, 1892–93.

Miller, J., U; Jordan; Knights of Labor No. 3543 and District Assembly No. 205, 1887.

Miller, R. (Rasmus Nelson), ME; GC; 1846–99; Knights of Labor outing, Fidelity Assembly No. 3286, 1885.

Miller, W. (William), ME; GC; 1832–1910; Knights of Labor outing, Fidelity Assembly No. 3286, 1885.

Miracle, J. H., U; Og; Typographical Union No. 236, 1895.

Monroe, R. S., U; SLC; International Association of Machinists Lodge 106, 1894-95.

Moorcock, (?), U; plumbers and gasfitters, 1874.

Morris, E. T., U; SLC; Typographical Union Local 115, 1893.

Morris, T. (Thomas), ME; SLC; 1855-1930; stonecutter, 1874; Utah Federated Trades and Labor Council, 1889.

Morris, Thomas C., U; Og; Builders and Contractors Exchange, 1892-93.

Morro, R. S., U; SLC; International Association of Machinists Lodge 106, 1896.

Munson, B., U; SLC; Tailors Union, 1890-92.

Naismith, Andrew B., M; SLC; 1853-1922; Moulders Union, 1890.

Neilson, Peter (Peter Matthews), ME; SLC; 1864 or 1867-1946; Harness Makers Union, 1890.

Nelson, Olof, U; Og; Tailors Union No. 111, 1892-93.

Newton, S. (Sam Smith or Samuel), ME; SLC; 1858-1954; Labor Day parade, 1889.

Nichols, Robert F., M; SLC; resolutions committee, protest meeting 1874.

Norton, W. S.; U; Og; Brotherhood of Railroad Trainmen, Salt Lake Lodge 68, 1892-93.

Oberg, C. J. (Carl J.), U; SLC; ——1914; Association of Stationary Engineers, 1890.

O'Connell, P., U; Og; Plasterers Union No. 1, 1890-91.

Odell, Joseph, ME; Og; 1870-1952; Typographical Union No. 236, 1891.

O'Fallon, John, U; Og; Plasterers Union No. 1, 1890-91.

O'Leary, E. T., U; SLC; Plumbers, Steam and Gasfitters Union No. 19, 1896.

Oliver, H. P., U; SLC; United Brotherhood of Carpenters and Joiners of America No. 267, 1893.

Oliver, W. B., U; SLC; United Brotherhood of Carpenters and Joiners of America No. 489, 1891-92; United Brotherhood of Carpenters and Joiners of America No. 263, 1893.

Olsen, C. M. (Carl Magnus), N; SLC; 1857-1915; Utah Federated Trades and Labor Council, 1889.

Olsen, T. M., U; SLC; Labor Day parade, 1889.

Ostby, Karl, U; SLC; Utah Board of Labor, 1896.

Oswald, John R., ME; SLC; 1832 or 1834-1908; Moulders Union, 1890.

Ovard, J. (John Alma), ME; GC; 1861-1933; Knights of Labor outing, Fidelity Assembly No. 3286, 1885.

Palmer, Frank, U; SLC; Street Car Men's Union, 1st Division, 1890.

Parimore, G. (Paramore, George), ME; SLC; 1828-1916; Utah Federated Trades and Labor Council, 1889.

Parker, George (Parkes), U; SLC Utah Federated Trades and Labor Council, 1890; Tailors Union, 1890-92.

Smith, Sherden (Sheridan), ME; SLC; 1867–1961; Association of Stationary Engineers, 1890; National Association of Stationary Engineers, Salt Lake City No. 1, 1896.

Smith, Theo A., U; SLC and Og; Deseret Typographical Union Local 115, 1868; Ogden Typographical Union No. 236, 1893–1901.

Smith, William, U; Murray; Knights of Labor No. 6854 and District Assembly No. 205, 1887.

Snyder, J. T., U; SLC; Typographical Union Local 115, 1888.

Snyder, S. H., U; SLC; Salt Lake Union No. 1, 1884.

Spanner, S. K. (Spann, S. K.), U; SLC; ——1957 Federated Trades and Labor Council, and Typographical Union Local 115, 1890.

Spencer, Pomeroy, U; SLC; Plumbers, Steam and Gasfitters Union No. 19, 1896.

Springer, Dr. W., U; Og; Brotherhood of Railroad Trainmen, Salt Lake Lodge 68, 1892–93.

Stack, E. D., U; Og; Typographical Union No. 236, 1894.

Stamm, C. M., U; SLC; United Brotherhood of Carpenters and Joiners of America No. 263, 1893.

Stenberg, O., U; SLC; painters, 1874.

Stenhouse, S. (S.M., Serge M.), U; SLC; Typographical Union No. 115, 1888–93.

Stephens, H. H., U; SLC; Utah Federated Trades and Labor Council, 1889.

Stevens, James (James W., Sr., James W., Jr.), M; SLC; carpenters, 1874.

Stewart, J. W. (John W.), U; SLC; Brotherhood of Locomotive Engineers, Wasatch Division No. 222, 1890.

Stoll, E. J., U; SLC; Cigar Makers Union, 1893.

Stover, David B., U; Stockton; Knights of Labor No. 6162, 1887.

Sylvester, Mrs. E. E. (Ethan), U; SLC; Typographical Union Local 115, 1892.

Taylor, George G., ME; Og; 1852–1904; International Typographical Union convention, 1889; Typographical Union No. 236 and Labor Day parade, 1889–93.

Taysum, A. F. (Alonzo Frank), N; SLC; 1860–1929; Typographical Union Local 115, 1886, 1888.

Taysum, R. G. (Rollo George), M; SLC; 1858–1901; Deseret Typographical Union Local 115, 1881–86, 1879–80.

Tenny, C. W. (Charles W.), N; SLC; Brotherhood of Locomotive Engineers, Wasatch Division No. 222, 1890–92.

Thomas, Arthur L. (Lloyd), U; SLC; Salt Lake Union No. 1, 1884.

Thomas H. (Henry or Hank), U; GC; ——1912 Knights of Labor outing, Fidelity Assembly No. 3286, 1885.

Thompson, Ed (Edward), U; SLC; ——1893; Cigar Makers Union No. 224, 1890.

Thompson, O. S. (Orson Spencer); ME; SLC; 1855–1944; Typographical Union Local 115, 1880; Pressmen's Union, 1890.

Thompson, W. W., U; SLC; United Brotherhood of Carpenters and Joiners of America No. 263, 1893.

Tibbs, C. T. (Peter T.), M; SLC; 1853–1919; Brotherhood of Locomotive Engineers, Wasatch Division No. 222, 1890–95.

Tisdale, Thomas (Thomas K. or R.), U; SLC; Pressmen's Union No. 41, 1893; Pressmen's and Stereographers Union, 1896.

Torfierson, G., U; Og; Tailors Union No. 111, 1890–91.

Toronto, J. B. (Joseph B.), ME; SLC; 1854–1933; Salt Lake County People's and Workingmen's parties, 1890.

Tracy, S. H., U; Og; Order of Railway Conductors, Wasatch Division No. 124, 1890–91.

Treboul, G. L. (Gustav L.), U; SLC; Cigar Makers Union No. 224, 1890.

Tretheway, John U; SLC; Clerks Union 1894–95; Retail Clerks Union No. 27, 1896.

Tuttle, J. C., U; Og; Brotherhood of Painters and Decorators No. 100, 1890–91.

Tyne, Stephen, U; SLC; Board of Labor, 1894–95; Building Trades Congress, 1894–95; Utah Board of Labor, 1896; Stone Masons International Union No. 1, 1896.

Tyson, Edward (Elwood), U; SLC; plasterers, 1874.

Ule, Frederick, U; SLC; Harness Makers Union, 1890.

Van Gilder, I. N., U; Og; Brotherhood of Railway Conductors, 1892–93.

Van Gorden, J. B., U; SLC; Salt Lake Typographical Union Local 115, 1893.

Vaughn, C., U; GC; Knights of Labor outing, Fidelity Assembly No. 3286, 1885.

Veeser, Nicholas (Veiser, Nicolas), U; SLC; Brewers Union, Salt Lake No. 1, 1890.

Wadman, R. H., U; Og; Brotherhood of Painters and Decorators No. 100, 1890–91.

Wagner, E. M., U; SLC; United Brotherhood of Carpenters and Joiners of America No. 263, 1893.

Waldo, H. (William P.), U; SLC; Brotherhood of Painters and Decorators of America, Salt Lake City Local 98, 1890.

Wallace, Hugh (Hugh S.), U; SLC; Utah Federated Trades and Labor Council and Brotherhood of Painters and Decorators Local 98, 1890.

Wallin, William, U; Og; Typographical Union No. 236, 1890–91.

Ward, M. A., U; SLC; Brotherhood of Railway Car Men, 1896.

Warmbath, Max, U; SLC; Barbers Protective Union, 1890–92.

Warren, G. G., U; Og; Knights of Labor Local Assembly 3533, 1886.

Waterfall, John, M; SLC; 1836–1902; Association of Stationary Engineers, 1890.

Watson, C. G. (Charles), U; SLC; Pressmen's Union, 1893.

Watson, James, ME; SLC; 1833–89; Stone Cutters Union, 1874.

Webly, J. F. (Fred), U; SLC; Typographical Union Local 115, 1884–86, 1888.

Webster, S. (Samuel), ME; GC; 1854–1939; Knights of Labor outing, Fidelity Assembly No. 3286, 1885.

Webster, W. (William), ME; GC; 1842–1906; Knights of Labor outing, Fidelity Assembly No. 3286, 1885.

Weightmen, W. C., U; SLC; 1868–1933; Brotherhood of Locomotive Firemen, 1890–92.

Welles, George (George G. Wells), U; SLC; Typographical Union Local 115, 1894–95.

Welsh, W., U; GC; Knights of Labor outing, Fidelity Assembly No. 3286, 1885.

Welty, A. J., U; Og; Hod Carriers Union and Central Union, 1890–91.

Wheelwright, John, U; Og; Inter-Stone Masons Union No. 3, 1890–91.

Whitaker, George A., U; SLC; 1820–1907; American Federation of Labor, 1896–99; Cigar Makers Union No. 224, 1893–96.

White, A. M., U; Og; Brotherhood of Railway Conductors, 1892–1893.

White, David (David H.) M; SLC; 1860–1941; Hod Carriers and Labor Union No. 1, 1890–92.

White, H. L. (Harry L.), U; SLC; Typographical Union Local 115, 1879–86.

White, William, U; Og; Brotherhood of Railway Car Men, Ogden Lodge 76, 1892–93.

Whiting, John (Whiteing), N; SLC; 1821–82; bricklayers, 1874.

Wiggins, W. W., U; Og; Brotherhood of Railway Car Men of America Lodge No. 76, 1892–93.

Wignant, William, U; SLC; Brewers Union, 1891–92.

Willard, H. M., U; SLC; United Brotherhood of Carpenters and Joiners of America No. 263, 1893; Federated Trades and Labor Council, 1893.

Williams, A. D., U; SLC; International Association of Machinists Lodge 106, 1896.

Williams, F. B., U; Og; Brotherhood of Painters and Decorators No. 100, 1890–91.

Williams, H. (Henry Thomas or Henry Benjamin), M; GC; Knights of Labor outing, Fidelity Assembly No. 3286, 1885.

Williams, W. (William or William Walter), M; GC; Knights of Labor outing, Fidelity Assembly No. 3286, 1885.

Williamson, C. S. (Charles), U; SLC; ——1926; national convention of International Typographical Union 1890; Typographical Union Local 115, 1888–90.

Williamson, I. (Ivan), U; Og; Inter-Stone Masons Union No. 3, 1890–91.

Willis, Jesse, U; SLC; 1858–1933; Brotherhood of Railroad Trainmen, 1890–92.

Willis, W. S. (William), U; SLC; Typographical Union Local 115, 1896.

Wilson, A. R. (Alexander Kennedy), M; GC; 1843–1905; Knights of Labor outing, Fidelity Assembly No. 3286, 1885.

Wilson, Robert, U; Og; Knights of Labor Local Assembly 3533, 1886.

Wilson, William, M; SLC; Bricklayers Union, 1874.

Wiseman, Frank H. (Frank A.), U; SLC; 1862–1907; Hod Carriers Union, and Utah Federated Trades and Labor Council, 1890.

Wolf, C. C., U; Og; Typographical Union No. 236, 1892–93.

Woodburn, John U; SLC; Plumbers Union, 1893.

Woodruff, George C., U; SLC; Brotherhood of Locomotive Firemen, 1893–95.

Woody, J. O. U; Og; Typographical Union No. 236, 1890–91.

Woolf, John A. (Andrew), M; SLC; Stone Cutters Union, 1874.

Wright, A. G. (Albert), U; SLC; Typographical Union Local 115, 1893.

Wyatt, James, U; SLC; plasterers, 1874.

Wyne, G. M., U; SLC; United Brotherhood of Carpenters and Joiners of America No. 263, 1893.

Yeats, J. A., U; SLC; Brotherhood of Locomotive Engineers, Wasatch Division No. 222, 1893–95.

Young, Ben, U; GC; Knights of Labor outing, Fidelity Assembly No. 3286, 1885.

Young, Charles W., U; SLC; Pressmen's Union No. 41, 1890.

Young, E. D., U; SLC; Deseret Typographical Union Local 115, and International Typographical Union convention, 1873–74.

Zeidler, William, U; SLC; Typographical Union Local No. 115, 1885–88.

Zitzman, Fred (Frederick Adolph), N; Og; Typographical Union No. 236, 1890–91, 1903–04; International Typographical Union convention, 1892.

General Index

Index of Personal Names

Cummings, James Willard, 35, 229
Curtis, Theodore, 42, 229
Cushen, M. C., 236
Cushing, George R., 210, 236
Cushing, George W., 195, 201, 236
Cushing, James, 139, 141, 236
Cushion, Henry A., 106, 236

D

Daniel, F., 178
Daniels, M. H., 183
Dangerfield, John S., 204, 205
Dangerfield, Thomas, 201
Dankers, G. B., 188
Dart, Robert, 41, 229
Daveler, J. S., 178, 237
Davis, A. L., 237
Davis, Edward, 237
Davis, John S., 58, 60, 63, 69, 229
Davis, Walter, 71, 76, 237
Debs, Eugene V., 212
Derr, William, 35, 61, 42, 229
Derrick, Z. W., 41, 229
Devine, James, 204, 237
Dexter, Richard, 119, 237
Dickson, James, 107, 237
Dixon, George H., 237
Dodds, J.J., 204, 205, 237
Dofflemyre, I. J., 205, 237
Dolan, John, 237
Donkin, T. J., 75, 77, 78, 237
Donnelly, Joseph R., 237
Doremus, John Henry, 229
Dower, James, 237
Dowlin, J. C., 201, 237
Drennan, James, 237
Drinkwater, J. R., 139, 140, 237
Driscoll, James P., 139–41, 237
Duckworth, J. J., 122–23, 237
Duffy, James F., 139, 237
Duggan, John, 139, 237
Dunbar, W. C., 95
Dunn, William, 237
Dunne, Daniel, 237
Dusenberry, Warren N., 49, 229
Dusenberry, Wilson H., 49, 229

E

Eardley, John, 41, 229
Edmond, Alfred, 237
Edwards, Joseph, 237
Ellerbeck, J. W., 35, 43, 229

Ellsworth, Edmund L., 41, 229
England, J., 119, 237
Erickson, John, 237
Ester, B. F., 237
Evans, David, 36, 238
Evans, H. F., 139, 238
Evans, H. L., 178, 182, 238
Evans, J. Allen, 122
Evans, John, 41, 71, 75, 77, 229
Evans, John E., 71, 238
Evans, Richard, 238
Eynon, Thomas, 120, 238
Eynon, Thomas F., 120, 238
Eyring, Henry, 97

F

Faddis, David, 120, 238
Faddis, J., 120, 238
Faddis, Robert, 120, 238
Fagan, J. W., 106, 238
Fenstermaker, H. C., 182, 238
Ferguson, Fergus, 209, 210, 238
Ferguson, Henry A., 58, 229
Ferguson, J. D., 188
Ferguson, James, 33
Fisher, H., 204, 238
Fitzsimmons, 112, 238
Fletcher, Francis, 34
Fletcher, J., 114
Fluellen, M., 238
Flynn, Z. M., 238
Foreman, M. W., 120, 238
Foster, E., 238
Fowler, F., 120, 238
Fowler, William, 120, 238
Fox, J. W., 41, 229
Freeman, H. R., 182, 238
Frey, Henry, 238
Fuller, William, 71, 74, 76, 238
Fullman, George, 195, 239
Fumerton, J. G., 239

G

Gallup, Oliver, 183, 239
Gavagan, James, 239
Gilberg, C. D., 239
Gilbert, E. S., 239
Gillchrist, A., 120, 239
Glassman, William, 139–41, 239
Glenn, H. E., 178
Glover, William, 33, 229
Godby, Wm. H., 146

762 : DESERET'S SONS OF TOIL

Pratt, Arthur, 112
Pratt, Orson, 38, 231
Pratt, Orson, Jr., 231
Pratt, Parley P., 112, 231
Preday, Charles, 246
Price, William L., 71, 72
Priestley, John, 71, 75, 77, 78, 167–71, 174, 183, 246
Probst, D. W., 190, 246
Probst, Robert, 189, 246
Pugmire, Jonathan, 40, 43, 231
Pugsley, George, 247
Pyper, A. C., 41, 42, 231

Q

Quinn, Maurice, 247

R

Rabb, John A., 247
Raddon, W. R., 247
Randall, Joseph H., 103, 189, 190, 247
Raymond, C. H., 139, 247
Rawlins, Joseph L., 49, 231
Reardon, John, 247
Reed, John W., 247
Rice, C. P., 178, 247
Rice, R. L., 247
Richards, Henry P., 34, 231
Richards, S. W., 59, 231
Richards, Willard, 231
Richardson, A. B., 150
Riding, Henry, 231
Riggs, Obadiah H., 49, 231
Riser, G. C., 94, 95
Rivers, A. L., 182, 247
Roberts, Joab S., 71, 72
Roberts, Samuel, 71, 79, 247
Robertson, Charles, 125, 247
Robins, E. J., 247
Robinson, J., 120, 247
Robinson, John G., 247
Robson, James, 42, 231
Rodgers, John, 41, 231
Rollo, A. H., 190, 247
Romney, George, 95
Romney, Miles, 41, 44, 95, 96, 231
Romney, Miles P., 44, 96, 150, 231
Romney, William George, 150
Root, Frank, 178
Ross, A. M., 201, 247
Rost, T. H., 247
Rowe, Watkin L., 177, 247

Rowland, T., 195, 247
Rumell, John H., 41, 231
Rumell, John H. Jr., 247
Russell, A. N., 247
Russell, Joseph S., 106, 247
Ryan, John, 204, 247
Rystrom, Al (Rystram, F. C.), 247

S

Sage, Frank, 195, 247
Sager, Emil, 247
Salisbury, Joseph, 107, 247
Samuelson, A., 247
Sands, Frank, 248
Sanford, Samuel S., 248
Savage, C. R., 150
Sawyers, E., 41
Sayers, E. M., 231
Schaekelford, J. F., 178
Schaff, A. F., 178
Scheideler, F. J., 248
Schettler, B. H., 95
Schneider, Emil, 248
Schmol, Christ, 248
Schultz, Robert G., 248
Schwenk, N. F., 248
Sconberg, Henry (Skonberg or Schoenberg), 78, 167, 170
Scott, John, 40, 231
Scott, Wm., H., 71
Sharkey, W. H., 248
Sharp, Adam, 41, 231
Sharp, John, 95
Sharp, S., 120, 248
Sheets, John, 201, 248
Shepherd, Rensford, 248
Sherlock, James, 106, 248
Shupe, Hyde, 248
Shupe, P. R., 248
Sills, M. W., 189, 248
Silvers, Joseph M., 103, 248
Simmons, E. L., 120, 248
Simpson, John, 248
Simpson, Joseph, 248
Skilicorn, James, 248
Sleater, Robert Gibson, 12, 14, 15, 39, 70, 71, 74, 76, 77, 78, 103, 104, 114, 143–66, 170–71, 174, 176–84, 193–95, 196–201, 204, 209–11, 213, 222
Sloan, R. W., 248
Smedley, J., 248
Smiley, J. J., 248
Smith, Elias, 60, 231